ST KILDA AND THE WIDER WORLD

St Kilda and the Wider World

Tales of an Iconic Island

Andrew Fleming

WIND*gather*
PRESS

St Kilda and the Wider World: Tales of an Iconic Island

Copyright © Andrew Fleming 2005

Published by: Windgather Press Ltd, 29 Bishop Road, Bollington,
Macclesfield, Cheshire SK10 5NX

Distributed by: Central Books Ltd, 99 Wallis Road, London E9 5LN

British Library Cataloguing-in-Publication Data

A catalogue record for this book is available from the British Library

ISBN 1-905119-00-3

Designed, typeset and originated by
Carnegie Publishing Ltd, Chatsworth Road, Lancaster
Printed and bound by CPI Bath

for Mireille

Contents

List of Illustrations

Abbreviations

DCRO	Devon County Record Office
MM	MacLeod Muniments, Dunvegan, Skye
NAS	National Archives of Scotland, Edinburgh
NLS	National Library of Scotland, Edinburgh
NSA	New Statistical Account (Edinburgh, 1845)
NTS STK	St Kilda Archive, National Trust for Scotland
PSAS	Proceedings of the Society of Antiquaries of Scotland

Preface

This book, the first general history of the remote Hebridean archipelago of St Kilda to be published for over 30 years, has been ten years in the making. It is based partly on my own archaeological fieldwork (1994 to date) and has been inspired by a growing conviction that the conventional wisdom developed by mid to late twentieth-century commentators needs to be challenged. The Hirta community was over-mythologised during the last two centuries of its existence; since its evacuation in 1930, St Kilda has become something of a historical drama queen. Its history and culture have often been treated allegorically and in isolation, creating the iconic island of today, a World Heritage site which is still of absorbing public interest despite the difficulties of access. In this book I want to question the St Kilda mythologies and 'de-isolate' the archipelago, considering its history in the context of the wider geographical region and broader historical trends. Hence my title. My contention is that the lives and culture of the St Kildans were not particularly exceptional within northern Scotland; but I am not making this point in order to develop a prosaic, mundane version of St Kildan history. Given the awesome landscape and seascape of the archipelago, its striking archaeology, the richness and range of the literature, and the remarkably varied reactions which these islands provoked among visitors and residents originating from outside, to make this book boring would be a difficult task. I hope I have failed to achieve it!

St Kilda and the Wider World is intended for the general reader. It is based on a good deal of documentary and archaeological research, and I have tried to provide as many end-notes as possible as authority for statements made. Inevitably there will be some annoying omissions, for which I can only apologise; the fault is carelessness or undue haste rather than an attempt to mislead or evade responsibility. I am conscious that there are sources out there which I have not consulted, for various reasons. Hard choices have had to be made; this is just one of several books which might be written from the extensive St Kilda literature. I hope the distinction between fact and interpretation will be clear to the reader; I take responsibility for the interpretations offered here.

I owe thanks to several institutions, and to more people than there is space to list here; deciding whom to leave out has involved invidious and sometimes arbitrary choices. If you have contributed and your name is omitted, please consider yourself also thanked, not slighted.

I thank Robin Turner, chief archaeologist at the National Trust for Scotland, without whose encouragement and support I might now be pondering what might have been; also Jill Harden and several other NTS staff. I thank Mark Edmonds and Ann Clarke for their stimulating contributions as collaborating archaeologists; for academic and archaeological advice I thank Susan Bain, Colin Ballantyne, Bob Dodgshon, Kevin Edwards, Pat Foster, Jacqui Huntley, Fraser MacDonald, Mary MacLeod, Andy Meharg, Dick Merriman, Alex Morrison, Mike Parker Pearson, Andrew Reynolds, Niall Sharples, Alison Sheridan, Domhnall Uilleam Stiubhart, Bob Will and Alex Woolf. For excavation and survey work, and related skills, I thank Bill Bevan, Chris Fenton-Thomas, Richard Jones, Jamie Lund, Colin Merrony, Joe Nikel, Graham Robbins, Helen Smith, Heidi Taylor, and especially Quentin Drew. Among librarians and archivists I owe special thanks to Kathy Miles at University of Wales Lampeter, Isla Robertson, photographic curator at NTS, and Willie Johnston of the Royal Highland and Agricultural Society of Scotland; also staff of the National Library of Scotland, the National Archives of Scotland, the School of Scottish Studies (University of Edinburgh), the Royal Commission on the Ancient and Historical Monuments of Scotland (RCAHMS), the Library of the Royal Museum of Scotland, the Scottish Life Collection at the RMS, the Shetland Record Office, and Andrew Cordier for material from his personal library. I thank the NTS and fellow members of SKARC (St Kilda Archaeological Research Committee), Historic Scotland, Scottish Natural History and RCAHMS (permission to work on Hirta and related matters); and for financial support, the University of Wales Lampeter, the Pantyfedwen Fund (UWL), the University of Sheffield, Society of Antiquaries of Scotland and the Russell Trust. I thank Patrick Foster for his skilled drawing. Many people have made my stays on Hirta enjoyable – including Gill Pilkington, Claire Deacon, several rangers, archaeology wardens, independent researchers, staff of Glasgow University Archaeological Research Department (GUARD), and those who have personned 'the base' – staff from the Royal Artillery, Serco, QinetiQ and the rest. Finally I owe much to Richard Purslow, my editor and publisher, for encouraging me to write this book and for seeing it through the production process.

I have been so fortunate.

Talsarn, Ceredigion   September 2004

CHAPTER ONE

Prologue: Reopening the Inquest

....

The St Kildians may be ranked among the greatest
curiosities of the moral world.

Kenneth MacAulay, The History of St Kilda *(1764), p. 278.*

FIGURE 1.
Finlay MacQueen.

FIGURE 2.
Approaching the
archipelago: Hirta on
the left, Boreray on
the right.

On a clear day in the Western Isles of Scotland, one does not have to climb
much of a hill to catch sight of the islands of St Kilda, 40 miles (*c.* 65 km) out
in the north-east Atlantic. Just two shapes are silhouetted where the sky meets
the sea – the sharp crags of tall Boreray, and the hills of Hirta which occupy
a broader stretch of the horizon (Figure 2). These islands were once the home
of the most remote community in Britain, dispersed for ever when Hirta was
evacuated on Friday, 29 August, 1930. The main and only permanently habit-
able island is called Hirta (*Hiort*); *Hiort* is pronounced 'Heersht', like the
sighing of the sea. On the map, these islands look small; it is less than six
kilometres from the north-west end of Hirta to the south-east tip of Dun.
Together, Hirta, Boreray and Soay (Figure 3) – the third sizeable island – cover
an area comparable to Richmond Park or Heathrow airport. But Hirta's cliffs
are the highest in Britain, and walking its high central spine, from Ruaival to

FIGURE 3.
The isle of Soay.

Oiseval, is a strenuous task. It is hard to find words to describe these islands; adjectives lose themselves in a blizzard of seabirds, superlatives fly away on the wind like the cries of distant seals. In this book, photographs will have to do much of the work of description; but they convey little of the *experience* of being here, the encounter with the wildness of Earth at the edge of the ocean – spray on the face, heaving lungs, green slopes dropping vertiginously to seething waves far below. But there is more here than awesome scenery. The crowded buildings at Village Bay and the ruined stone structures scattered across the hills are powerfully evocative of a vanished community.

In the early 1950s, the archipelago belonged to Lord Bute, whose ancestors had made a fortune from the Cardiff coal trade; St Kilda was managed as a private nature reserve. Seals lay around in the grassy meadows at Village Bay, their slumbers disturbed only by the occasional visit of a yacht crew, a group of naturalists, or trawlermen in quest of shelter and drinking-water. Lord Bute had a vision for these islands. His ideal was expressed by the distinguished naturalist James Fisher: 'St Kilda *is* a safe place for life. It *is* a sanctuary. The Marquis of Bute ... himself a naturalist, keeps it so ... he wishes it to be left as a perfect sanctuary, where wild animals and plants may go the ways of nature, without any trace of the influence of man ... Man's future on St Kilda is in one role only – the role of *observer*. He is miscast, now, in any other part'.[1] These words were written only a couple of years after Hiroshima, at a time when governments were beginning to prepare for a Third World War which would probably be fought with nuclear weapons. So perhaps it is not surprising that in 1955, when the British government proposed to construct a

2

radar station on Hirta to support a new rocket range on South Uist, Lord Bute does not seem to have put up much resistance. Perhaps conscious of his impending death, he bequeathed St Kilda to the National Trust for Scotland. The military leased the land they needed from the Nature Conservancy, which in turn leased the archipelago from the Trust.[2] So when the RAF arrived on Hirta in April 1957, to initiate what they called Operation Hardrock, the advance party included naturalists, who would take stock of the nation's new inheritance – and, as it soon turned out, dissuade the military from bulldozing standing buildings for roadstone.[3]

To judge from the entertaining account written by Kenneth Williamson and John Morton Boyd, Operation Hardrock was a classic 1950s-style adventure. Had they filmed it, there would certainly have been roles for the likes of Kenneth More and John Mills. 'Tent city' was established at Village Bay (Figure 4); in their free time, personnel sunbathed in their khaki shorts, or played cricket in Glebe Meadow. After church parade, the church was swiftly converted into a cinema. No doubt Operation Hardrock involved the usual clash between official pomposity and real life, a familiar mixture of fiasco and ingenuity. A naturalist's work at St Kilda could be great fun, with opportunities for climbing rock-stacks, operating boats in challenging conditions, hitching rides in planes and flying-boats. There must have been laughter and good conversation in the evenings, in the afterglow of long days in the open air, a briar pipe or two being savoured as observations were written up and samples sorted. Some of the work continued the studies of earlier scientific

FIGURE 4.
Operation Hardrock, 1957. Note the connecting passage between manse and church and the long 'coffin cleit' opposite the church door.

3

expeditions. But as far as the history of the islands was concerned, little had been written recently; the latest archaeological overview had been published in 1928.[4] Although the Hardrock naturalists were accompanied by a young archaeologist, this did not inhibit them from pronouncing upon archaeological matters themselves; indeed their published interpretations were influential for the next 40 years. And it was the naturalists, with the support of a geographer, who started what I call the Hardrock Consensus, a view of St Kilda's history which has come to dominate the late twentieth-century literature; it is a perspective which I intend to challenge in this book.

What is the Hardrock Consensus? Put simply, it is the idea that the key to St Kilda's long-term history is embedded in the 'causes' of the 1930 evacuation. This may seem surprising. After all, many other islands in the west of Scotland and in Ireland have been abandoned without generating much historical discussion; why should the 'death' of a community say something profound about its life? A man may smoke heavily, and eventually die from lung cancer; yet his life is not defined by his addiction to tobacco, and he might in any case have met his end by falling under a bus. Perhaps members of the Hardrock party were more deeply affected than we realise by their frequent encounters with roofless houses full of broken and rotting furniture and the poignant relics of a once vibrant community.[5] Be that as it may; in any event, the quest to explain the abandonment of St Kilda, which started in 1957, plunged historical commentators into deep philosophical waters. Their 'explanations' are deeply entangled in several powerful and emotive concepts – the Fall of Man, classical tragedy, ecological Armageddon, the crisis of modernity, and the role of humanity within the natural world – more than enough intellectual baggage, one might think, to explain the iconic status which the archipelago enjoys today.

The Hardrock Consensus

E. M. Nicholson, in 1957 Director of the Nature Conservancy, told a humorous and revealing story. While taking the 1939 bird census, the biologist Julian (later *Sir* Julian) Huxley poked his head through the window of one of the old houses. He was greeted by 'a flood of Gaelic oaths', having disturbed a 'returned native' who happened to be asleep. Huxley was equal to the occasion. Turning to his colleague, he called out '*Homo sapiens*, one!'[6] For the naturalists, Man was simply an advanced primate, an outcome of evolutionary forces designed by God (in Boyd's view[7]) or Nature, with that revealing capital N. The former inhabitants of St Kilda were essentially part of its natural history. And perhaps it should come as no surprise that one of them, the most impressive summer migrant to the nature reserve in the 1930s, old Finlay MacQueen (Figure 1, page xiv), was 'on show' at the great Glasgow Empire Exhibition of 1938. At the opening ceremony he was presented to the King and Queen (whose hand he kissed);[8] he murmured (in Gaelic) 'God bless you both and your family'.[9] MacQueen could be viewed at the highly popular *clachan*, the 'Highland village', which featured reconstructed croft houses, a kirk, an inn and a formidable-looking castle.[10] (A generation earlier, at the Glasgow Exhibition of 1911, some black Rhodesians had actually been exhibited under a 'natural history' heading.[11])

The naturalists of the 1950s tended to regard the former St Kildans as members of a species whose extinction had been caused by the destructive power of modern humanity. In this sense St Kildan history was essentially natural history, and the St Kildans had been part of a world subject to Darwinian principles, before the intervention of 'modern' outsiders who imagined that they had suspended the laws of nature. For Williamson and Boyd, the 'great personal integrity' of the St Kildans had been corrupted 'by growing contact with the outside world' and Hirta became the showplace of 'poverty, squalor, disease and famine'. The islanders' existence 'became an anachronism, and a degraded one at that'.[12] These people had lost their innocence; no wonder the naturalists were enthusiastic about the re-creation of St Kilda as an unsullied natural paradise.

A participant in this conversation was the historical geographer D. R. MacGregor, who was also on Hirta in 1957, partly on behalf of the National Trust; he carried out a survey of earthworks and structures at Village Bay. MacGregor's exploration of the 'failure' of the St Kilda community was contained in an article on the history and geography of the archipelago, published in 1960. He argued that isolation was the most powerful factor in the human occupation of St Kilda, and that 'the resource base of the St Kildans was at all times meagre and limited'.[13] Problems were caused by the islanders' 'rather ineffective farming', their refusal to develop a proper commercial fishing industry, their destructive use of turf rather than peat, and their habit of procrastination.[14] Although they were 'dependent upon outside influence and example', 'close contact with the Scottish mainland produced fatal changes in the outlook and structure of the community', and eventually the donation of gifts and outside relief led to a disastrous loss of self-reliance.[15] It was 'the bigoted impositions of the Free Church', rather than material want, which mostly led to their 'unhappy state' in the late nineteenth century.[16] As we shall see, these notions are all to be found in earlier literature. MacGregor's overall view was that the St Kildans were to be admired for 'defying the elements' on an isolated, rocky outpost 'in the deeps of the Atlantic'. But as to the final fate of the community – *che sera, sera*; one should accept the march of events.[17]

And then in 1965 Tom Steel, barely into his twenties, published *The Life and Death of St Kilda*. This highly readable book is regarded by many as a classic; a revised version (1994) is still available. For many people – including me – *The Life and Death* has been an essential introduction to St Kilda, and also the main instrument of their conversion to the contagious enthusiasm of Hirtophilia. Evidently Steel was heavily influenced by the ideas in MacGregor's article, as these quotations from the 1994 paperback edition of *The Life and Death* show:

'throughout their history they possessed a sense of community that was to show itself increasingly out of place';

'Like many Celts, they were dreamers rather than men of action';

'As contact with the mainland increased ... the St Kildans were incapable of adapting to a more complex set of rules of behaviour and became introverted';

'the stern faith of the Free Church ... made slaves of the people of St Kilda ... religion in the hands of some was to stifle what little initiative existed among the inhabitants';

'they lacked the ability to take up the challenge of free enterprise'.[18]

So for Steel, the islanders' 'socialism', their failure to embrace free enterprise and their Celticity contributed to their downfall. The 'anti-socialist' view had been expressed by Robert Connell in 1887, at a time when socialism was winning increasing acceptance in Britain: 'after fifteen days stay on St Kilda I came to the deliberate conclusion that this nibbling at socialism is responsible for a good deal of the moral chaos which has so completely engulfed the islanders'.[19]

What makes Steel's book so compelling is that he wrote it as tragedy (there is an explicit mention of Aristotle in the last paragraph of the 1994 edition).[20] He picked up on two classic tragic themes. The first is the doomed struggle of the hero against his fate, an archetypal idea even older than Aeschylus, who set it at the heart of tragedy. The second features a hero who has the world at his feet, until his flawed character (or a fatal mistake), sweeps him inexorably to his doom (as in Othello, or Michael Henchard, the mayor of Casterbridge). From an early stage in the narrative, a tragic end is foretold and foreshadowed. In history, too, we know the end; particular events may have immediate causes, but for a deeper understanding we have to reach further back in time. The temptation to write history as tragedy is obvious – particularly when the 'end' involves the 'death' of a community. It is a temptation which Steel did not resist; he made use of both tragic themes. We have already noted his enumeration of the St Kildans' 'character flaws'; the other theme, the hand of Fate, is best expressed by his epitaph for the islanders on the eve of evacuation, composed for *The Life and Death*'s first edition:

The attempts made by the few to stave off evacuation were noble and well-intentioned but bore marks of the pathos and futility of working against the inevitable. St Kilda stood in the Atlantic, the changeless amid the changed. All that could be done was to wait and allow the men and women of Village Bay the courtesy and privilege of making for themselves the decision that would make Nature's defeat of man a reality.[21]

Whether we take Nature or Fate to have been the ultimate cause of St Kilda's 'death', Steel created a striking cosmic drama, spinning the Hardrock Consensus out into the book-shops. Tragedy is a powerful expression of the human condition, and the tragic themes of *The Life and Death* have helped to create St Kilda's iconic status. As I write these words, the archipelago seems set to join the select band of World Heritage Sites which have won their status on the basis of both natural *and* human history.

Tragic consequences

There is nothing like a 'decline and fall' story to make history readable. But unfortunately neither of Tom Steel's tragic themes stands up to close examination. As his own account reveals, it simply isn't true that the 'failure' of the St Kildan community was caused by the islanders' rigorous observance of the Sabbath, their 'socialism', their failure to embrace the spirit of capitalism, or their refusal to engage with the modern world. The people and their culture did *not* 'stand still for centuries' whilst all around was changing;[22] rather than being inflexible and incapable of adaptation,[23] the St Kildans' economy was highly diversified and their lifeways were notably responsive to outside influence. Culturally speaking, the islanders were not 'remote from the rest of society'.[24] The community may be absolved of its character flaws, and helped off the psychiatrist's couch.

But what of the doomed struggle of Man against Nature at the edge of the Ocean? By common consent, the lifeways and material culture of the *Hirteach* were well adapted to their environment; as we shall see, plenty of mechanisms were in place to buffer their economy against risk. The idea that the St Kildans were 'doomed'[25] and could not 'win' their 'struggle' against Nature amounts to little more than rhetoric. But in any case, for those who created the Hardrock Consensus the most compelling explanation of St Kilda's demise was not Fate, nor yet cultural flaws, but rather the impact of modernity. For Steel, the damage was done by the growth of tourism, the introduction of an extreme and damaging form of Sabbatarian Christianity, an inappropriate education system, the rise of a cash economy, increasing dependence on charity, and the misconceived interventions of 'amateur sociologists and do-gooders'.[26] As we have seen, for Boyd and Williamson the history of St Kilda was an allegory of the Fall of Man; the sooner the archipelago was returned to the wild the better. This recalls words also written in the mid-1950s, by the landscape historian W. G. Hoskins, who famously decried 'the obscene shape of the atom-bomber ... the high barbed wire around some unmentionable devilment ... barbaric England of the scientists, the military men, and the politicians'.[27] Those who had to live with the St Kilda radar station belonged to the generation which had known Auschwitz and Belsen, Dresden and Hiroshima, Guernica and the gulag; the emergence of a consensus on the meaning of St Kildan history had a great deal to do with the *angst* of the 1950s.

Charles MacLean, another young writer whose *Island on the Edge of the World* first appeared in 1972, took these ideas to their logical conclusion.[28] For him too, 'in evolutionary terms St Kilda was out on a limb', and the community's adaptive system could not cope with the increasing rate of change in the modern world. MacLean expressed alarm about ecological catastrophe and alienation in the later twentieth century, noting the 'dissatisfaction with existence in the modern age' and the attractiveness of the ideal of the commune. Warning against 'puritan wistfulness and the sentimental verbiage of nature worship from afar', MacLean suggested that there must nevertheless have been *something* behind the frequent claims that St Kilda was the lost Utopia. For him, the island republic seemed a good model for an utopian community whose hopes for success were based on isolation and smallness. This 'archaic social type' might well prove to be 'the most adaptive response' after the impending ecological and social Armageddon. 'The utopian dream', wrote MacLean, 'begins to look less ideal and more realistic'.

Wider perspectives

Between them, the influential writers Steel and MacLean, in their expression of the Hardrock Consensus, have endowed the history of the archipelago with tremendous symbolic significance. But then distant islands have often been mythologised, and conversely, traditional story-tellers have frequently created imaginary islands. Otherworlds beneath the ocean have long been envisioned by people in western Britain and Ireland.[29] The more optimistic, dominant strand of this tradition portrayed an island with a sunlit central plain – a land of plenty, full of heavily laden apple trees, in which birds sing all day, and the tired hero is sumptuously fed and caressed by beautiful women at bathtime and bedtime. But there was also a darker world of Death, a realm beneath the sea, reached from *underneath* an island rather than located upon it.

Authors of books dealing with political, ethical and philosophical issues – from Thomas More's *Utopia* to William Golding's *Lord of the Flies* – have appreciated imaginary islands as microcosms, rich in allegorical potential.[30] This tradition has touched St Kilda. Martin Martin, whose wonderful *Voyage to St Kilda* was first published in 1698, travelled here in the spirit of science. He contended it was 'weakness and folly to value things merely on account of their distance'.[31] Nevertheless, the blurb on his title page claimed that: 'The inhabitants of St Kilda are almost the only people in the world who feel the sweetness of true liberty; what the condition of the people in the Golden Age is feigned to be, that theirs really is'. Martin the scientist was also offering his readers an island Utopia. And many subsequent visitors assumed that a trip to Britain's most remote inhabited island must involve an encounter with the exotic (Figure 5). As their writings reveal, they were not disappointed. But this was to some considerable extent because the St Kildans learned to collude with their expectations. Rev. Neil MacKenzie, who spent 14 years on the island (1829–43) is worth quoting at length on the subject:

> Encouraged by the amazing credulity of the ordinary tourist, the natives have got to be very successful in imposing upon them. The tourist comes with a certain idea in his mind as to what the native is like, and would be

disappointed if they did not find him like that; this the natives have been shrewd enough to discover and turn to their own profit. For example, when they went on board a yacht they would pretend that they thought all the polished brass was gold, and that the owner must be enormously wealthy. Yet, when in a few minutes after they might be offered the choice of several coins, selecting not the gold but the largest as if they had no idea of the relative value of the different metals. At the very same time some of them would be below with the steward showing the keenest knowledge of the value of the supplies which they were trying to sell and of the value of every several coin. Again, they would pick up pieces of coal and affect surprise at not being able to eat them; and when they would come in front of a looking-glass they would start back and express great surprise at not being able to find the person who appeared to be behind it; and yet a moment's observation would have shown anyone that they had that very morning shaved before a looking-glass ... all the time they would be saying to themselves in Gaelic ... "if we seem to be paying great attention and make them believe that we are simple, they will be sure before they go away to give us something much better".[32]

The St Kildans had understood all too well that the most significant mirror proffered by the tourists was the one which already reflected their own preconceptions.

Islands have often paid high scientific dividends. Charles Darwin learnt a great deal on the Galapagos Islands, initiating the fascinating subject known as island biogeography. Historians and archaeologists have sometimes been stimulated to attempt the same line of enquiry. An archaeologist once wrote

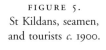
FIGURE 5.
St Kildans, seamen,
and tourists *c.* 1900.

an article entitled 'Islands as Laboratories for the Study of Culture Process',[33] and the remarkable history of Easter Island, another World Heritage Site, has been held to carry a profound message for humanity.[34] There is something irresistible about the idea of a world in microcosm, small and simple enough to be thoroughly understood, an island where the infrequency of outside interference has placed its inhabitants largely in charge of their own destiny. And the more 'exotic' the islanders' lifeways seem, the more their history appears to depend upon remoteness and insularity. However, even on remote islands, human history cannot really be treated as an exercise in biogeography. Archaeologists working in the Pacific and the Aegean now recognise that the sea is more significant as a highway than as a cause of 'isolation'; they have become much more interested in the *connectedness* of islands, even in great expanses of ocean.[35]

A comparison between Martin's account of St Kilda and his general description of the Hebrides, published five years later, reveals more similarities than differences between St Kildan lifeways and those of the region in general.[36] Much the same point could have been made in the eighteenth and nineteenth centuries; for example, the white linen 'mutch' worn on the forehead by married women was to be seen on the mainland as well as on St Kilda.[37] The St Kildans' well-known interest in the outside world ('Are there any wars going on?' 'Is the king still on his throne?' and so on[38]) turns out to be just as prevalent, perhaps even more so, in places not served by a regular steamer service, such as parts of the Highlands.[39] In Shetland, news of William of Orange's landing arrived six months late and was not believed.[40] In the late eighteenth century, Highlanders 'most curious after the politicks of the world' avidly devoured the content of old newspapers.[41] Tourists from Glasgow or Edinburgh usually travelled by sea, and were familiar mostly with 'must see' sites like Fingal's Cave or Loch Coruisk; so they may not have been aware that St Kilda was not all that exotic, in a Hebridean context. In any case, by the mid nineteenth century, the Clearances had destroyed many traditional communities. As a matter of fact, a tourist from Iceland who had sailed via the Faroe Islands and Shetland would probably have found Hirta more familiar than would someone from the Central Lowlands of Scotland. Ethnographic literature suggests that the lifeways of St Kilda were as much north-east Atlantic as Hebridean.[42] This partly reflects the ecological characteristics and opportunities of the region – wild-fowling, hunting marine mammals, wind-drying meat, and so on; certain points of comparison probably derive from contacts between these island groups, particularly during the period when Norsemen ruled the waves.[43] Like most islanders, the St Kildans were curious about the world outside and receptive to its influences; Martin noted that 'both sexes have a great inclination to novelty'.[44] I tend to agree with the geologist John MacCulloch, who wrote in the early nineteenth century: 'in truth there appears no difference between the present inhabitants of St Kilda and those of the neighbouring islands ... they have sailed down the stream with their neighbours'.[45]

FIGURE 6.
North-west Scotland, to show location of St Kilda and places mentioned in text. A: Ardnamurchan; AO = A t-Ob (Leverburgh); BL = Barpa Langass; E = Ensay; K = Killegray; U = The Udal.

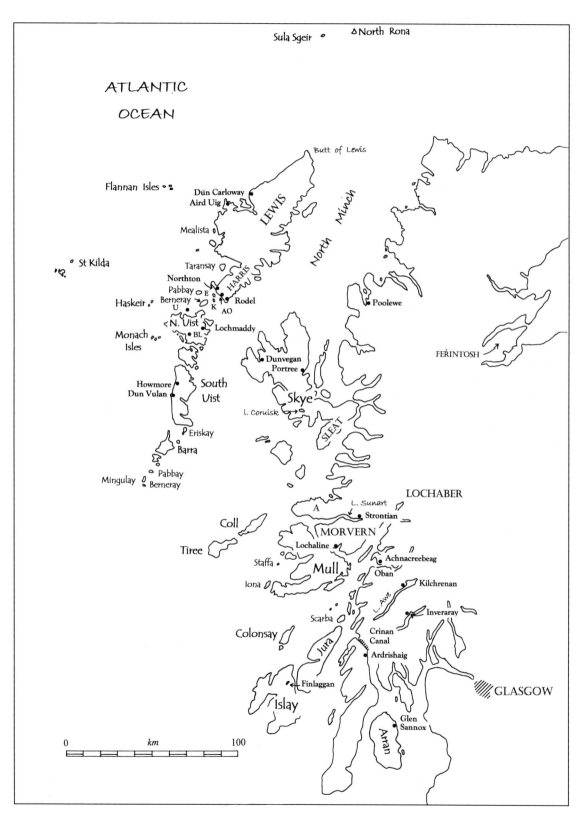

ATLANTIC

OCEAN

Sula Sgeir ○   △ North Rona

Butt of Lewis

Flannan Isles ● ⦂   Dūn Carloway ●
Aird Uig
LEWIS
North Minch

Mealista ○

● St Kilda

Taransay ○
HARRIS
Northton
Pabbay ○ ● E
Berneray ⦂ ● Rodel
Haskeir ○   U ● K
AO
N. Uist   ● Lochmaddy
Poolewe ●

Monach ○○○
Isles
● BL

FERINTOSH →

Dunvegan ●
Portree ●

Howmore ● ○
Dun Vulan   South
Uist
Skye
L. Coruisk →
SLEAT

Eriskay ●

Barra ○

Mingulay ○   Pabbay ○
Berneray ⦂

LOCHABER

A   L. Sunart
● Strontian

Coll
MORVERN
Tiree   Lochaline ●

Staffa ●   Achnacreebeag ●
Mull   Oban ●
Iona ○   Kilchrenan ●
L. Awe
Inveraray ●
Scarba ○
Colonsay ○   Crinan
Canal
Jura   ● Ardrishaig

GLASGOW

Finlaggan ●

Islay   Glen
Sannox
Arran

0   km   100

II

A common theme among more recent commentators has been St Kilda's 'marginality'. It is probably because they have perceived these islands as 'marginal' – geographically, ecologically, and culturally – that professional historians have shown little interest in them. If anything, however, St Kilda's 'remoteness' paradoxically made it more conspicuous, more of a desirable destination, and in that sense quite frequently brought the archipelago into the mainstream of both historical processes and external perceptions. The notion of marginality – which is usually ill-defined by its proponents, and sweepingly applied – is essentially a red herring. And its more focused version, *ecological* marginality, essentially resolves itself into the question of how *any* community protects itself against risk. What is at issue is not marginality as such – and still less the attachment of 'marginality' as a defining label – but rather questions of cultural competence. The St Kildans were no different from other people in risk-prone environments – kelpers and fishermen in the north of Scotland, miners and mill-workers in the factories and slums of industrial England, for instance – in their need to find cultural strategies which allowed them to cope with the manifold problems which they encountered. The *Hirteach* engaged vigorously with the world, and their lifeways had been ingeniously and collectively developed over centuries.

The Hardrock Consensus, which read 'pre-modern' human history as natural history, regarded the culture of the St Kildans as well adapted to 'the struggle against the elements' and also 'unchanging'. (There is a contradiction here, in the sense that adaptation implies a recurrent capacity for change.) From this perspective, history becomes almost synonymous with lifeways, and the historian should prioritise the description and cataloguing of St Kilda's 'cultural tradition'. But rural ethnography, even when labelled 'folk tradition', is not history. In St Kilda's case we should try to avoid weaving information stretching over two and a half centuries into a timeless ethnographic tapestry which is all about 'adaptation' to a 'marginal' existence. Such an approach minimises the significance of changing historical conditions and treats the St Kildans as 'culture bearers' rather than active participants in their own history. Perhaps the best antidote to this tendency is to try to make individual people stand out against their ethnographic background, something I will try to do in this book.

'Islandness', remoteness, exoticism, and 'marginality' are parts of more general mythologies of islands which always deserve to be challenged. If these factors have played significant roles in St Kilda's history, it is mostly because they have come to preoccupy the mindsets of outsiders.

A rich resource

The historian of Hirta has one supreme advantage. I doubt if there is another rural community in Europe which has been so frequently documented in so much detail. Over the best part of three centuries, we have quite a number of eye-witness accounts, some written by people who lived on Hirta for extended periods of time. They wrote down songs and stories, they made sketches, took photographs. Nor did the evacuation stem the flow of books and articles. We are, however, dealing here with the perceptions of outsiders; although the words of some of the people evacuated from Hirta in 1930 have been recorded,[46] the viewpoint of the islanders often has to be deduced by reading between the lines, or picking up on the significance of particular anecdotes. Much information has been recycled, not always accurately. Many of the commentators were concerned, educated people. However, in evaluating their remarks, one has to ask – how long were they there, to whom did they talk, and what were their preconceptions? Generally, the shorter the stay, the more opinionated the tale. Often the greatest significance seems to derive from the most casual comment, or the most apparently trivial anecdote.

Hirta is first mentioned in the thirteenth century;[47] in local terms, then, prehistory lasted until the later Middle Ages. This, of course, is why the record of archaeology is so important. Fortunately, Hirta is archaeologically rich and crowded, with well-preserved standing structures, mysterious ruins, and numerous 'humps and bumps', otherwise known as earthwork features. Such archaeology is not altogether straightforward; on this small island we should, for instance, expect considerable recycling and reuse of building stone. When I first visited Hirta, and started looking around with the restless, reflective gaze of the landscape archaeologist, I felt challenged, keen to relate such traces of human handiwork to information contained in documents, and even more curious to know what light they might shed on the island's prehistory. My own discipline of landscape archaeology has now made some progress here, and so has conventional archaeological excavation, which has already disproved Steel's contention that 'it is unlikely that the thin stony soil has many secrets to give up when archaeologists ultimately dig'.[48] At present St Kilda is under intensive archaeological and palaeo-environmental investigation, and I am very aware that the results of ongoing archaeological excavations, survey work and the remarkable applications of soil science recently developed by Professor Andy Meharg of Aberdeen University may make it necessary to revise the archaeological story in this book in the not too distant future.

In what follows, I will make a reasonable attempt to 'cover the ground' – but choices have had to be made. The reader in search of more detail is advised to consult Mary Harman's book, *An Isle called Hirte* (1997), an excellent work of reference (although unfortunately it has no index). I will try to illuminate Hirta's history by placing it in a wider context – sometimes regional, sometimes intellectual. I intend to read between the lines and think more anthropologically than previous commentators have cared to do. The past is over and done with. However, such is not the case with *history*, which is constantly under revision and review, as new information comes to light and new perceptions evolve. The iconic status of this island group owes much to the way its history has been written – and its history has been written in the service of its iconic status. It is time to re-examine the Hardrock Consensus, and to question the way St Kilda's history has been singled out and treated as an allegory illustrating high philosophical propositions.

CHAPTER TWO

The Qualities of the Isle

....

... this truly romantic place ... that always presents grand objects
and strange landskips, a boundless ocean, immense precipices, hills
unsung, whose summits are lost in the clouds, a prodigious variety
of birds, and these beyond the reach of numbers ...

Kenneth MacAulay, 1764 (1974), p. 218.

FIGURE 7.
'Some of them would
be reckoned
extraordinary beauties';
Annie Gillies at the
well.

Nowadays, the journey to St Kilda only takes 20 minutes by helicopter. One
is whisked through the air and plonked down on Hirta like one of the
chessmen in *Alice Through the Looking Glass*, though after watching the safety
video and struggling into his survival suit, the White King might have been
even more disconcerted. On a boat there is a more human sense of scale and
distance, as one's braced body feels the pitch and roll on the surface of the sea,
underlain by the more measured swell of the ocean. The sense of anticipation
will be sharpened by the occasional sight of a snow-white gannet. Perhaps the
skipper will take you close to Boreray (Figure 8) and past its dark, intimidating
outriders, Stac Li and Stac an Armin, former hunting-grounds of the St
Kildans, where seabirds whirl like snow-flakes – a tourist spectacle which nineteenth-century steamer captains liked to stimulate by firing small cannons.[1]
Village Bay, the point of arrival on Hirta (Figure 9), will not look strange to
visitors familiar with photographs of the abandoned village – the line of
roofless houses facing the sea, the green of once-farmed land cradled by an arc
of hills. Newcomers may also recall the sepia images of the people who lived
in these houses, above all the much-reproduced photograph of the 'St Kilda
Parliament', taken in 1886 – a group of redoubtable-looking men, bearded,
bewhiskered and tam o'shantered, who have gathered in the street on a foggy
morning to discuss the business of the day (Figure 10). It is a compelling image
of the 'island republic'. Steep, bulky hills beset the enclosed land at Village
Bay (Figure 11). There is the great mass of Oiseval (East Fell), its profile
sweeping down to the Gap and then steeply upwards to Hirta's highest
summit, Conachair. West of Conachair, the skyline falls to the shoulder of
Mullach Mór, then down to the high ridge of Mullach Sgar, and down
again, out to rocky Ruaival (Red Fell). The hills carry screes – white or
oatmeal-coloured granophyre (granite) at the foot of Conachair, and below
Mullach Sgar a grey-buff dolerite which sometimes turns a shimmering blue
when the sun catches it after rain. Across the bay is the jagged skyline of Dun,

FIGURE 8.
View of Boreray from
Hirta, with Stac Li
whitened by gannets.

FIGURE 9.
Village Bay from the
slopes of Oiseval.

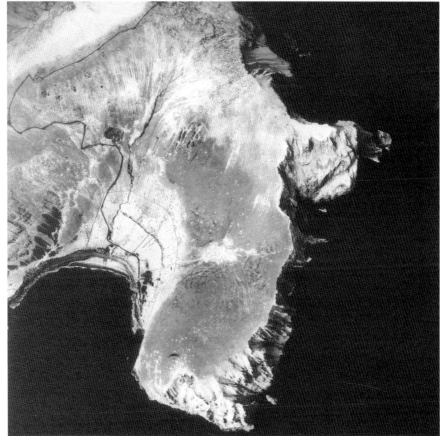

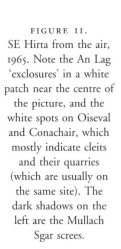

FIGURE 10.
The St Kilda
'Parliament'; Norman
MacLeod's classic
photograph, taken in
1886.

FIGURE 11.
SE Hirta from the air,
1965. Note the An Lag
'exclosures' in a white
patch near the centre of
the picture, and the
white spots on Oiseval
and Conachair, which
mostly indicate cleits
and their quarries
(which are usually on
the same site). The
dark shadows on the
left are the Mullach
Sgar screes.

17

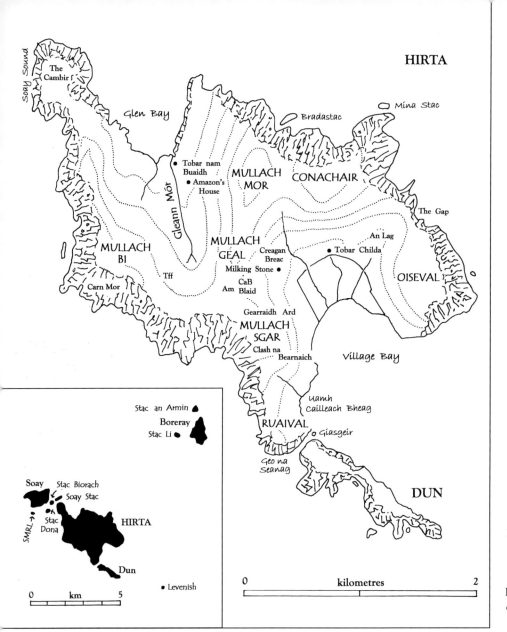

HIRTA

Soay Sound
The Cambir
Glen Bay
Mina Stac
Bradastac
Tobar nam Buaidh
MULLACH MOR
CONACHAIR
Amazon's House
Gleann Mór
The Gap
MULLACH GEAL
An Lag
Creagan Breac
Tobar Childa
MULLACH BI
Milking Stone
CaB Am Blaid
OISEVAL
Tff
Carn Mor
Gearraidh Ard
MULLACH SGAR
Clash na Bearnaich
Village Bay
Uamh Cailleach Bheag
RUAIVAL
Giasgeir
Geo na Seanag
DUN

Stac an Armin
Boreray
Stac Li

Soay   Stac Biorach
Soay Stac
SMRL
Stac Dona
HIRTA
Dun
Soay
Levenish
0   km   5

0   kilometres   2

*St Kilda and the
Wider World: Tales
of an Iconic Island*

FIGURE 12.
The St Kilda
archipelago (inset,
bottom left) and the
main island of Hirta.
CaB:Cnoc a
Bheannaichta (Hill of
Blessings); Tff = Tighe
an fhair faireadh
(Watchman's House);
SMRL = Sgeir Mac
Righ Lochlainn (Skerry
of the Son of the King
of Norway).

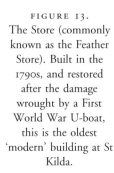

FIGURE 13.
The Store (commonly
known as the Feather
Store). Built in the
1790s, and restored
after the damage
wrought by a First
World War U-boat,
this is the oldest
'modern' building at St
Kilda.

FIGURE 14.
General map of Village
Bay. Black spots
represent cleits, circles
are houses of 'Calum
Mór's House type'.
BH:Bull's House;
CMH = Calum Mór's
House; H = helipad;
LGH = Lady Grange's
House. With some
omissions and
simplifications.

an island separated from Hirta only by a narrow channel (Figure 36, page 64).

Averting one's eyes from the sprawl of functional, unprepossessing structures making up 'the base' (Figure 84, page 192), one turns to look at the line of single-storey houses facing the bay, tar-black roofs marking the six at the east end of the street which have been restored by the National Trust for Scotland. The other ten have been 'consolidated' as standing ruins. Further east, beset by the paraphernalia of the base, are other 'modern' buildings. There is the single-storey white-washed manse, almost at the edge of the sea (Figure 59, page 124); behind it, the dull church, slate-roofed and grey-rendered, with an annexe which was once the school. Still further east, and even closer to the sea, is the sturdy Feather Store (Figure 13). Believed to date from the 1790s, it is the oldest of the 'modern' buildings. Here were stored the produce and manufactured goods which the laird's factor took away; some of their value was credited against rents or other charges levied by the estate.

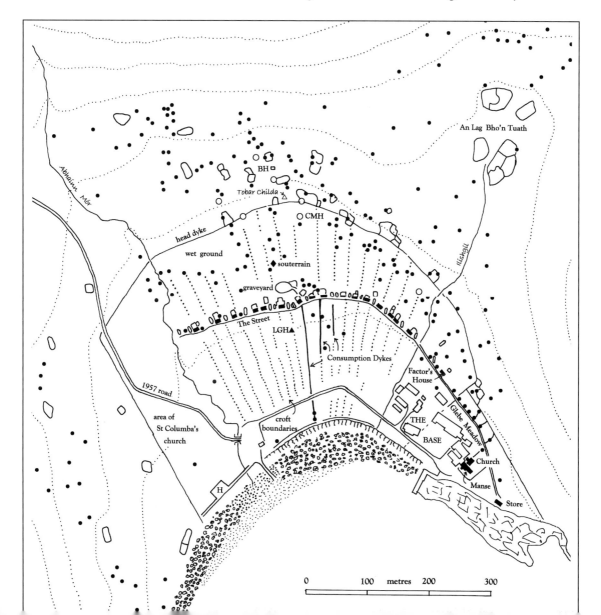

The fireplaces on the ground floor suggest that the factor stayed here when he came, at least before the construction of the Factor's House in the 1860s. The latter, now partly obscured by the horrendous 'Ablutions Block', is a handsome white rendered building with a slate roof, porch and an upper floor of sorts; it was a useful multi-purpose facility (and it continues to play this role today). It was sometimes used to house guests; in the late 1880s it accommodated the teacher and the school.[2] Nurses also stayed at the Factor's House. It was here in April 1930 that a fateful meeting took place, at which the islanders, over tea, scones and cakes made by Nurse Williamina Barclay, were finally persuaded to focus their minds seriously on the idea of evacuation.[3]

A prominent feature of the Village Bay landscape is the head dyke, a well-constructed stone wall enclosing the crofts of the abandoned village. This layout dates from the 1830s. The croft boundaries take the form of low banks, some incorporating sporadic large stones. In plan, they make a pattern like the folds of an open fan, each croft becoming gradually wider from coast to head dyke (Figure 14). Near the centre of the village, below the houses, three adjacent croft boundaries carry 'consumption dykes', thick walls intended to 'consume' cleared stones; one runs to the edge of the sea (Figure 36, page 64). Behind the houses, mostly, stand the massed ranks of the cleits (the Gaelic plural is *cleitean*, although the word is Norse in origin). Stone-built, part-corbelled, slab-roofed and turf-capped, these celebrated structures (Figures 48 and 49, pages 93 and 96) have been kept in good repair by National Trust work parties. James Fisher called them stone age drying machines.[4] They also stored a wide range of commodities; Hirta could truthfully be described as the Island of a Thousand Sheds. On the north-west slopes of Oiseval, or the top of the Mullach Geal spur further west, you will see cleits on the skyline, looking like

FIGURE 15.
An intriguing cluster of cleits near the roadstone quarry at Creagan Breac.
See also Figure 25.

FIGURE 16.
The central part of the
Street; note the near-
circular graveyard, and
the roofs renovated by
late twentieth-century
work parties.

small, mysterious towers. Their turf roofs long gone, they are tumbling gradually into ruin. Soon you will notice that degraded, ruined cleits are dotted all
over the western flank of Oiseval, white spots on the hillside. Opposite them,
on a little green shoulder near the gash of the modern quarry, is a concen-
trated group of 15 cleits or so (Figure 15). Some of the hilltop cleits were
already in being when Martin Martin came here in 1697; on his map he
marked 'stone pyramids', as he called them, on Oiseval and Mullach Geal.[5]
Sixteenth-century references to dried mutton[6] imply that cleits almost
certainly were in use at least two centuries before Martin's visit.

The long, grassy street (Figure 16) runs from the Feather Store, through the
Glebe, past the Factor's House and then in front of the houses, from No. 1 to

St Kilda and the
Wider World: Tales
of an Iconic Island

No. 16. It has been constructed as a paved causeway, carefully edged with stone. Neat, slab-covered drains run between the houses and then under the street, some still quietly gurgling with water. In front of some of the houses there are broad, stone-faced benches; these were used to display tweed and knitwear for sale to tourists. Beside the houses are the remains of more primitive-looking buildings, end on to the street. These are the 'blackhouses', the first dwellings to be built on the crofts, in the 1830s. When the 'modern' houses were constructed, in the early 1860s, the blackhouses usually became byres. Most of the houses have small walled yards or gardens behind them, and pits in which compost was made; these are usually circular, and faced with stone. At the east end of the street, each house tends to be accompanied by a small thatched barn or cottage (sometimes used as a 'granny flat'), as well as a byre. Scattered through the crofts are little square or circular enclosures, without gateways – 'plantie-crues' where people grew vegetables such as cabbage. In the distance, there are much larger 'exclosures', above and beyond the head dyke, or attached to it; some of these were once cultivated (Figure 17; Figure 11, page 17). Many walled structures are frequented by wrens, which scutter about among the stones, and charm the air with their loud, liquid song. Long isolation has led to the evolution of a local sub-species, *Troglodytes troglodytes hirtensis*.

Halfway along, the street is joined by a short spur road leading to the graveyard – a small, almost circular space, defined by a well-built wall, neatly battered around its southern half to contain the thrust of the deep earth within (Figure 62, page 132). Most of the memorials are simple stone slabs, unworked and uninscribed, placed side by side in irregular rows. There is now no trace of the tiny Christ Church which once stood here. But at the western end of the street, a large cross is inscribed on a jamb of the eastern window of House 16, and there is another on the underside of one of the roof-slabs of cleit 74, just west of the graveyard (cleit numbers are marked in white paint).

A visitor with a little more time may walk over to the north-west side of the island, tackling the steep tarmac road which climbs to the modern quarry and then snakes up to the ridge of Am Blaid. Up here, on a clear day, there is a fine sense of being among hills and at the same time in the midst of the ocean (Figure 18). To the east, the hills of the Long Island may appear as grey, distant silhouettes – or sometimes dark blue and much closer. They form a hundred-mile panorama, the distance from the lighthouse on the Butt of Lewis to its counterpart on Barra Head being the same as that from London to Sheffield or Shrewsbury. On an exceptionally clear day, the mountains of Skye may be seen.[7] From the ridge, the scenic route takes you higher, along the narrow spine of Mullach Bi, bristling like a hog's back with rocks and cleits – a walk above the sea, out to the Cambir, to look across to the high, hunched island of Soay (Figure 3, page 2), and marvel through binoculars at the precipitous positions of its cleits (if you can spot them). In places this walk will take you to the vertiginous edge of the island, sheer grassy slopes plunging between the crags to the swirling ocean far below.

From the Cambir, you may return to Village Bay through Gleann Mór (Figure 19, Figure 50, page 97 and Figure 81, page 185). The Great Glen is a quiet, peaceful place, though to come here in summer is to court the territorial aggression of the bonxies – the great skuas which started to colonise Hirta in the early 1960s and now number 200 pairs or so. It is worth flying a pennant a couple of feet above one's head to keep them (sometimes literally) off one's back, for there are some interesting ruined stone structures to visit at the lower end of the glen. In recent history, Gleann Mór was where women and girls grazed their cattle and sheep in summer, and made butter and cheese. They lived in complex stone structures, sleeping in little corbelled chambers, 'wall-beds' opening off small enclosed courts. There are about a dozen of these structures; from a distance, they look half sunk into the ground (Figure 81 page 185 and Figure 80 page 184). They are evenly scattered over the lower part of the glen, respecting each other's space (Figure 35, page 62). The most celebrated one is the *Taigh na Banaghaisgeich*, translated by Martin as the 'Amazon's House'. When Martin saw these structures they were believed to be 'some hundred years old'.[8] The likelihood is that they are unusually well-preserved 'Pictish' houses, dating from within the period between roughly AD 400 and AD 900;[9] they are well-preserved because they were re-occupied and refurbished, with the addition of 'horns' – low walls, in plan like the pincers of a lobster, creating forecourts for handling livestock.

Everywhere on the island you will encounter sheep living wild – the ancient Soay breed (Figure 20). Once they were to be found only on Soay – the name means 'Isle of Sheep'. But in 1932 a balanced flock of 107 Soays was transported to Hirta, replacing the blackfaces evacuated in 1930.[10] They are now the subject of a long-term study.[11] Soays are nowadays a familiar sight at rare breed centres. They look much better in their homeland, grazing at the island's edge, their black and ginger bodies standing out against the deep blue of the ocean. Sometimes they may seem to have blended quietly into the Hirta landscape, but then suddenly an ovine drama will be played out, as the brittle sound of clashing horns breaks the silence, or an uxorious ram hustles a line of ewes along a scree-path.

To anyone familiar with the St Kilda literature, there is something quite bland about Village Bay today. It takes effort now to visualise the crofts as they were in the nineteenth century. There would have been scruffy thatched roofs, rope-netted and half-covered in sorrel, and lines of puffins hanging from strings. Numerous dead sea-birds were stuck by their bills into crevices of the walls, to dry before being plucked.[12] At some seasons feathers were everywhere;[13] smells of dung, offal and peat-smoke and many other things – not to mention people – would have assailed the nostrils.[14] There would have been many dogs in the village, an array of comical-looking mongrels and mutts ('one universal cross of Coally, Terrier, Dutch Pug, Lurcher and yellow old wife's dog', says Atkinson helpfully[15]); they were not usually encouraged to pose for photographs. The dogs were pointers,[16] terriers and retrievers rolled into one,[17] and they barked furiously at new arrivals. Every house had a cat,

FIGURE 17.
The 'exclosures' at An Lag. Note the tendency for the cleits to be set in lines.

FIGURE 18.
Hirta's central spine, looking south from near the watchman's house, with the cone of Conachair and the hulking mass of Oiseval in the background.

and there were feral cats among the rocks; yet ravens and hooded crows wandered largely unscathed among the houses.[18] Today the sheep operate like lawn-mowers, and one struggles to envisage patches of corn and potatoes, croftlands dark with freshly-dug earth, and vegetation shaggy enough in summer to conceal the corncrake, with a wide range of 'weeds of cultivation', most visibly 'a splendid crop of corn marigolds'.[19] At some times of the year (though not the season when photographs were taken) straw ricks would have been noticeable.[20] The wildlife has changed; one has to imagine a sea eagle's eyrie on the cliffs of Conachair (but not in later years)[21] and also peregrine falcons and kestrels[22] – and think away recent arrivals like the bonxies, not to mention the most recent newcomers, the even more aggressive arctic skuas. Most of the smaller relics of human habitation have now vanished. In the 1950s, despite a couple of decades of looting, it was still possible to come across piles of equipment and furniture, heaped up within the houses – before over-zealous work parties chucked them into 'huge pits' in the lower meadows.[23] Ironically, the interior of the little-used church is now smart, clean and well

FIGURE 19.
Gleann Mór from the
sea.

FIGURE 20.
A Soay ram.

maintained; in its heyday, before refurbishment in 1898 and 1919,[24] it had an earth floor and benches bodged together from termite-infested driftwood.[25] Gaelic is not often heard on Hirta nowadays, nor the carrying sound of men or women singing in unison, as they often did when they were working.

The most difficult task for the imagination is to visualise the people. Now they stare from the pages of the St Kilda literature, grey-scaled in solemn sepia, faces frozen in deference to the requirements of early photography, masks of Victorian and Nonconformist respectability. Looking at the faces of these adherents of the Free Church, who lived their lives at the edge of the Atlantic, it is easy to recall the peasant images of the mid twentieth-century black and white cinema, and to reach for words like bleak, austere, stoical, unforgiving. But those who knew the St Kildans in the era when these arresting black and white photographs were taken describe them as a courteous, warm-hearted and emotional people, lively and disputatious. Robert Connell was hardly the most objective observer, but his description of the St Kildans as 'an excitable, emotional people' rings true.[26] John Ross, who taught there in 1889–90, described them as 'as nice civil kind and honest a people to live amongst as can be found anywhere'. He mentioned their elaborate emotional displays when parting and when re-united (even when the absence only lasted a week or involved a 'routine' trip to Boreray), and the 'rather lively' Parliament, in which 'all seem to speak at one and the same time'. Ross wondered at times how the women, despite the rigours of their work, 'could have so much time for *ceilidh* going from house to house'. The people were, he said, 'of a very affectionate nature and would do anything for one they liked well'.[27] We cannot hear the shouting, the crying, the chatter and the laughter now; it takes some effort to resist seeing the St Kildans in the photographs as icons of Hirta's history, the particularities of their own lives forgotten.

Early history

The first episode in St Kilda's history which connects with familiar cultural horizons is represented by the simple carved crosses already mentioned, which are currently believed to be 'probably of pre-Norse date'; similar examples occur on Taransay, and at Howmore on South Uist,[28] which has recently, thanks to an excellent piece of architectural analysis by Andrew Reynolds, been revealed as the most important early Christian site in the region.[29] The Hirta crosses are said to reflect the presence of early Irish monks, who would have come here to find peace and solitude, although there is no particular reason to assume that the island was uninhabited at this time. The three churches or chapels mentioned in the literature may well have been constructed at this early period. It is curious how they have vanished so comprehensively. If we take recorded measurements at face value,[30] Christ Church measured 8 m by just under 5 m, rather larger than the small early chapels at Howmore.[31] It was set within a walled enclosure whose perimeter length in paces, quoted by Martin, suggests that the present-day boundary wall, constructed in the 1830s, is on much the same line as the one Martin saw.[32] Apparently the other chapels were also within enclosures;[33] St Brendan's was apparently associated with 'almost entire' 'monkish cells'.[34] It is sad – but not entirely unexpected on a small island where building stones are constantly recycled – that we can no longer see such an interesting triad of early Christian chapels. Before the Reformation, the *Hirteach* celebrated both St Brendan's and St Columba's festivals, in May and June.[35]

Then came the Norsemen, whose presence is demonstrated both by place-names and by some rather elusive archaeological evidence. The first mention of Hirta occurs in an Icelandic saga, which tells how, in the summer of 1202, an Icelandic cleric, on his way to Norway to be consecrated as a bishop, took shelter on 'the islands that are called *Hirtir*' after being blown off course in a storm.[36] (One wonders how closely he resembled the bishops in the famous walrus-ivory chess-sets from Lewis, now exhibited in the British Museum, which date from around this time.) This event occurred only a few decades before the Scandinavians lost control of their Hebridean lands, in 1266. The region was subsequently ruled by various chieftains who were nominally subordinate to the Lords of the Isles; like their predecessors, they exercised their power mostly by sea. There is little in writing to tell us directly about medieval Hirta, Norse or Gaelic, although a few sixteenth-century documents are helpful.[37] By the mid sixteenth century the island was the property of the MacLeods of Skye and Harris, who sent out a 'steward' every summer to collect the rents (paid in kind) and also a priest. The islanders were exempt from military service, and were described as 'a poor barbarous people', 'scant learnit in ony religion'. Sixteenth-century accounts are explicit about the fertility and productivity of Hirta. Mention of sea-birds and seals, and the collection of eggs, implies that the St Kildans were skilled rock-climbers and boatmen. They sometimes used their boats (supplied by the MacLeods) for hunting seals, though they were not keen on using them much for fishing, an attitude which persisted throughout the history of the community. By this time the people must have been using cleits for wind-drying meat and storing eggs. They were cultivating with spades, not ploughs, and they brewed a lethal ale flavoured with nettles.[38] The island's sheep are mentioned with respect; in the late fourteenth century they were described as 'wild sheep ... which can only be caught by hunters',[39] a description which will be readily recognised by anyone who has ever tried to herd Soays.

It was this period which saw the creation of the name 'St Kilda'. There was, in fact, no such saint. If there had been, she might be the patron saint of the misunderstood, for the name derives from early map-makers' mistakes.[40] Eight miles (*c.* 13 km) west of North Uist lie the Haskeir islands. The Norsemen called them *Skildir*, because from afar – and indeed as glimpsed through the window of a distant helicopter – they look like domed shields, floating on the surface of the sea. With the inadequate knowledge and plagiaristic tendencies of late sixteenth-century cartographers, it was easy, given the scale and character of contemporary maps, for 'Skildar' to be read and copied as 'S. Kilda', and for the name to be later misplaced and attached to a different group of islands – the one which included Hirtir, not far away. The pre-Norse name for Hirta seems to be unknown; 'Gaelic' readings of the name *Hiort* as 'the western island', or 'death island', are apparently too problematic to be trusted.[41]

In the sixteenth and seventeenth centuries, Hirta was part of a maritime Hebridean chiefdom – the realm of the MacLeods of Skye (who lived at Dunvegan Castle – Figure 37, page 68) and Harris (where they erected the imposing church (and sea-mark) at Roghadal). In his excellent book, *From Chiefs to Landlords*, Robert Dodgshon has explained how the chieftains of the Highlands and Islands were locked into an intensely competitive system, involving the 'uplifting' of food rents, the maintenance of large retinues of followers, the extortion of forced hospitality from local communities, the promotion of chiefly displays, and fights with neighbouring clans, with cattle raids and seizures of territory. After the demise of the Lordship of the Isles, the dominant political structure in western Scotland from 1266 to 1493, such behaviour seems to have increased. The late sixteenth century was a particularly bad time for inter-clan feuding. In April 1615 Hirta was raided by Coll MacDonald of Colonsay and his crew; they helped themselves to 30 sheep and a considerable quantity of barley, probably the stored rents.[42] The islanders dreaded this kind of attack. They kept a sea-watch from the *Tigh an Fhairfaireadh*, the Watchman's House, on the saddle below Mullach Bi, and had hiding-places among the screes of Mullach Sgar (Figure 41, page 76).

Times were changing. The Scottish Crown – which after 1603 was also the English Crown – was trying to get a grip on the situation in the west. Statutes issued in 1609 and 1616 were designed to civilise the chieftains of the Highlands and Islands, and their henchmen, and to control their exactions by encouraging them to participate more in the cash and market economy.[43] From now on, they were expected to receive rents and other payments in cash rather than food; if this was not possible, they must stick to the agreed amounts. The new statutes banned the practice of sorning – that is, turning up with a large retinue, living off local communities, and carrying away as much food as galleys could hold. But issuing laws was one thing, enforcing them quite another – especially on the outermost islands. Eighty years later, when Martin visited Hirta, he noted that the 'steward', MacLeod's tacksman, who came from the island of Pabbay in the Sound of Harris, had brought a retinue of 50 or 60 people with him.[44] This was illegal as well as burdensome for the Hirta community. Martin claimed that those who had come with the steward, together with the people on the minister's boat, on which Martin had travelled, got through 16,000 seabirds' eggs in three weeks![45] This may be an over-estimate.[46]

A Voyage to St Kilda is an outstanding book – a sympathetic, unsentimental and anthropologically credible portrait of the Hirta community. Martin was well educated, had lived in London and knew the scientific and intellectual agenda of his day. His party's mission was to rid Hirta of 'Roderick the Imposter', a sort of charismatic Christian shaman. Martin was interested in many things – geography and natural history, the lifeways of the people, and their relationship with the steward and the wider world. As a medical man he was interested in the St Kildans' general state of health, which he pronounced good. He noted, however, that when the steward's boat arrived they always succumbed to an infection – the *cnatan nan gall*, the strangers' cold. Having observed its behaviour in various circumstances, the islanders had deduced that the cold was caused by some kind of infection; by the same token, they knew that going abroad was not good for their health. Martin was unjustifiably sceptical: 'I told them plainly, that I thought all this notion of infection was but a meer fancy'.

Hirta apparently contained some 180–200 inhabitants at this time, as well as about 2,000 sheep, 90 cows, and up to 18 horses, which were used mostly for hauling peat. The people liked tobacco, music, dancing and poetry. They were Protestants, although Martin recorded folklore and ritual which owed little to Christian belief. He was fascinated by the communitarianism of the islanders, which found expression in a myriad rules and regulations; and he was enthusiastic about the fertility and productivity of Hirta ('the soil is very grateful to the labourer').

It is as just well that we have Martin's account, because 30 years later the community was almost wiped out by what was probably smallpox. The early years of the eighteenth century were evidently a time of hardship.[47] By 1727, the year of the epidemic, it seems that the population had fallen to a figure of around 120–130. The people may have been without a boat for much of the first decade of the eighteenth century; this would have cut them off from the gannet harvest on Boreray and the adjacent rock stacks, not to mention opportunities for killing seals. The weather cannot have helped. Hirta was not subjected to the massive influxes of sand which blanketed many coastal areas in western Britain in the last decade of the seventeenth century, from Cornwall to the Western Isles. It has been suggested, however, that its disastrous effects in Pabbay may have triggered the illegal sorning expedition to Hirta which Martin witnessed.[48]

There were years, and sometimes runs of years, when the timing of multiple episodes of bad weather affected not only the harvest, but also the success of wildfowling (in terms of the loss of eggs and chicks as well as the difficulties of using boats and scaling stacks). Continuous bad weather sometimes prevented the steward from turning up to reprovision the island. In the early eighteenth century the people may have been suffering from the effects of malnutrition and inadequate food supplies, making them more vulnerable to infection. To make matters worse, this was probably the time when infantile tetanus made its first appearance on Hirta – the dreaded 'sickness of the eighth day'; it led to lockjaw and rapid death in new-born babies.

The arrival of smallpox in 1727 was devastating. Apparently only four adults and 26 children or adolescents survived, and that was partly because three men and eight boys were away fowling on Stac an Armin; they were stranded for nine months over the winter. But the chiefdom soon resettled

Hirta with people from Skye and Harris. It is not obvious that this major repopulation episode led to any great loss of continuity in traditional knowledge and ways of living. Perhaps this shows how fully the children of Hirta had absorbed what their parents had taught them. But in any case, immigrants and 'natives' already had a good deal in common, as I have explained.

Into the modern era

For a long time, the finances of Hebridean chiefs had been on something of a knife-edge. They were under pressure from the Crown, the traditional expectations of their clansfolk, and the costs of their increasingly extravagant lifestyles. In 1773, Samuel Johnson and James Boswell visited Dunvegan Castle and stayed a week, enjoying plenty of wine, venison and good conversation.[49] The chief's immediate predecessor ('The Red Man') had had expensive tastes. A keen gambler, and 'notably intemperate in a hard-drinking age', in 1769 he had raised his tenants' rents by more than 300 per cent. Many threatened to emigrate. At his death, the year before Johnson and Boswell's trip, he had left debts of £40,000.[50] No wonder the visitors were told that 'a Highland chief should now endeavour to do everything to raise his rents, by means of the industry of his people'.[51] The St Kildans' rents were apparently doubled in 1754, and again in the 1760s,[52] though since much of the rent was paid in kind, various concessions were made, and the attitude of the tacksman was critical, how far the St Kildans really felt the impact of the Red Man's financial problems is not clear. But soon more drastic measures were taken to ease the financial problems of the new chief, who was a big spender, a hard drinker and a gambler who once flounced out of Harrogate 'because the stakes for which the people played there were not high enough'.[53] In 1779 the Harris part of the Dunvegan estate, including St Kilda, was sold for £15,000.

The new proprietor was Alexander MacLeod, a former sea captain who had made a fortune in the East, and intended to invest it in his Hebridean estate.[54] During the 1780s he revolutionised the little port of Roghadal at the south-east corner of Harris – improving the harbour, building a capacious boathouse, constructing new port facilities to promote fishing and the cloth industry, and investing in the social infrastructure.[55] He was also keen to develop commercial fishing on St Kilda. Having made his money elsewhere, he was more interested in improving the local infrastructure and promoting the general prosperity of the area than in extracting short-term profits. Captain Alexander was almost certainly responsible for the erection of the Feather Store, which looks like a smaller version of the storehouse which he built at Roghadal, depicted on a contemporary illustration[56] and still standing today. Taking some expert fishermen, he made a successful trial of 'the banks of St Kilda'[57] and the steward's custom of obliging the St Kildans to make salt in a small underground kiln, recorded in 1799,[58] may reflect one of the Captain's projects (they were still doing it in 1815, using a good deal of high quality peat[59]). Perhaps the three boats recorded in 1799 also represented the

Captain's investment.[60] But in 1790 death put an end to his plans; the estate passed to his son, who chose to concentrate on his work with the East India Company. In 1804 St Kilda was sold to Lieutenant-Colonel Donald MacLeod and then in 1813 it passed to Sir John MacPherson MacLeod, who had a distinguished career in India before returning to live in England.[61] In 1804 St Kilda and Pabbay were sold separately from Harris, although Lord Dunmore of South Harris remained the feudal superior of St Kilda – a role which bemused Lord Leverhulme when he took over the South Harris estate in the early 1920s.[62]

In the closing years of the eighteenth century, rich tourists started to arrive. In 1797 the son of Lord Uxbridge came here in his 'gap year' with his tutor, the future Professor of Mineralogy at Cambridge University.[63] The party had guns with them; they shot a fulmar and a puffin (on the wing!) and tried for a gannet; the St Kildans were terrified and impressed.[64] In 1799 young Henry Brougham, later to become Lord Chancellor of England and also inventor of the French Riviera, brought a party of friends, including Charles Stuart, one of the Bute family.[65] The young Sir Thomas Dyke Acland, a country landowner from Devon, first visited Hirta in 1812 with his wife Lydia, after whom he later named his yacht, *The Lady of St Kilda*. He returned in 1834, on the *Lady's* maiden voyage. One year later, this boat, caught on a sandbank on an Australian beach, was to lend its name to a suburb of Melbourne.[66] Acland did some rather vague sketches of St Kilda.[67] The year 1834 also saw the visit of the *Glenalbyn*, the first steamship to come here, its passengers bearing gifts of tobacco and brightly-coloured cotton handkerchiefs for the natives.[68]

Decisive change was on the way. During the 1820s, Hirta was visited by a passionate missionary from north-east Scotland, John MacDonald, alias 'the Apostle of the North'. It was he who raised money to build a church and a manse, and in 1829 introduced Rev. Neil MacKenzie as the new resident minister. This was the Age of Improvement, when many lairds, keen to address their financial problems and make more money from their lands, broke up systems of communal farming in order to create large, profitable farms for rent. People surplus to requirements were settled on holdings too small to support them; they were expected to work in industries such as kelping or fishing, and most of their wages were clawed back as rent. It was MacKenzie who persuaded the St Kildans to abandon the old-established cluster of houses at Village Bay, and the intricate, shifting patchwork of small fields, gardens and hay meadows. Now they would live in 'black-houses' of improved standard, set along a street. New fittings and furniture, including essential tokens of civilisation such as bedsteads and windows with wooden frames and glass panes, were bought with money donated by Sir Thomas Acland, as well as the laird and other well-wishers. In principle, each house stood on its own croft, and the crofts were collectively enclosed within a head dyke cum sea wall, to create the pattern of land enclosure and subdivision which we see today.

In comparison with most north-west Scottish communities, St Kildans were fortunate. They were not forced to work in the kelp or fishing industries. Nor were they evicted to make room for a sheep farm, re-settled on rocky, thin-soiled, ill-drained land, or dragooned into emigrating to north America.[69] Catching sea-birds gave them a cash-producing export – feathers for stuffing eiderdowns. St Kilda's lairds lived far away, with limited opportunities for direct interference. And throughout the nineteenth century numerous 'amateur sociologists and do-gooders', as Tom Steel called them,[70] intervened to ensure that St Kilda moved with the times.

Having set up a demanding programme of religious observance and instruction, by 1838 MacKenzie felt able to bring in a couple of ecclesiastical heavyweights to admit some of his flock to full membership of the Presbyterian Church.[71] But then in 1843 came the Disruption; numerous Scottish Presbyterian ministers broke away to form the Free Church. MacKenzie found himself in a dilemma. Despite his Evangelical enthusiasm, and the fanaticism of some of his flock – who had recently been through a religious revival – he decided not to 'go out'; he left Hirta, and sought a new ministry within the Established Church. The islanders, who wanted to join the Free Church, were faced with obstruction by the laird's factor, who locked up church and manse for several years. It seems that it was partly the issue of religious freedom which persuaded a party of 36 St Kildans to emigrate to Australia in 1852, on the barque *Priscilla*. This was disastrous; 18 of them perished on the voyage, mostly from measles. Of the 12 adults who died on the ship, 10 were St Kildans. Their lack of immunity to mainland diseases had proved fatal.[72] This emigration episode reduced the population from about 110 to around 75.

The year 1860 was eventful. Two naval captains, Thomas and Otter, who were charting the local waters, had started to take an interest in the welfare of the Hirta community. At the same time, a bequest which became known as the Kelsall Fund offered opportunities for improving the island's infrastructure. Work commenced on the construction of a pier. But at the beginning of October there was a ferocious and highly destructive storm. Otter, teaming up with the administrator of the Kelsall Fund, acted quickly and decisively, raising money by public subscription and seeing that the island was resupplied as quickly as possible. The response of Sir John MacPherson MacLeod, the laird, had been inadequate, and it was largely embarrassment and annoyance which led him to pay for the construction of 'modern' houses, with their revolutionary zinc roofs.

For much of the nineteenth century, a major preoccupation of the St Kildans and their well-wishers was the acquisition of a boat big enough to allow the islanders to get to Harris under their own steam (or rather, by sail and oars). This might have enabled them become less dependent on the factor, who controlled the 'price' of almost all of St Kilda's import and export products – or rather, set the exchange rate, since these were not cash transactions. It must have been around this time that better looms were developed, enabling the islanders to produce more tweed cloth for sale (Figure 74, page 164). The new houses made the weaver's life easier; they had larger windows, and no longer contained livestock. Later in the nineteenth century the St Kildans sometimes stayed up most of the night weaving. In 1892 the young A. G. (Alexander) Ferguson, one of the most remarkable of the documented St Kildans, went to Glasgow, soon to set up a shop which sold tweed and other St Kilda products.[73]

In 1863 a trip to Harris ended disastrously, when the islanders' new boat, the *Dargavel*, went down with the loss of eight lives. Getting a good boat was still a priority for the St Kildans in 1875, when John Sands came to Hirta to improve his Gaelic. When he returned the next year, bringing a boat, the factor failed to make the autumn visit, leaving Sands marooned on the island for the winter. While he was there he formed an unfavourable impression of the way the St Kilda was managed (in 1871 it had been bought back by the MacLeods of Dunvegan). Sands got on well with the islanders, and promised to help them. When he got home he wrote to the press, chased up the administrator of the Kelsall Fund, and managed to get the island resupplied. In the columns of *The Scotsman*, and other newspapers, he argued that the winter food supplies were often inadequate, especially after a poor harvest; he accused the factor of exploiting his monopoly trading position to fix the values of St Kilda's imports and exports to the estate's financial advantage (and perhaps his own) – a situation which had attracted adverse comment a century earlier.[74] The debate which followed drew public attention to St Kilda, and sparked a swift commercial response; July 1877 saw the first summer excursion of the *Dunara Castle*, carrying numerous representatives of the professional classes. From now on, the St Kildans enjoyed better communications (at least in summer), and the growing tourist trade (Figure 5, page 9) meant that they did not have to rely on the factor to market everything they produced. A regular summer steamer service was what Sands and the islanders had been asking for.

The 1880s were a pivotal decade in the history of the Hirta community. Infantile tetanus continued to be a problem, keeping the population down and operating unevenly to create a shortage of marriageable young men. The unprogressive 25-year reign of the elderly minister, John MacKay, continued until 1889. The laird and his factor were becoming increasingly conscious that when things went wrong on Hirta, the matter could no longer be concealed; it became a subject of concern and debate. The islanders had learnt how to use their well-wishers to play upon the sympathy of the wider world; at Dunvegan they came to be seen as spoilt darlings. Now the tourists bought the St Kildans' tweed and knitwear, as well as other products such as birds' eggs and postcards. Tourism encouraged the diversification of an already flexible economy, and increasing amounts of cash were in circulation. It looked a better bet to use the earnings from weaving to pay for imported food and other modern household 'necessities', rather than relying upon the increasingly undependable produce of croft and garden. This was the age of

Mr. Gladstone, late Victorian ideas of progress, and a more inclusive electorate. Government and other agencies were increasingly trying to promote the social and economic welfare of outlying regions. From 1884 there was usually a resident teacher on Hirta, though there were a few intermissions; during the last 40 years of the community's existence the role of teacher was sometimes taken by the minister and/or his wife. The purpose-built school (Figure 75, page 164) was constructed in 1898 as an annexe of the church. Pupils learnt to speak and write English, allowing them to communicate better with the tourists and potentially to make their way in the outside world.[75] A Post Office was established in 1900, initially in the manse.[76] In 1901–2 the Congested Districts board built a concrete jetty.[77] From the 1880s there was a resident nurse on Hirta (though with a gap between 1892 and 1914).[78] The islanders were vaccinated against smallpox in 1873.[79] And in the early 1890s, the scourge of infantile tetanus was at last overcome, thanks largely to the energy and intelligence of the new minister, Angus Fiddes.

Numerous scientists arrived, by steam or sail.[80] There were naturalists, like the Kearton brothers who came here in 1896, or geologists like Sir Archibald Geikie (whose studies took place in 1895 and 1896).[81] Others took an interest in the physical and mental health of the islanders, the state of agriculture on Hirta, and the economic and social welfare of the community. There was also the vexed question of its future. In June 1883 the minister and two islanders gave evidence to the Napier Commission, which was concerned with the condition of crofters and cottars; a one-day session was held on Hirta itself. In October 1885 Malcolm MacNeill, Inspecting Officer of the Board of Supervision, visited on HMS *Jackal*, on behalf of the Government, producing his official report a few months later.[82] Potentially, various individuals and public bodies were in a position to promote progress and development. The Navy was involved in several supply missions[83] and several celebrated London entrepreneurs got in on the act – Sir Thomas Lipton, Gordon Selfridge, and Joe Lyons of Corner House fame.[84] A *Daily Mirror* campaign led to the establishment of a radio station in the Factor's House; it was used during the winter of 1913–14.[85]

During the First World War the Royal Navy established a radio station on Hirta; armed trawlers and whalers sheltered in Village Bay, sometimes steaming out to engage German U-boats, one of which came in and shelled several buildings in an unsuccessful effort to destroy the radio station (the islanders received no compensation). The St Kildans had a good war; they were paid a daily allowance for manning lookout posts on Oiseval and Mullach Geal (in both locations, cleits proved useful) and digging trenches for telephone lines.[86] But at the onset of the conflict the market for Harris tweed collapsed. The community was already in demographic decline, which was irreversible without fresh immigration. The naval personnel were lively emissaries of the modern world, with their urban outlook, fascinating possessions, and talk of life-styles of which the St Kildans could only dream. The older people were reluctant to leave; their children were torn between looking after their parents and attempting to make their way in the world. At the 1921 census the population was still 73, including the nurse and the family of the minister. But by 1925, emigration had brought it down to 46.

I will not dwell here on the poignant story of the evacuation of the community, at the end of August 1930; it has been well told elsewhere.[87] I take the view that people – and communities – are best remembered for the times when they were at the height of their powers, not for their deathbed performances.

CHAPTER THREE

Men of Stone

....

I was supplied with a light and boldly crawled in, and sketched, and
measured, &c., not without a consciousness of that stern joy which
the prospect of becoming a victim to archaeology must ever produce.

Captain F. W. L. Thomas (1870) p.158, on visiting a St Kilda wall-bed.

FIGURE 21.
Finlay MacQueen
exhibits a triumph of
the taxidermist's art.

The earliest inhabitants of the Western Isles are archaeologically elusive.
Around 6000 or 5000 BC these islands were quite well wooded, mostly with
birch and hazel.[1] Analyses of sequences of pollen grains preserved in peat
bogs have picked up changes in vegetation cover, and also layers containing charcoal, which have been interpreted as possible evidence for the activities of
Mesolithic hunters and gatherers.[2] But no stone tools from these times have
yet been discovered. The period of the earliest farming – the Neolithic – which
began somewhat before 3500 BC, has left more tangible traces; approximately
50 chamber tombs (also known as 'megalithic tombs') can still be seen.[3] They
were built mostly of large slabs and covered by round or sometimes long
cairns. Most of them are in the Uists; Barpa Langass on North Uist is the most
striking example. These megalithic tombs would have contained bones of the
(selected) dead; they were powerful reminders of ancestors who had first
claimed these lands. The southern part of the Long Island was evidently an
attractive area for settlement, for there are far more chamber tombs here than
anywhere else in the Hebrides, Inner or Outer. Pollen analysis on South Uist
and Barra has demonstrated declining tree cover and spreading bog in different
places at various times, including during the Neolithic and Bronze Age.[4] The
spread of bog at the expense of woodland was a natural process, but browsing
livestock also prevented the regeneration of trees, and people may also have
been burning heathland to improve pasture quality.[5] Not very many Neolithic
settlement sites are known, and the few excavated ones may not be 'typical'.
A major problem for archaeologists is that numerous sites must lie below the
peat, or under the blanket of blown sand on the machair (the coastal plain).
Around 7000 BC the sea was at least 4–5 metres below its present level, and
the coastal plain was a good deal wider in Mesolithic and early Neolithic times;
then the sea started rising rapidly, and some places occupied in the Neolithic
will have been submerged.[6]

We do not know whether farming was introduced by boatloads of immigrants, or whether contact with farming people across the Minch would have

*St Kilda and the
Wider World: Tales
of an Iconic Island*

been enough to change the lifeways of local hunters and gatherers. It is probably wrong to think in terms of these simplistic alternatives. But it does seem that the Neolithic peoples of the Western Isles had far-reaching cultural connections; paradoxically, they were probably not a notably 'insular' people. There were links, for instance, with Orkney and Shetland. The chamber tombs of the Western and Northern Isles show certain similarities,[7] and some of the pottery found in the Western Isles is made in a style called Unstan Ware, which was first recognised as characteristic of the Orkney Neolithic. Recently, striking similarities detected by Alison Sheridan[8] between sherds of a pottery vessel from a chamber tomb at Achnacreebeag, just up the coast from Oban, and pottery from north-west France, dating from around 4000 BC, have reanimated prehistorians' long-standing belief in the antiquity and importance of the seaways of western Britain. Some northern Scottish chamber tombs, the passage graves, represent a tradition with roots much further south, in Ireland and north-west France. There can be little doubt that Neolithic Hebrideans understood the sea and its ways, and knew how to stretch hides over wooden frames to make sea-going currachs.

The Western Isles were attractive to settlers. Small islands provide longer stretches of accessible resource-rich coastline than many coastal locations on the mainland. Hunting large mammals such as deer should have been easier here (once they had been imported[9]). There was the broad western coastal plain, and plenty of woodland. How soon would Neolithic people have reached St Kilda? The distance is about twice that from Skye to the Long Island. Sailors would have waited for settled anticyclonic conditions, and they could take advantage of prevailing winds and currents for the return journey. I do not think it would have taken them centuries to pluck up their courage. In any case we now have concrete evidence that Neolithic people did reach Hirta. During one of my early fieldwork campaigns, trying to get a look at the soil profile at the top of the low cliff at Village Bay, I discovered a spot not far east of the main consumption dyke where a large dump of earth and stones, shoved over the edge by a military bulldozer, gives the archaeologist a leg up. It was here that I came across the first sherds of Neolithic pottery to be found on Hirta – incised rim sherds of 'Hebridean Ware', sticking half-exposed out of the section.[10]

Experts used to be cautious about the idea that Hirta might have been settled in the Neolithic. A case in point was Mike Walker's interpretation of a pollen sequence from Gleann Mór, which he analysed in the early 1980s. At a depth of about 180 cm, ribwort plantain starts up, and is continuously present thereafter, higher up the profile. Walker noted similar sudden appearances of this plant in Lewis and Shetland, which probably indicate the beginnings of farming in those regions. But as he pointed out, there was no other evidence to support a similar interpretation at St Kilda.[11] Conventional wisdom at the time suggested that the earliest settlement on Hirta was represented by some stone settings known as 'boat-shaped structures', situated above the 1830s head dyke and near An Lag. These were thought to have contained human burials and to date from the Bronze Age;[12] it was said that there were good parallels for them on the west Scottish mainland. Nowadays they are interpreted as small cleits which have been partly dismantled, and they are probably more recent than the Bronze Age. To the north-west of the 'exclosures' at An Lag some of them are arranged in short lines extending up the lower flanks of Conachair (Figure 17, page 24), just like the lines of *intact* cleits beside the paths to the Gap and down into Gleann Mór.

Discovery: working with stone

As a result of recent discoveries, the early prehistory of Hirta now looks much more interesting. The story starts in August 1994, when I joined work party no. 6, organised by the National Trust for Scotland. There are six work parties every summer. Each consists of a dozen volunteers, who stay in the re-roofed houses for a fortnight, working on an archaeological excavation, or doing maintenance work. Not wanting a busman's holiday, I had signed up for a maintenance party.

Our working hours gave me time to explore. To help find my way around, I taped the Royal Commission's archaeological plan[13] to a piece of hardboard. The most obvious object of interest was a complex of large banks and robbed-out stone walls located in the area near the spring at Tobar Childa (Figure 22). They looked like the boundaries of quite an old field system – although they were largely ignored in the St Kilda literature. And then something else attracted my attention. In the little museum in House 3, I noticed a small case containing three or four chunks of stone, labelled 'stone implements'. These looked interesting; shouldn't they be prehistoric? And then one evening, I spotted a small piece of dark stone protruding from the eroded turf cap of a cleit. In shape and size it was like the cross-section of a mackerel, not far from the tail. Was I perhaps looking at a fragment of something larger – maybe the profile of the tip of a pointed stone implement, shaped by striking flakes off a core, like the ones in the museum? I reached up and pulled the stone out; that was exactly what it was! And then a thought struck me: what if there were more stone implements – or fragments of them – in other cleits? It took only 15 minutes or so to establish that this was indeed the case. Amongst the oatmeal-coloured stones of the cleits, dark implements stood out. Even though they were virtually all broken, it soon became clear that they had once been quite large – 20 or 30 cm long, 8 or 10 cm wide, and 2–3 cm thick (Figure 27, page 48 and Figure 33, page 56). Some were quite crude, but others had beautifully flaked surfaces; in terms of the balance and distribution of weight, they felt good to hold in the hand.

This was exciting. Nothing in the museum display or the literature had suggested that stone tools were so widespread, or so well made. The next question was – what was the source of the dark stone? In geological terms, the answer seemed obvious; it occurs on the western side of Village Bay, and forms the screes below Mullach Sgar. The geological map on display in the museum

*St Kilda and the
Wider World: Tales
of an Iconic Island*

FIGURE 22.
The Street from the
south. Note the banks
of the Tobar Childa
field system, beyond
the 1830
head dyke.

called it Mullach Sgar dolerite, and showed that it gives way to the oatmeal-coloured granophyre of Conachair and Oiseval along a line running beside and just east of the Abhainn Mór burn. This line shows up as a colour change in the boulders on the beach (Figure 23).

The tops of the Mullach Sgar screes form an array of strange shapes which, to judge from old photographs, have been stable since at least the late nineteenth century. (A few modern denizens of Hirta have given them names; The Cat (or Sooty), The Coffee Pot (or the FA Cup), Robert Morley Smoking a Cigar.) Some way above these, and on either side of the great central cleft now known as The Chimney (though its old name is Clash na Bearnaich) the bases of the crags lie at much the same level on the hillside. At the north end of these, I had noticed a couple of dark openings, looking like the tops of blocked-up caves. But could natural caves occur in dolerite? I was reminded of an exhilarating day spent visiting the stone axehead quarries at Great Langdale in the English Lake District, which date from the Neolithic, around 3500 BC. I had had the good fortune to be shown round by an expert – Mark Edmonds, who was doing his doctoral research there and also co-directing some excavations. After negotiating mildly dangerous terrain, with piles of sharp-edged stone waste flakes ringing beneath our boots, Mark took me to see a kind of 'cave' – actually a little Neolithic quarry, with room for only one excavator, who was uncovering layers of charcoal which revealed that fire had been used to break up the rock. This was flaked to make 'rough-outs', and then taken off the mountain to be ground and polished into finished axe-blades. So perhaps the Hirta 'caves' were ancient quarries too?

During the three or four days which remained, I searched a sample of cleits at Village Bay, to get some idea of how widely the implements were distributed. I found them as far east as cleit 1, which is close to the Feather Store, and as far north as cleit 145, outside the head dyke and near Tobar Childa. I also looked on the steep lower slopes of Mullach Sgar for evidence of their manufacture. The screes were obviously natural, having formed from the crags above; many critical areas, including the mouths of the 'caves', had an almost unbroken grass cover. However, some small outlying rock outcrops at the northern end of the area had a 'bashed' appearance, with scatters of sharp-edged chunks of rock below them. In this zone I found a fist-sized beach-pebble. This was highly indicative. Only a human could have brought this stone up here – intending to use it to work stone? Closer to The Chimney, there were small, sheep-eroded pockets of bare ground. And in one of these, I discovered sharp stone flakes, the debris of tool-making. There is no mistaking the ringing sound made by waste flakes disturbed by boots or scrabbling hands; it is quite different from the dull scrunch of natural scree. And among the flakes – yes, a beautifully shaped stone tool! Two or three hours' exploration was all I had time for. But I had found enough to suggest quarrying and implement manufacture at Clash na Bearnaich, and to persuade Mark Edmonds – who had become a leading expert on stone tools since my visit to Langdale – to join me in a four-year campaign of fieldwork.[14]

We carried out a systematic survey of the Mullach Sgar screes, often using the terrace-like paths created by many generations of sheep. Only in one or two places did we find patches of waste flakes. But we did come across more fist-sized stones derived from the beach. The stone in the screes would have been too weathered to provide good knapping material; the tools must have been made from dolerite quarried higher up. And then we started to find one or two larger 'beach-pebbles', about 30 cm in diameter. These we interpreted as mauls for use in quarrying stone – and indeed one or two of them have clearly suffered impact damage. We began to explore further up, at the level of the 'caves', which were at the northern end of a long, narrow, grassy 'shoulder' which continued south of The Chimney. We were cautious at first, wondering how far the 'caves' might have been created by natural weathering. But then we found a flaked tool roughout actually protruding from thick grass

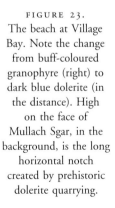

FIGURE 23.
The beach at Village Bay. Note the change from buff-coloured granophyre (right) to dark blue dolerite (in the distance). High on the face of Mullach Sgar, in the background, is the long horizontal notch created by prehistoric dolerite quarrying.

cover, high on the hillside, just below the shoulder and some way south of the Chimney. There was no doubt about it; tools – or more likely 'blanks' destined for finer working at home – had been made up here, high on the shoulder; sporadic waste flakes can still be found in this area, despite the general cover of thick grass. One day we spotted what looked like a new 'cave'. But this one was halfway up The Chimney, on the south side. Lungs heaving, braving the chattering fulmars with their potential for pestilential puking, we investigated. Again, only the upper part of the 'cave' was open to inspection. However, thrusting a ranging pole deep inside convinced us that this cannot be a natural feature.

The most dramatic view of these quarries comes when the sun is high in the western sky, for instance at four or five o'clock on a July afternoon. The main quarry level is highlighted by the shadow which captures the sharpness of the long notch cut along the face of the crags (Figure 23). And the sun has made more critical contributions to our archaeological understanding. In 1994 I found myself wondering about the humps and hollows to the north of the Clash na Bearnaich crags, on the steep but less precipitous hillside of Gearraidh Ard. The pitted surface reminded me of prehistoric quarries which Mark had shown me in the Lake District. I noted this in the article announcing these discoveries.[15] Later, however, Mark and I convinced ourselves that we were probably looking at natural features – variations in the character of the bedrock, combined with centuries of gulley erosion, landslips, peat growth, and so on. And then one day at the end of August 1997, around six or seven in the evening, as the sun was just about to dip behind the high ridge to the west, I looked up and was astonished. The Gearraidh Ard hill-slopes were casting some extraordinary shadows (Figure 24). Their vaguely undulating surface was transformed. It looked as if numerous bites of different sizes had been taken out of the hillside. There was no time to stand and stare; the image had to be captured on film immediately, before the sun disappeared over the hill. When my slides came back from processing, I was able to study the image in detail. There seemed no doubt about it; the hillside was covered in quarries.

In 1998 I went back with a small team, to make a plan of these newly-discovered features (Figure 29, page 50). It was a difficult task; outlines once sharp are now masked by soil and unbroken grass cover. Erosion, land-slips and the growth of peat have indeed helped to confuse matters. In some places, however, it seems quite easy to pick out small, distinct quarries, each with a definable low 'face' and a 'floor'. There are also areas where a long, low, face seems to have been worked, a less developed version of the notch cut at Clash na Bearnaich. Most of the quarries are quite high on the hillside, and they also occur on the flatter area of Am Blaid, just over the skyline seen from Village Bay.

One major quarry is no longer with us. In 1957, after the RAF had been talked out of bulldozing the abandoned houses,[16] they needed a quarry for roadstone. As it happens, the location they chose at Creagan Breac was on the site of a much older quarry. Ironically, we know this because it is visible on the RAF's own vertical air photos, taken only nine days after the start of Operation Hardrock (Figure 25). The old quarry was a long, grass-covered bench, just like the one at Clash na Bearnaich. In the photo, its face is in shadow, but closer inspection reveals a series of bite-like features which would be consistent with stone-getting. In photographs taken before 1957, looking west, the ancient quarry is visible in the background. On an early colour photograph taken from an aeroplane in July 1947 by the naturalist Eric Hosking, the gash in the hillside can clearly be seen.[17]

There may be further revelations to come. I have noticed that evening shadows in mid-July are subtly different from those cast at the end of August. Occasionally one catches a glimpse of what looks like a pathway, or part of one, zigzagging or going straight up the hillside. Could these paths be old ones, serving the quarries? In 2003, the mid-July sun was picking out quarry pits much higher on the shoulder of Mullach Sgar, near the top of The Chimney. I had not noticed them before.

We should excavate a sample of the quarries. So far, we have only dug three test pits, each one metre square. The most revealing one, Pit C, was dug on the Gearraidh Ard hillside, on what looked like a spur of untouched ground between two small quarries with distinctive apron-like floors; we expected to find a pile of quarry waste sitting on an undisturbed natural profile. What we actually found was a 35–55 cm layer of earth, highly mottled and containing rounded and weathered stones and others which were sharp and spall-like, as well as voids; we interpreted this as mixed, dumped material. It was sitting on top of a developed soil, whose upper (A) horizon was represented by a very dark, humus-rich clay, some 6–12 cm thick, a horizon much too coherent to represent simply the downward leaching of humus through the soil. It looks as if this soil had developed over time, probably on a pre-existing quarry floor; if this is the case, our 'untouched spur' was really a long pile of waste, deposited on the floor of an older quarry. More importantly, this profile suggests that in some places there could have been many years between episodes of quarrying, time enough for soil to build up on old quarry floors.

Stone tools at Village Bay

What about the stone tools for which the quarries were created? Mark and I decided to make a thorough search of all structures at Village Bay, and also piles of cleared stone. It was tough going at times, particularly inside the cleits, where we encountered dead sheep, sheep-shit, mud and water, not to mention fulmars retching ominously and entrances constricted enough to evoke the travails of Winnie the Pooh. Some of the stone tools were loose and could be handled, but others were firmly wedged in place. When our work was over, we had a map which showed how many stone tools we had found at each search location, and also sites where we had drawn a blank (Figure 26).

We had to think about the uses of these tools. We knew that Hirta had always been virtually treeless, so they were not primarily axe- or adze-blades, though some could have been used for working imported wood.[18] They might have been employed to some extent for butchering seals or livestock. But it is hard to avoid concluding that they were mostly used as hoes or mattocks (Neil MacKenzie, writing of the 1830s, described a heavy, adze-shaped hoe called a *caibe* as a multi-purpose tool, used for breaking clods, improving the seed bed, destroying weeds, and making rigs.[19]) Cultivating the land, year after year – and regularly *breaking* hoe-blades in the process – is the only activity which would account for the sheer number of tools found at Village Bay, and the sustained demand reflected by the extent of quarrying (though a few hoe-blades were made from beach-pebbles, and a few from granophyre rather than dolerite). It is worth emphasising that hardly any of them are undamaged. Some have been made with narrow haft-ends, making it easier to bind them to wooden handles. The requirement for wood poses interesting questions; it probably implies regular contact with the Long Island, although driftwood from North America would also have been available.[20] Sometimes there is quite a sharp distinction between the body of the tool and the hafting tang, and occasionally the 'shoulder' between the tang and the body of the implement is very pronounced, demonstrating that a few blades were shaped rather like narrow, heart-shaped table tennis bats.

Our trickiest task was to interpret our map of the distribution of hoe-blades at Village Bay. Archaeologists' training in sampling theory does not prepare us for situations where artefacts can be picked up in standing stone structures set in undisturbed grassland. Mark and I had to consider how far our map represented the 'original' distribution of stone tools, and how far it reflected the availability of sampling points. Areas with numerous cleits and walls may produce high numbers of stone tools – or much lower frequencies. In zones with few search opportunities, just a few artefacts may be highly meaningful.

FIGURE 24. Shadows cast on the slopes of Gearraidh Ard at the end of August 1997 reveal numerous ancient dolerite quarries.

FIGURE 25.
The ancient quarry at
Creagan Breac (from an
RAF photograph taken
in April 1957) just
before it was
obliterated by the
roadstone quarry. The
cluster of cleits is
illustrated on Figure 15.

FIGURE 26.
The distribution of
dolerite hoe-blades at
Village Bay.

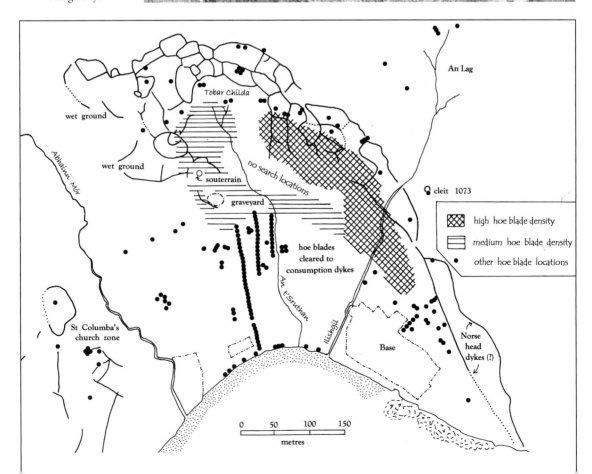

An Lag

Tobar Childa

wet ground

wet ground

Abhainn Mór

souterrain

graveyard

no search locations

cleit 1073

high hoe blade density

medium hoe blade density

other hoe blade locations

hoe blades
cleared to
consumption dykes

An t-Sruthan

Ilishgil

Base

Norse
head
dykes (?)

St Columba's
church zone

0   50   100   150

metres

We also had to consider how and why these implements have arrived at their present locations, mostly nineteenth-century structures. How much have the hoe-blades been moved around? Were they perhaps cleared from land some distance from where we recovered them – as might be the case for the ones in the consumption dykes? And how many of them had once been incorporated in earlier structures, now demolished? We think this has happened in the zone where the density of implements is greatest – in the upper parts of the crofts just below the 1830s head dyke, in a belt stretching from the House 8 croft to the area behind the Factor's House. Here many tools are in cleits, which are perched as high as possible, on well-drained sites, the better to wind-dry their contents. Many sit on platforms cut into the tops of the massive banks of the Tobar Childa field system. Immediately behind the houses, these old field banks have been truncated in an attempt to get rid of them. Further back, on higher, rockier ground, they were left intact, perhaps deliberately, in order to serve as high stances for the cleits. The obvious conclusion is that when field-banks were demolished, mostly in MacKenzie's time, their stone content, including broken hoe-blades, was re-used for building cleits. A few of the hoe-blades may have come from local cultivated surfaces and small clearance cairns, but probably not many were actually dug up in the nineteenth century; cultivation would have taken place mostly on raised, manured beds, or in plantie-crues, without deep disturbance of the soil.

All this considered, there are hoe-blades throughout the area enclosed by MacKenzie's head dyke, apart from the north-western zone, which I am inclined to believe has always been wet, peaty ground, best avoided by cultivators. What happens *above* the head dyke, in the area where the Tobar Childa field system is best preserved? In the zone nearest to the Conachair screes, Mark and I found no implements. Here the cleits are quite 'pure'; it made sense for their builders to take stone from the screes, or to lever up boulders, put chocks under them, and break them up (plenty of evidence for this can be seen on the ground). But further east there *is* a scatter of tools beyond the 1830s head dyke. Some must have been found by people gardening in exclosures in the nineteenth century, and put in or onto walls. As the map shows, there are a few tools in the walls of the exclosures at An Lag, and even one or two in the cleits which run in a line from here up to The Gap.

Dating the hoe-blades

But how old were these hoe-blades? Did they occur in seriously old structures, such as the *Taigh an t-Sithiche*, the Fairies' House, not far from the graveyard (Figure 69, page 152)? This is an Iron Age souterrain – a stone-lined, slab-roofed 'underground passage' just below ground surface, which should date from somewhere around the time of Christ, give or take the three or four centuries.[21] The Fairies' House came to light during cultivation in the early 1840s, probably after one of its roof-slabs fell in. The area was under potatoes in the summer of 1876 when John Sands carried out an 'excavation' here; he had to compensate the tenant.[22] Later, Kearton dug here in 1896, Mathieson in 1927, Ritchie in 1974. In spite of their efforts, we know little of the souterrain's history. As one might expect, it has produced Iron Age pottery. Mark and I found one or two broken hoe-blades in the fabric of the structure, and there is a complete one from the souterrain in the Royal Museum in Edinburgh. So we know that the hoe-blades date from at least the Iron Age. Probably they were already around when the trench for the souterrain was dug, and got casually incorporated into its structure.

Most of the hoe-blades are probably a good deal older than the Iron Age. Identical tools have been found, oddly enough not in the Western Isles but in Orkney and Shetland, where they are known as flaked stone bars. While I was making these discoveries on Hirta, Ann Clarke was putting the finishing touches to her thesis on the 'coarse stone tools' of northern Scotland.[23] She had a fairly limited number of sites to work with. The earliest 'flaked stone bars' known so far were found in considerable numbers at the Neolithic site of Scord of Brouster, in the Walls area of the west Mainland of Shetland, where they date from about 3400 BC. The site consists of a fairly discrete cluster of six or seven walled 'fields', covering an area only about 150m across, as well as numerous clearance cairns and three stone-walled, roughly circular houses (which seem to have been occupied in sequence rather than all at the same time[24]). Here, the hoe-blades ('flaked stone bars') were accompanied by ground and polished stone ard-tips (an ard is a simple form of plough). Many of these implements were broken, and had been incorporated into the walls of houses and fields. It seems that hoe-blades and ard-tips went together as tools of cultivation, as one might expect, for they were found in similar numbers relative to each other all over this site and others. Many of these stone tools have been found in Shetland, in association with prehistoric fields and houses;[25] one or two small quarries are known, though beach material was sometimes used. In Orkney, flaked stone bars tend to be found on sites of the Early Bronze Age, after 2000 BC, especially in the earlier phases. They are present, although not dominant, on later Bronze Age and Iron Age sites, although it seems that their use was tailing off by that time.[26] In some cases they may have been 'residual' on these late prehistoric sites – that is, just kicking around, left over from earlier times, or perhaps still in sporadic use. So the quarries and hoe-blades on Hirta are likely to be prehistoric – at least Iron Age, but more likely Neolithic and/or earlier Bronze Age, if we also take into account the finding of Hebridean Ware on Hirta and the Neolithic links already mentioned between the Western Isles and the Northern Isles.

A new prehistory for Hirta

As relics of Hirta's early prehistory, the quarries and broken hoe-blades bulk large, in terms of sheer physical presence. But the standing structures at Village Bay contain other interesting stones. Many of these are beach cobbles imported by humans ('manuports'). The majority are dolerite, and they have

FIGURE 27.
The three most common prehistoric stone tools at Village Bay – a hoe-blade, a pounder/grinder, and a Skaill knife.

come from quite a restricted zone in the centre of the beach, around the mouth of Abhainn Mór (the eastern and western flanks of the beach are composed of larger, squarer, more angular boulders, the product of relatively recent coastal erosion). Most manuports seem to have been used without modification – perhaps as loom-weights, or thatch-weights, for example – but some have clearly been employed as tools, and shaped or damaged in the process; others have been cracked and split by fire. With Ann Clarke, I have recently been investigating them.

If the hoe-blades reflect sustained prehistoric agriculture, there must have been stone querns and rubbers for grinding grain into flour. The most conspicuous finds are 'pounder/grinders' – almost cylindrical pebbles, rounded and shaped by wear at one or both ends, so that they look like pestles (Figure 27 and Figure 33, page 56). These too are good to hold in the hand; the even distribution of weight makes them feel ready for use. The heaviest weigh just over 2 kg, and are about 20 cm long (though there are a few even heavier ones); one or two are slightly 'waisted' with scratches around the circumference, which may suggest the chafing of string, and/or attempts to make a notch to secure a haft or binding. More common are smaller ones, presumably hand-held, weighing around 500 gm and not much more than 10 cm long. In general these tools must have been used mostly in food preparation, or for softening various materials. In the Faeroes they were traditionally used to grind the root of tormentil,[27] which was used in the tanning of sheepskin – as it was on St Kilda.[28] Some have chipped edges, evidently caused by hammering against a resistant surface. It must have been annoying to have a favourite pestle damaged; but one could always use the other end, and there were – literally – many other pebbles on the beach. At Village Bay, pounder/grinders are quite scarce compared with broken hoe-blades, but their distribution is just as widespread. In the Northern Isles, as far as we know at present, they first appeared in the Bronze Age, and were very common in the Iron Age. Once there were deep mortars, trough querns as they are sometimes called, to go with them. A century ago Richard Kearton illustrated a possible example,[29] and noted that old 'querns' were to be seen around the village; it's clear that he did not mean the rotary querns then still in use, which he called 'mills'.[30] These trough querns have gone now. They were sold as souvenirs to tourists in the twentieth century; Alasdair Alpin MacGregor describes the St Kildans on the eve of the evacuation, 'searching the old byres and houses for querns and cruisies and the like, in anticipation of the visit of the last batch of tourists'.[30] Any querns which remained were probably looted more recently. So in the summer of 2004 it was exciting to discover one survivor – half a trough-quern, languishing just above high water mark, at the bottom of a pile of stones pushed over the cliff in 1957 by a military bulldozer knocking out a gap in the long consumption dyke at Village Bay, to make room for the new road (Figure 28).

After hoe-blades and pounder/grinders, the next most conspicuous stone tool is another one familiar from the Northern Isles – the Skaill knife. A Skaill knife is a flake tool, manufactured by throwing a beach-pebble against a stone anvil to create a flake which forms a near-circular butchering-tool, with a sharp cutting edge where the external surface of the pebble meets the flat side where the flake has been detached (Figure 27). Skaill knives are numerous in the Orkney Neolithic (around 3700–1800 BC) but they do occur considerably later, and they are also found on a Shetland Bronze Age site.[32] There are also a few 'flaked cobbles' on Hirta – beach-pebbles with maybe three or four flakes struck off them (so that they look like the early pebble tools from Olduvai Gorge). Flaked tools also occur on Neolithic and Bronze Age sites in the Northern Isles. And sometimes Hirta beach-pebbles were used as cores, from which small flakes were struck for use, presumably as tools too small to be incorporated into walls and discovered by landscape archaeologists. And there are a few distinctive 'Hirta tortoises'. A Hirta tortoise was made by splitting a beach cobble in half and then knocking flakes off its circumference; it may be no more than a distinctive form of core.

Among the most intriguing finds at Village Bay are larger, heavy 'boulders' which resemble small, slightly domed pouffes, or roughly cylindrical pillows. The larger ones, those over 30 cm in length or diameter, are quite numerous and widespread, and there are some above the 1830s head dyke. What were these large beach stones used for? Quite a lot of them are undamaged, or

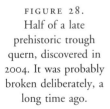

FIGURE 28. Half of a late prehistoric trough quern, discovered in 2004. It was probably broken deliberately, a long time ago.

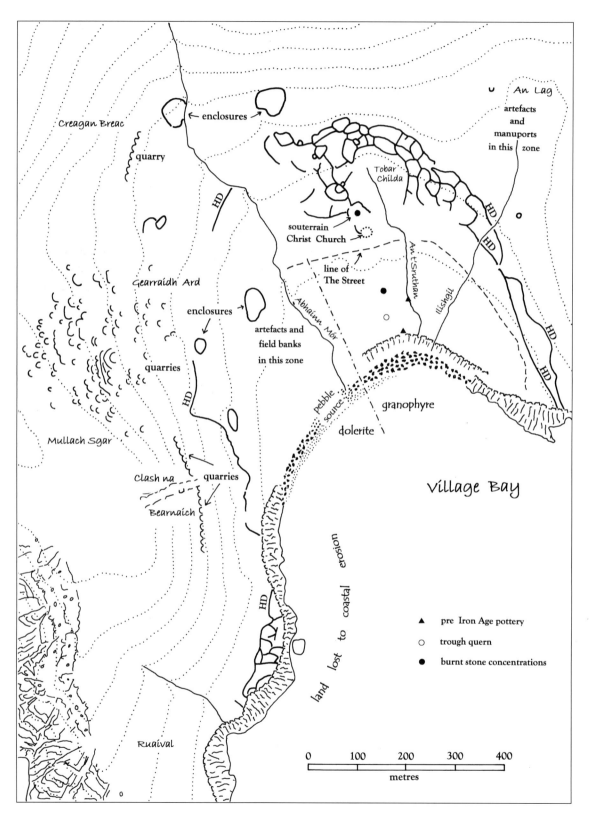

Creagan Breac

quarry

enclosures

An Lag

artefacts
and
manuports
in this zone

Tobar
Childa

souterrain
Christ Church

line of
The Street

Gearraidh Ard

enclosures

artefacts and
field banks
in this zone

quarries

Mullach Sgar

Clash na

quarries

Bearnaich

Abhainn Mòr

An t-Sruthan

Uishgiu

pebble
source

granophyre

dolerite

Village Bay

land lost to coastal erosion

Ruaival

▲ pre Iron Age pottery

○ trough quern

● burnt stone concentrations

0   100   200   300   400

metres

50

apparently so (some are only partly observable because they are wedged tight within walls). Were they used as seats, pillows, or perhaps as anvils or mauls? All these suggested uses are 'domestic' rather than agricultural. Such very large beach-pebbles are too heavy to have been casually moved around like smaller stones, in baskets of compost; most of them should be quite near the places where they were originally used. Because of their distribution, it is tempting to conclude that they belong to the same phase of prehistory as the hoe-blades. If this is true, and their uses were 'domestic', houses must have been dispersed across the landscape, like the ones associated with Neolithic and Bronze Age settlement in Shetland.[33]

Fields and enclosures

More potential evidence for prehistoric settlement is provided by primitive-looking field systems and enclosures (Figures 29, 30). The most obvious field system is the one around Tobar Childa (Figures 29, Figure 22, page 40). It consists of a network of small, irregular 'fields', occupying an arc which extends from just north of the souterrain, runs above the Tobar Childa spring, and continues probably as far east as the Ilishgil burn. The northern, upper edge of the system is clear-cut. It seems that the lower edge was wrapped around an unenclosed zone (of meadow?) around Tobar Childa and the An t-Sruthan burn. The 'fields' are edged by thick stony banks (though in places these take the form of 'robber-trenches' where stone has been grubbed out in later centuries). The pattern incorporates ovoid, D-shaped or roughly circular 'enclosures' of varying size; these were probably built at an early stage, since the field-banks tend to run up to them. Further east, the southern edges of the fields have been truncated, almost certainly in the 1830s. Stone tools have been found in varying numbers throughout the area covered by these fields (Figure 26). Further primitive fields occur on the south-west side of Village Bay, beside the cliffs on the way to Ruaival; their distinctive thick banks have provided most of the boundaries of a set of more recent cultivated fields. In 2004, in a tumbled modern wall here, I found two pounder/grinders and two beach-cobble manuports. Prehistoric artefacts and beach cobbles have also been found on the knoll above the helipad (where there are stretches of old-looking walls). The other interesting area lies above the head dyke, stretching up to the An Lag corrie, Glen Beag as it was sometimes known.[34] There are a few artefacts and manuports in this zone; we found a hoe-blade in cleit 1073, which post-dates a very small walled enclosure. We also found two hoe-blades and a beach cobble on the surface west of the An Lag exclosures, close to a semi-circular wall, presumably the remnant of an enclosure which should be relatively early, because it was almost certainly uncovered, and then partly robbed out, after peat had been stripped from this zone (Figure 30).

The Royal Commission has mapped a cluster of similar primitive-looking walled fields in Gleann Mór, on the east bank of the burn, and mostly north of the famous 'Amazon's House'[35] (Figures 35 and 50). Here there are at least

FIGURE 29.
Map of early Hirta, to show quarries, probable prehistoric field systems and enclosures, and finds of prehistoric material. HD: pre-1830s head dyke (probably of medieval date).

51

FIGURE 30.
Remains of a probable
prehistoric enclosure at
An Lag, uncovered by
relatively recent peat-
stripping.

two ovoid enclosures, perhaps more; these too are 'primary', in that they have field walls running up to them. As at Tobar Childa, the longer, straighter boundaries occur on the periphery, and thus may be relatively late – they look like *divisions* of land, rather than accumulations of enclosures. So did *two* communities once inhabit Hirta at the same time, one at Village Bay and the other in Gleann Mór? It seems clear that the 'Amazon's House' and similar structures are later in date than the field walls, and unconnected with them. Mark Edmonds and I have looked for stone tools in Gleann Mór, and failed to find them. However, this is not too surprising. The structures of 'Amazon's House' type, and the nearby cleits, are not constructed from stones dug out of old field-walls, nor is there any sign here of recent cultivation episodes which might have uncovered broken hoe-blades.

To what extent can we link the hoe-blades directly with the 'old-looking' fields and enclosures? There is a substantial area to the south of The Street which has plenty of hoe-blades but virtually no old field banks. But this could easily be explained. On the sloping ground around Tobar Childa, it was necessary to build walls in order to absorb cleared stone and arrest soil creep; in areas where soils were deeper and slopes gentler, there may have been little need for them.

Mark Edmonds and I got permission to excavate a short stretch of old field-bank. The bit we chose contained one or two large facing-stones, and ran roughly east-west just inside the 1830s head dyke, at the rear of the croft behind House 6. At this point the Royal Commission plan shows a short bank approaching from the north, to join the larger one. We thought this might have been the edge of a small recent garden, but our excavation showed that there was an old wall along this line, which must have helped to trap a depth of up to 35 cm of soil behind the main wall. This wall was skilfully constructed. A narrow terrace had been cut for it, with a stone revetment on the lower side. The basic structure was a broad, low wall, like many prehistoric walls in the British uplands – two lines, usually one to two metres apart, of big facing-stones, revetting a core of smaller stones (Figure 31). Over the years, the wall was thickened, and a new set of facing stones was placed along the north side, one of them on a bed of carefully arranged small stones. A lot of stone was cleared onto the area just below the wall – at first, rounded, weathered stones from the exposed land surface, and then more angular stones from lower down in the soil. We found plenty of hoe-blades, some of them complete, *in* the wall, in the cleared and tumbled stone beside it, and low down in the deep soil just above it. It would still be possible, on the evidence, to claim that this is a relatively late wall, incorporating hoe-blade fragments from an earlier period. We would argue, however, that cultivation on this slope would not have been undertaken without some soil-trapping mechanism such as a wall. The blades and spalls found low down in the wall would have come from digging tools broken during the wall's construction, whilst the others – especially those found low down in the deep soil behind the wall – would reflect cultivation episodes. The wall was partly robbed out, probably in the age of MacKenzie; a great bite had been taken out of the western end of the north face, presumably to remove some facing-stones. It is interesting to look at other walls in the Tobar Childa field system in the light of our findings. Despite later stone-robbing (Figure 32), in places it is still possible to spot two or three thicknesses of chunky facing-stones, which represent the gradual increase in size of these boundaries. In some of these 'fields' we think that cultivation may have been confined to the areas of deeper soils along the lower edges. In any case, we assume that such fields were peripheral to the main cultivation areas which would have occupied gentler slopes and deeper soils.

The Village Bay area also contains several primitive-looking enclosures, roughly circular or kidney-shaped in plan. They are defined by low stony banks, and mostly located to the west of the Abhainn Mór (Figure 29) – perhaps set along the edge of a livestock-rearing zone. There is no proof yet that they are prehistoric, but they *look* ancient, and they seem to complement the areas of enclosed fields. In Gleann Mór there are two or three similar enclosures on the floor of the glen – also at some distance from the fields.

Getting these fields, quarries and enclosures dated more precisely will be a time-consuming task for archaeologists. It may well turn out that not all of the features I have mentioned belong to the same time horizon, even if we date that as broadly as sometime within the Neolithic and earlier Bronze Age (*c*. 3500–1500 BC). Nevertheless, in archaeology as in medieval philosophy, we try not to multiply hypotheses beyond what is necessary. Technically, St Kilda prehistory is very poorly dated; yet the fact that it hangs together, as an assemblage with a recognisably 'Northern Isles' character, means that

FIGURE 31.
The excavation of an ancient wall at Village Bay. At top right, part of the wall has been demolished, probably in the 1830s.

it will not do to think of it as some late, decadent phenomenon arriving here in the Iron Age or even later. Furthermore, it is now clear that we are no longer dealing with a prehistory which is elusive and fragmentary, the impression conveyed by recent St Kilda literature.[36] It is obviously wrong to think of the archipelago as so 'marginal' that it was settled reluctantly and late, or so remote that any prehistoric culture must necessarily have developed an eccentric character. With its fields and enclosures, a hillside covered in quarries and a highly recognisable set of distinctive, abundant and accessible artefacts, Hirta's prehistory stands out on the northern Scottish map. More dramatically, even after we have taken into account the fact that knowledge of the Long Island Neolithic and Bronze Age is rather limited, pre-Iron Age St Kilda resembles not so much an out-station of the Western Isles but rather an outpost of the Northern Isles. Perhaps this explains why there is as yet no evidence that Mullach Sgar dolerite reached the Long Island; indeed, as far as I know, artefacts made from Hirta dolerite have not yet been identified anywhere else in Scotland. Living as they did in a landscape of uncompromising pre-Cambrian gneiss, the peoples of the Western Isles would surely have given their eye teeth for good, workable stone; although absence of evidence may not be evidence of absence, given that, as I have explained, land surfaces relating to the Neolithic and earlier Bronze Age are hard to locate on the Long Island. Prehistorians will have to think long and hard about why St Kilda was apparently so closely linked to the Northern Isles, and what this may mean for our understanding of maritime skills and long-distance contacts four or five thousand years ago.

Burnt mounds

Small beach-pebbles, mostly dolerite, which have been split, cracked, crazed or darkened by exposure to heat, are widely distributed at Village Bay, in small

FIGURE 32.
Hirta's ancient walls have been robbed out in many places; where they survive, the massive stones which revetted them testify to the hard work invested in the enclosure and clearance of land.

numbers. There are one or two in the head dyke, but they are rare. Occasionally one finds fire-cracked fragments of hoe-blades. Things got interesting when I started searching the long, westernmost Main Consumption Dyke in 20 m sections, starting at the north end. At first, counts of fire-cracked stone per section were modest – 6, then 14, then 25. But then numbers rose sharply – 58, 63, and then 72. In the final section, south of the modern road, I only counted 17 fire-cracked stones. On a search of the Central Consumption Dyke, which is shorter, the numbers per 20 m section (from north to south) run like this – 21, 3, 29. In the fourth and final section, which is only 16 m long, I counted 48 fire-cracked stones. Thus a distinct zone with a high density of fire-cracked stones has been identified. It was tempting to wonder whether one or more 'burnt mounds' once existed in this area. And in the zone where fire-cracked stones are most numerous, the Main Consumption Dyke does indeed climb over a roughly circular mound, about 10 m across (Figure 36, page 64). To the west of the dyke it seems to have been badly damaged; it is much better preserved on the east side, where there is a flattened area where people have started to demolish it.

'Burnt mounds' occur in many parts of Britain and Ireland; where reasonably systematic surveys have taken place, they are quite common. They consist of heaps of fire-cracked stones, often close to streams; sometimes they are horse-shoe shaped, suggesting that the stones have been discarded and accumulated around something, probably a tank of some sort, in which water (or stew?), was heated by adding hot stones. Most burnt mounds – but not all of them – date from the later Bronze Age or Iron Age, roughly the last thousand years before the birth of Christ,[37] although in Scotland the custom of cooking with hot stones in a hide or a wooden trough apparently survived into the early eighteenth century 'in some of the islands'.[38] Fire-cracked stones have been found in the souterrain,[39] so some date from at least the Iron Age.

There may have been a burnt mound just west of the souterrain. Here, a neatly-faced pile of stones contains numerous fire-cracked stones, and broken hoe-blades. Possibly this is a stone-pile from one of the archaeological excavations at the souterrain. However, the croft boundary bank here is unusually high, and structures nearby have a 'perched' appearance, suggesting that they were built on some kind of mound which was later cleared away around them. This may have been what Sands interpreted as the 'midden' of the souterrain.[40]

The presence of small numbers of fire-cracked stones over much of the Village Bay area gives rise to interesting questions. It might simply suggest that prehistoric houses were widely dispersed, and that every hearth contained a few beach-pebbles, which eventually broke up in the fire. One hypothesis is that there were once several burnt mounds, located in areas where compost and manure were later made, and that fire-cracked stones (Figure 33) found their way into baskets of manure spread throughout the cultivated area; eventually they found their way into the structures of the nineteenth century.

There is no problem about the existence of burnt mounds on small, treeless Scottish islands. For instance, on Fair Isle, midway between Orkney and

Shetland, some 28 have survived, including one covering an area of 20 m x 30 m which may be the largest example in Shetland. John Hunter, who has recently investigated them, regards them as 'part of the infrastructure of prehistoric settlement'.[41] On the Western Isles, very few burnt mounds have been identified so far, though one was recently excavated on North Uist,[42] and many fire-cracked stones have been found at two double roundhouses on South Uist, dating from around 400 BC, and interpreted as buildings where smoking fish and meat, as well as boiling, took place.[43] On St Kilda it is tempting to interpret piles of fire-cracked stones as residues of communal feasts, or corn-drying – or both. In the early nineteenth century a single hot stone was dropped into a tub of grain and moved around to produce small-scale, temporary grain-drying in advance of grinding.[44] There is a school of thought which sees burnt mounds as evidence for 'sweat-houses' or 'saunas', places where the sick 'sweated out' various ailments, and shamans may have seen visions and undertaken 'spirit journeys' to other worlds.[45] On Hirta the situation is complicated by the fact that the two 'hot spots' identified, one near the souterrain and one further south, are both associated with the spur of stony, raised ground which may often have held houses and associated structures. So the burnt stone concentrations might simply represent the former presence of domestic middens.

Structures of the Iron Age?

It is now time to focus more specifically on the Iron Age (roughly 500 BC to AD 500), a time when the peoples of north and west Scotland expended a good deal of energy on the creation and maintenance of a dynamic new order, in which sea traffic played a key role. Highly distinctive new structures – brochs, duns, souterrains, wheelhouses – were built all over the Hebrides, the Northern Isles, and adjacent coastal areas. There is much debate about what these represented in social, economic and political terms. One current view is that around 500 BC people started to aggrandise their circular, stone-footed houses, which increased in size, height and complexity, eventually evolving into 'duns' and 'brochs', including famous ones like those at Mousa in

Shetland and Dun Carloway in Lewis. This is known as the Atlantic round house tradition.[46] We still have a limited understanding of its chronology, but broadly speaking the broch period is from about 400 BC to about AD 400,[47] with wheelhouses and souterrains occupied mostly in the two or three centuries on either side of the birth of Christ.[48] Ian Armit has recently argued that brochs and duns were not 'high status' residences, but belonged to extended families composed of perhaps 30–60 individuals, the equivalent of the tenant farmer class of much more recent times. The distribution and impressive appearance of these complex Atlantic round houses would have reflected the whereabouts and extent of agricultural land – and competition for it. The minimum amount of land exploited from a complex round house was about 3 sq km, the size of the island of Pabbay (south of Barra), which has one.[49]

No dun or broch has been recorded on Hirta, although on the basis of Armit's argument there should have been one. Early accounts tell of a 'little old ruinous fort' on Dun, called *Dun fir Bholg*.[50] This has never been convincingly identified – although it is of course conceivable that there was once a complex Atlantic round-house on the south-west side of Village Bay which has been lost to coastal erosion. However, it is much more probable that Dun did not need a separate name until it became an 'island' in the later Middle Ages (see below, Chapter Four), and that 'dun' refers to its jagged, rocky skyline (Figure 36, page 64), more than one stretch of which could easily be imagined as a ruined stone tower, built by the legendary *fir bholg*, whose ancestral identity would have needed reaffirming and celebrating with the demise of Norse rule. However, it *is* quite likely that some sort of Atlantic round house, now completely dismantled, stood somewhere near the souterrain. Roger Miket has argued persuasively that souterrains were probably intended mainly as cold-stores, and that for the most part their doorways were not originally concealed; many souterrains were located within settlements and may have been entered from within buildings.[51] Mathieson claimed that Christ Church once had a tower with an internal stair. But as his celebrated map shows, the interesting thing is that he believed (surely erroneously) that the site of Christ Church was near the souterrain.[52] Did his 'excavations on the site of Christ Church' in 1927[53] uncover part of a ruined broch? A detailed contour survey might provide evidence for the former existence of a major Iron Age round house in the area around the souterrain. A curious discovery was reported a long time ago; apparently during the works initiated by Neil MacKenzie, two men found a 'fairies' residence', stone-built with wall-niches, in a knoll which must have been somewhere along the line of the village street.[54] Could this have been an Iron Age wheelhouse? (Some wheelhouses, like the one at Cill Donnain on South Uist, can be quite small.[55])

Then there is the case of the *Tigh an Stallair*, the House of the Steward, on Boreray. It was mentioned by various writers from Martin[56] onwards. Between them, the accounts of MacAulay and Anne Kennedy[57] seem to establish that it was circular, dug into the ground, and corbelled, with a roof apex 18 feet

(6 m) high, closed by a single stone, and 'pillars' 'on which clothes might be hung' separating six 'beds'. The 'beds' could accommodate significant numbers of people, and it was possible to pass from one to another without passing through the central area, which evidently contained a large hearth. The structure apparently collapsed in the 1840s. As Captain Thomas was the first to point out,[58] it sounds very like what we would now call an aisled wheelhouse, dating from the Iron Age.[59] About 30 wheelhouses are known to have existed in the Western Isles, with a comparable number in the Northern Isles and along the north coast of Scotland.[60] A recent estimate is that there may have been over 50 of them in South Uist alone.[61] Wheelhouses are very distinctive, circular in plan with stone partitions radiating from the centre, supporting complex, partially-corbelled roofs; they are often set below the ground surface, like the Boreray wheelhouse, which was evidently reoccupied in the Middle Ages and later (when each 'bed' had its own name[62]).

The presence of a wheelhouse in such an extreme location poses challenging questions for Iron Age experts. It is hard to believe that people lived permanently on Boreray. We may have to consider the possibility that hunting sea-birds was a high-status activity, and that the wheelhouse was effectively an Iron Age 'fowling lodge'. A glance at reports on seabird bones found on contemporary archaeological sites shows that gannet occurred at the brochs of Dun Vulan on South Uist, Dun Mor Vaul on Tiree, Bu in Orkney and Crosskirk in northern Scotland, and also at the Udal (North Uist) in levels dating from AD 300–800.[63] According to Serjeantson, 'the gannet stands out as the seabird most commonly exploited in early historic times'.[64] Histories of the Bass Rock make it clear that young gannets, gannets' eggs, and gannet oil were prized resources from the time of Hector Boece (1526) (who considered that the oil was good for gout and diseases 'in the hanches and groines of mankind') until that of Thomas Pennant in the mid eighteenth century; interest declined over the course of the nineteenth century. In the 1660s the laird of the Bass Rock was making a considerable amount of money out of the young birds.[65] Gannets were not the only sea-birds hunted in the past. Scottish prehistoric sites have produced the bones of puffins and (now extinct) great auks, for instance,[66] and the Bass Rock was also valued for its kittiwakes. But the important point about gannets is that they live in colonies, often large ones. At present, the only gannetries near the Western Isles are those on the Flannan Isles, Sula Sgeir and St Kilda (the ratio between these three sites respectively, in terms of numbers of breeding pairs, is 1:23:121).[67] Over time, new colonies may be founded and established ones abandoned; but for the most part gannets wisely shun the regular haunts of humans. During the Iron Age, when the Western Isles were evidently well peopled,[68] and fowling a widespread practice, it seems unlikely that inshore colonies of gannets would have persisted for long; the gannetries targeted by fowlers would have been the distant and difficult ones known today.

The broad conclusion seems clear. In terms of the quantity and range of resources on offer, the St Kilda archipelago was easily the most promising of the offshore fowling stations. These islands offered the potential for a long summer of hunting (especially if their inhabitants proved accommodating) and a return to the Western Isles with as many spoils as a boat could carry, with tales of exploits to enliven many a winter evening. In this context, a wheelhouse on Boreray, and indeed a complex round-house on Hirta, with adjacent souterrain, would have represented a long-term social investment, reflecting and symbolising the incorporation of St Kilda within the wider world. In the longer term, the nature of the relationship between the St Kildans and those who made the trip would doubtless have varied, and it may well have lapsed and been interrupted at various times. The pattern of summer visits by groups of people intending to exploit St Kilda's special resources, which comes into rather fuzzy focus in the sixteenth and seventeenth centuries, may well have a long ancestry, extending right back to the Iron Age. Indeed, such activities may go back much further. The discovery of the bones of puffin, guillemot and gannet at the Neolithic site of Northton, in south-west Harris,[69] raises some intriguing questions; gannet bones were also found at the early Neolithic site of Knap of Howar, in Orkney.[70]

The significance of Hirta's prehistory

The prehistoric inhabitants of Hirta have left a much more impressive signature than we have previously recognised. Our discoveries suggest that this island was occupied by an energetic, viable community in later prehistory, cultivating an extensive area of land at Village Bay – a relatively sheltered low-lying plain, larger then the one we see today, which has suffered centuries of attack by the sea. Gleann Mór was evidently occupied too. The pre-Iron Age occupation of these islands is surely not now in doubt; the number, variety and quality of the stone tools left behind bear witness to that. The Northern Isles connections – which seem to operate to some extent throughout St Kilda's prehistory, not just in the later Neolithic and earlier Bronze Age – are intriguing. It seems impossible to isolate a definable area or time horizon in the Northern Isles which ticks precisely the same boxes as the Hirta material; there may have been no specific 'homeland' in the north, especially if maritime contacts endured over centuries.

It was once possible to take the view that the limitations of Neolithic mariners, or their lack of curiosity and enterprise, would have put these islands beyond the edge of the reachable world; that the St Kilda archipelago would have been unattractive to would-be colonists; and that any community established here would have been so isolated that it would necessarily have been destroyed by the effects of inbreeding. But the archaeological record suggests otherwise. Personally, I am inclined to believe that sustained settlement on Hirta goes back at least to Neolithic times, and that by about 3000 BC people had developed a viable way of life out here, and the means of maintaining regular and necessary contact with the outside world. Only time will tell whether I am right – if archaeologists are given the opportunity to investigate.

CHAPTER FOUR

The Interdependence of Islands

Islands, on account of the goodness of the soil, and the additional
subsistence they draw from the sea, are generally closer inhabited …
they are also more frequented by strangers; and therefore by a sort
of collision the men would polish one another into good manners.
Rev. Donald MacQueen (1774) A Dissertation on the Government of the People in the
Western Isles *(Pennant 1998) p. 746.*

FIGURE 34.
Grannie Gillies and her
knitting.

As we have seen, the late prehistoric period in north and west Scotland saw
strong cultural linkages and maritime connections between far-flung islands
and archipelagos, and St Kilda participated to the full. If we no longer expect,
in general, to find a strange, aberrant, 'insular' culture here, we should probably be prepared to identify the 'Amazon's House' type structures in Gleann
Mór as fairly normal houses dating from the Pictish period (Figures 80 and 81,
pages 184 and 185). They clearly post-date the probable Bronze Age fields in
the glen, and were old-looking when Martin Martin arrived, so they should
fall within the 500 BC – AD 1000 bracket, roughly speaking. Quite good parallels for the Gleann Mór structures would certainly include the buildings
excavated at Bostadh in Lewis, and the one found within the broch at Dun
Vulan on South Uist.[1] There is a respectable amount of evidence for 'Pictish'
material culture (*c.* AD 400–900) in the Western Isles.[2] (Incidentally, not many
archaeologists believe nowadays that the presence of this material is necessarily
evidence for people with a distinct ethnic identity.) The fascinating thing
about the 'Pictish' levels at Dun Vulan is that they contained the bones of
deep-sea fish – so it would not be surprising to find that the people of the
Western Isles were in regular contact with outlying islands at this period.
It seems that we must take a closer look at the structures in Gleann Mór
(Figure 35).

In the period of the Vikings, another time of long-distance relationships and
highly distinctive material culture, written documents improve our understanding. From around AD 800 the Western Isles came under attacks from
Vikings, and were ruled by Norsemen for several centuries until 1266, when
the Scandinavians lost control after the Battle of Largs and the consequent
Treaty of Perth.

According to popular belief, there is a profound difference between the
Western and the Northern Isles. The people of Orkney and Shetland like to

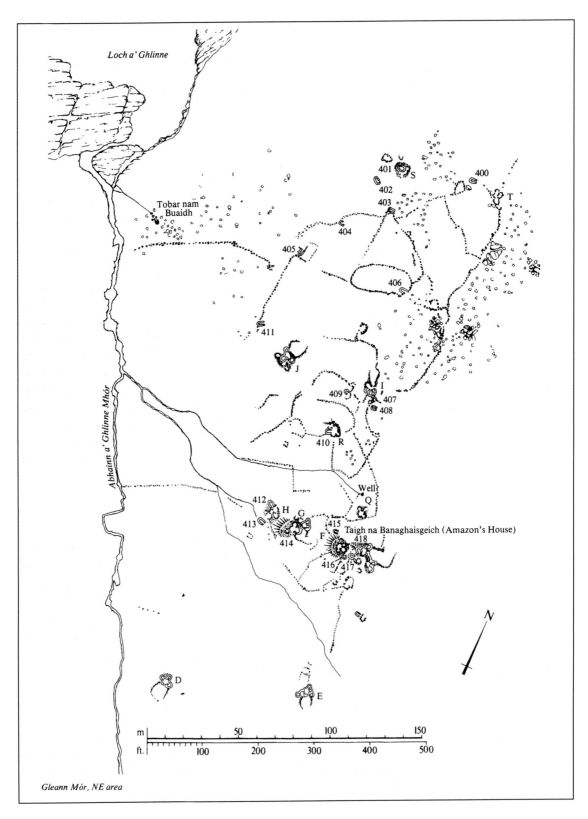

Loch a' Ghlinne

Tobar nam
Buaidh

Abhainn a' Ghlinne Mhór

401
402
403
404
405
406
411
J
409
407
408
410 R
411
S
400
T
Well
Q
412
H
413
G
414
F
415
416 417
418

Taigh na Banaghaisgeich (Amazon's House)

N

D

E

| m | | 50 | | 100 | | 150 |
| ft. | 100 | 200 | 300 | 400 | 500 |

Gleann Mór, NE area

celebrate their Norse heritage, whereas in the 'Gaelic' Western Isles the Norsemen tend to be regarded as foreign barbarians. How far these different perceptions reflect different genetic histories may eventually be demonstrated by DNA studies. But in any case the recent archaeological fieldwork of Niall Sharples and Mike Parker Pearson[3] has demonstrated that during the Norse period South Uist was extensively settled by a vigorous and capable people, skilled seafarers with a serious interest in deep sea fishing, specialising in herring, perhaps for distant markets as well as local consumption.[4] If South Uist is typical of the Long Island, it is likely that the integration of St Kilda into the wider world was as full as it was in the Iron Age. From a Norse perspective, of course, the Western Isles were the *Sudreyar*, the Southern Isles. Presumably the 'Norse' fishermen of Uist built on the sea-knowledge and long-distance connections of their 'Pictish' ancestors.

Place-names form the starting-point of our enquiry. St Kilda place-names tend to contain a mix of Gaelic and Norse words, and the forms which have survived are often distorted, having passed 'through the mouths of a people ... of very indelicate ears', as Kenneth MacAulay put it.[5] But there are a couple of dozen names which are genuinely Norse, in the sense that a Norse adjective comes *before* a Norse noun, and not after it in the Gaelic fashion; they include the names of Soay and Boreray as well as Hirta itself. More revealingly, there are seven tautologous names which have been adopted by Gaelic speakers who have not understood their Norse meaning. For instance, 'Tobar Childa' means 'spring' or 'well' in both Gaelic and Norse, and similarly 'Gob Scapinish' translates as 'Point Cavepoint'. Apparently Gaelic speakers also adopted – and mispronounced – Norse names for zones of arable land.[6] The point here is that such names were already in being, to be misunderstood or mispronounced by incoming Gaelic-speakers.

Early reports provide details of objects found long ago, and now lost. A pair of late ninth- or tenth-century 'tortoise' brooches implies the burial of a woman of high status. In MacKenzie's time, a mound in the Glebe apparently produced a male Viking burial, with a sword, spear, whetstone and various other pieces of iron. A spearhead found in the souterrain may reflect another Norse burial.[7] There is also a story about the finding of 'two antique urns' containing 'a quantity of Danish silver coin' in 1767.[8] Much more recently, excavations at House 8 uncovered fragments of vessels made of soapstone (steatite) and a spindle-whorl made of the same material, which was probably quarried in Shetland.[9] So both archaeological finds and place-names indicate a sustained Scandinavian presence on Hirta.

Reconstructing Norse St Kilda

How might we gain more understanding of the landscape of Norse *Hirtir* – The Stags, as the name may have been understood to mean? I have a few suggestions which are speculative, but I hope worth putting forward, in advance of the archaeological and palaeoenvironmental work which will ultimately be necessary.

FIGURE 35.
Plan of ancient field system, Gleann Mór. Note the position of *Tobar nam Buaidh*, commonly known as the 'Well of Virtues' (meaning 'supernatural powers'), and the relationship between structures of 'Amazon's House' type and the field system. Compare with Figure 50.

When the Vikings first arrived, they sailed into the kind of open bay which they liked to call a *vík* – as in Wick, and Uig. It seems likely that Dun (Figure 36) had not yet become an island. Probably the final breakthrough of the sea occurred in the fourteenth or fifteenth century, in one of the great storms of the Little Ice Age.[10] Had Dun already been separate when the Norsemen arrived, they would surely have named it as an island, as they did with So*ay* and Borer*ay*. An island accessible only at certain states of the tide was often called 'Orosay'. Giasgeir, a name at the east end of the channel between Dun and Hirta, means 'chasm skerry'; Coates therefore suggests that when the Norsemen named this spot there was an inlet, a *geò*, here, and not yet a channel;[11] at one stage there may have been a sea arch. The maps of Martin and MacAulay mark Dun as an island, but neither refers to it as 'the island of Dun'. MacAulay calls it the Peninsula; in his day, it was an island at high water.[12] By the end of the nineteenth century, according to Heathcote, it could only be reached dry-shod by leaping from stone to stone at low spring tides.[13]

We also need to consider the evidence of the celebrated St Kilda long-tailed field mouse (properly the St Kilda wood mouse, but we will keep the more familiar name here). This engaging little creature was almost certainly brought to Hirta as a 'stowaway' by the Norsemen, together, probably, with the house mouse.[14] Dun has had a colony of St Kilda field mice since at least the late nineteenth century.[15] They raise an interesting question. Which is more likely: that they were brought to Dun by boat, after it had become an island, or that they came across when Dun was still attached to Hirta? At the western end of

FIGURE 36.
The craggy skyline of Dun. This view along the longest of the consumption dykes also shows a mound (perhaps a burnt mound) underlying the dyke, in a zone where the count of fire-cracked stones reaches a peak.

Dun, near the narrow strait which separates it from Hirta, there is a set of prominent cultivation ridges. These already existed in the 1840s.[16] Possibly a pregnant field mouse *might* have been brought here when Dun was an island, in bags of seedcorn destined for this field (although, interestingly, Sands noted that 'the people are careful not to carry [mice] to Boreray or Soa',[17] and they apparently succeeded[18]). But there is another possibility. Over-ridden by the cultivation ridges, and at an angle of just off 90 degrees to them, is a bank defining the upper edge of a field. It has apparently been truncated by the channel between Dun and Hirta. Is it possible that this was once a Norse corn-field – an ideal place for a colony of Scandinavian field mice to establish itself, before being cut off from the mainland? It is interesting to note that there were 20 or 30 sheep 'of the native breed' on Dun in the nineteenth century.[19] Were sheep stranded too?

When I first arrived on Hirta, I was intrigued by two 'old tracks' marked on the Royal Commission plan in the zone of the 1830s head dyke – long narrow terraces cut into the hillside. The lower one is mostly *below* the head dyke; the upper one is mostly *above* the dyke, but is overlain by it at its eastern end. At this point, the 'old track' is truncated by the cliff edge, with a vertical drop to the sea (Figure 84, page 192)! The 'trackway' interpretation becomes frankly incredible. Even if there has been considerable coastal erosion since this 'track' was constructed, where could it possibly have been heading?

The 'old tracks' are actually abandoned, robbed-out head dykes. Each narrow 'terrace' was part quarry, part building-platform; the dyke was erected on its front edge. Livestock sheltering behind it would have compressed the earth and conserved the 'terrace' profile. Eventually the dykes were cannibalised for stone, although some sizeable boulders remain. This interpretation makes sense of the fact that each 'track' joins onto a large bank at its western end. As the plan shows, these banks belong to the Tobar Childa field system. It would make sense to see the early head dykes as either roughly contemporary with the fields, or joined to them at some later period, when they were still in being (or had recently been brought back into use). Just above the Factor's House, the lower head dyke is approached by a ramp, probably once leading up to a gateway, and the upper, later, head dyke curves south to join the lower one here, to form a kind of funnel entrance which would perpetuate the use of this passage to and from the hill ground.

To the west of the Tobar Childa field system, it is possible to pick up much of the course of what looks like a continuation of the upper head dyke. It disappears (removed by peat-cutters?) on the wet land beside Abhainn Mór, re-appears as a rather straggly 'wall' just east of the modern road, and then vanishes again before running persistently through the Mullach Sgar screes in the form of a rather damaged drystone wall – a very striking feature in some light conditions – and onwards to the cliff-edge, where it has been truncated by coastal erosion. If one looks across Village Bay from the crofted land, one can see where, further south-west, it resumes its course on the other side of this truncation.

There is, I must stress, as yet no evidence that these old head dykes date from the Norse period. However, the idea of a 'ring garth' enclosing the in-bye land is very much a Norse concept. For the pre-Christian Norse, it was a metaphor for their view of the cosmos, which distinguished between the *Midgardr*, the 'cultivated, inhabited, central world' inhabited by men and gods, and the *Utgardr*, the Out-Garth, an uncultivated zone of monsters and giants.[20] The sheer length and coherence of the upper head dyke reflects a serious, deliberate approach to the organisation of the Hirta community. By accident or design, this layout would have brought the chapels of St Brendan and St Columba within the enclosed land. The marine erosion of medieval in-bye land on the south-west side of the bay and the breakthrough which created the island of Dun may reflect the impact of the Little Ice Age, which commenced shortly after the end of Norse rule.

Strange-sounding names given to different parts of the cultivated land, and recorded in the seventeenth and eighteenth centuries, have been discussed by the experts.[21] Multum Agria, Multum Taurus and Multum Favere sound like cod Latin, but the first element in each is apparently Old Norse *moldu*, 'earth-mould', and presumably indicates that the making of deep 'plaggen' soils on Hirta, built up from applications of carefully-made compost, goes back at least to these times.[22]

The island of Boreray has rather more than its fair share of pure Norse place-names. Boreray itself means 'fortress island', which is taken to refer to the Iron Age wheelhouse, the *Tigh an Stallair* or 'Staller's House'.[23] A *stallari* was a steward or bailiff, or possibly a 'king's officer', and the expert consensus seems to be that the *stallarahús* was the old wheelhouse. In any case the suggestion is that the 'steward's visit' goes back to Norse times, and that the St Kilda archipelago played a significant role within the Norse realm.

Chieftains in action

After the demise of Scandinavian rule in the 1260s, the chiefdoms of the Hebrides were nominally under the control of the Lord of the Isles. In 1493 the Lordship was forfeited to the Scottish Crown, which then took various measures intended to control the lifestyles and activities of Hebridean chieftains – notably creating the Statutes of Iona in the early seventeenth century. During this period there was a resurgence of the Gaelic language. In general, however, late medieval Hebrideans drew on a cultural inheritance rich in hybrid vigour, partly Scandinavian and partly Scottish and Irish Gaelic.

The MacLeod of Skye and Harris, who eventually emerged as paramount chief of St Kilda, claimed ultimate descent from Leod, son of Olaf the Black, a ruler of the Isle of Man. Perhaps sometime in the early thirteenth century, Leod married the daughter of a half-Norse, half-Gaelic ruler of Skye, MacCrailt Armuinn, who was based at Dunvegan (the 'vegan' element is a Norse personal name, Began[24]). Leod died around 1280 and apparently was buried in front of the high altar at Iona.[25]

As Robert Dodgshon has recently explained, these west Scottish chiefdoms were dynamic and unstable; the chieftaincy was not an uncontested, static 'social institution'.[26] The power of chiefs was based on the uplifting, storage and distribution of food, which they used to maintain and reward retinues of fighting men and to support an impressive lifestyle, designed to instil loyalty, respect, fear and subservience. The chiefs (or sub-chiefs) and their retinues were often on tour, living off local communities. Their retinues included men with special roles – bard, spokesman, broadsword carrier, horse leader, baggage man, piper, assistant piper, and even a man to carry the chief over fords.[27] There were storytellers, clan genealogists, historians, musicians, and jesters, as well as falconers, fowlers, gamekeepers and a host of specialists in food preparation.[28] The chief's power depended on the regular exercise of violence (and threats of violence), and on his ability to settle or reactivate old feuds as strategically appropriate, in an atmosphere drenched in machismo. A story from the 1720s tells of a chief asking to be supplied with a large snowball to lay his head on, only for his followers to complain that 'our leader is so effeminate, he can't sleep without a pillow'.[29] It is this world which has given the English language the words 'henchman' and 'blackmail'.[30] It was normal for an aspiring young man from a chiefly lineage to lead a cattle raid, as a 'public specimen of his valour', as Martin puts it.[31] In essence, turning up mob-handed to collect food rents due by established custom is not very different from arriving in a galley and taking away food by force of arms. Last year's casual raid could easily become next year's incipient annual institution. Some of these relationships must have been little different from protection rackets.

These were maritime chiefdoms; Hebridean chiefs lived in 'sea castles' designed to command major seaways and shelter their galleys, or birlinns.[32] The lair of the MacLeods, Dunvegan Castle on the Isle of Skye, was expertly chosen (Figure 37). It dominated the head of a tidal inlet, on a rocky boss, which was strengthened by cutting back the natural channel separating it from dry land (which was not bridged until 1748). We must imagine away the big grey pile much visited today. Most of what we see now is post-medieval. The oldest parts of the castle are the curtain wall and the keep (but only its basic plan and the core of its masonry). It is possible that the earliest medieval stronghold consisted of these two features, constructed together in the fourteenth century, as a mainland-style 'tower-house and barmkin' as at Loch Leven (Kinross); the third chief, Malcolm, had strong mainland connections by marriage (his two successive mothers-in-law were sisters of Robert the Bruce). But perhaps it is more likely that the first castle was a rather basic 'Hebridean' structure, featuring a curtain wall enclosing a simple hall and other buildings – and a well – and that the keep was a slightly later addition.[33] Before 1748, access was only possible by sea, through a water gate in the thick curtain wall and then up a flight of steep steps (which can still be seen). The narrow entrance to the inlet would have sheltered and concealed any galleys anchored near the castle, and would have been highly defensible in the event of an attack from the sea. So much for control of the western sea routes, and the crossing to Harris. Galleys destined for the *southern* seaways (which the MacLeods took when they attended the Council of the Isles, at Finlaggan on Islay) could have beached on a sheltered tombolo only a couple of miles away, giving onto Loch Bracadale, or taken advantage of the well-protected anchorage at Pool Roag. One of the finest images of a birlinn (Figure 38) is carved on the monument to one of most celebrated MacLeod chiefs, Alastair Crotach ('the Hunchback') located in the church which he built (or rebuilt) at Roghadal on Harris in the early sixteenth century. In the latter part of the time of Norse supremacy, galleys took part in important sea battles.

During the period of the Lords of the Isles, Hebridean boat-building more or less stood still.[34] Soon the birlinns were no match for the more effective ships of the English or Scottish navies, and tended to avoid direct combat with them. However, not having to rely on sail, the oar-powered Hebridean galleys were faster and more manoeuvrable than more advanced craft; they could land on beaches, so they were well adapted to local weather conditions and the kind of raids carried out by chiefs and their henchmen. As late as 1545 the Hebrideans could assemble a fleet of 180 boats. They were used for the lucrative traffic in transporting mercenaries to fight in Ireland, and also for piracy, a crime for which Rory MacLeod of Dunvegan was fined heavily in 1604.[35] The nuisance value of the elusive birlinns was considerable. In the early seventeenth century, reducing the numbers and size of Hebridean galleys was a key

FIGURE 37.
Dunvegan Castle, Skye, located superbly as the hub of a medieval maritime chiefdom. Note the jetty, the dark archway marking the water gate (once the only access), and the strength of the rocky boss on which the castle stands.

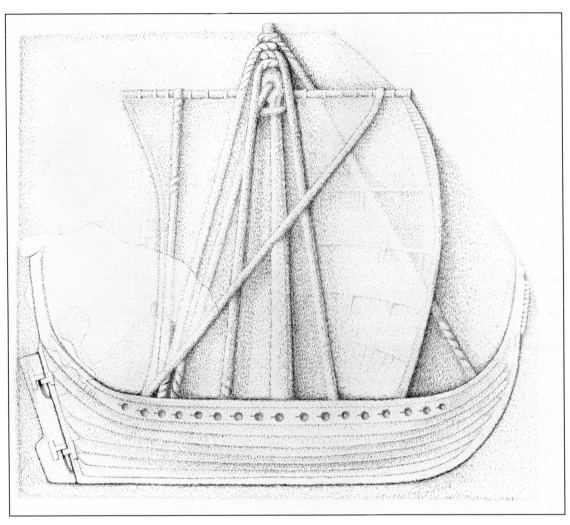

FIGURE 38.
A fine rendering of
MacLeod's best galley
carved on the
sixteenth-century tomb
of Alastair Crotach in
Roghadal church
(Harris), and displaying
a knowledgeable
attention to nautical
detail.

policy objective of the Scottish Crown – though enforcement was a different matter. In these times, threats came almost always from the sea. Keeping a sea-watch, and lighting signal fires when appropriate, were necessary practices which were evidently followed on St Kilda. Martin tells how the men of Hirta, stranded for ten weeks on Boreray, lit 'as many fires on the top of an eminence as there were men in number', a signal which was joyously understood by their womenfolk, who set about digging their arable ground with unprecedented energy.[36] The traditional beacon site on Hirta itself, for communicating with people at Boreray and the stacks, or even the Long Island, was at the top of Clash na Bearnaich.[37] The St Kildans also used turf-cutting for long-distance signalling. Three long strips cut out of the Boreray turf meant 'send the boat'; two marks meant that someone was sick or dead.[38] When ten men were stranded on Boreray in 1859, the people deturfed ten spots, a signal that they were not neglecting to cultivate their arable ground.[39]

The galley carved at Roghadal evokes the skills and energy of those who built, rowed and sailed the birlinns, men who knew the location of suitable timber on the well-wooded island of Skye, and the hazards of crossing the Minch. Not far away, in the nave of the church, is the recumbent effigy of Alastair Crotach's son William, who died in the mid sixteenth century; he is depicted traditionally, as a 'knight' in a suit of mail, a massive sword between his legs in the customary (not to say highly symbolic) position. Carved in black amphibolite, it is one of the most sinister images I have ever seen. It reminds us that the power of Hebridean chiefs was ultimately based on the use of force – and of the tales of violence in which the MacLeods and their adversaries were implicated, exploits which would grace any Icelandic saga. In the fourteenth century the wife of the fourth chief had her two daughters buried alive in the dungeon of Dunvegan, whilst the young men who had tried to carry them off were mutilated and flogged to death.[40] The fourth chief himself, Iain Keir ('Swarthy' or 'Gloomy'), missing a favourite white stag while hunting on Harris, had the man accused of taking it put to death by 'forcing the antlers of a large deer into his bowels'.[41] A Harris man came home and found the corpses of his family flung on a dunghill and the dismembered remains of his infant grandchild bubbling in a cauldron; his chief organised a revenge, setting fire to the thatched roof of a church occupied by members of the rival clan.[42] After a bloody battle fought in the late fourteenth century, at the head of Loch Sligachan, in Skye, severed heads of the hated MacDonalds were displayed at Dunvegan.[43] This was not the only head-hunting episode.[44] Another case occurred in the early sixteenth century, after a massacre of the MacDonalds at Loch Stockernish, five miles (*c.* 8 km) up the coast from Roghadal; the severed heads were delivered to Alastair Crotach's 'governor' of Harris. The MacDonalds took their revenge by incarcerating the crew of one of Alastair's birlinns, condemning them to death by cannibalism and starvation.[45] Mutilation was a favourite practice, MacCaskill of Talisker having his ears cut off after he had landed on the MacLeods' island of Eigg.[46] Iain Dubh ('Black Iain'), a sixteenth century usurper, ruled by hostage-taking; he hosted a banquet which culminated in the carefully choreographed massacre of his guests, and was eventually put to death in Ireland by having a red-hot iron forced into his bowels.[47] The autocratic behaviour of Hebridean chiefs persisted long after the Statutes of Iona. In the 1730s the young MacLeod chief who repopulated Hirta after the smallpox epidemic was complicit in the banishment of Lady Grange to the island and her eight-year exile there. And he was relaxed about the conduct of one of his tacksmen, who in 1739 loaded a ship, the *William*, with people from Skye and Harris, including many women and children, intending to sell them into slavery in America. The crime would not have been discovered if the *William* had not stopped off in northern Ireland.[48]

Acts of violence, oppression and generosity were often arbitrary, but they took place in a context of customary law and conventional behaviour, which chiefs were also expected to maintain and uphold. This is essentially the world of the Icelandic sagas, in which law is both a necessary form of social control *and* a resource to be used and manipulated by the powerful, a sphere of action which was an alternative to violence but sometimes a cause of further trouble. So how are we to characterise the relationship between an essentially exploitative, predatory chiefdom and a small, distant island community?

A programme of predation

There is no doubt what the chiefdom stood to gain. The annual visit of the sub-chief or 'steward', traditionally from Pabbay but sometimes from Berneray or possibly other islands in the Sound of Harris, brought to St Kilda a retinue of several dozen men. They lived off the fat of the land (not to mention the cliffs and sea stacks) and the hard work of the islanders, and then took away as much in food 'rents' as their boats could carry. If we assume that the basic rules of engagement did not change very much, Martin's account may help us to reconstruct the essentials. The retinue usually arrived in mid June[49] (though in 1697 the steward's party was already there when Martin arrived on 12 June[50]), and stayed until late August or early September.[51] When Martin was there, the islanders were feeding about 60 extra mouths[52] – which suggests that each birlinn had a crew of about two dozen. This would have been larger than the maximum size authorised by the Statutes of Iona (16 to 18 oars[53]). But then according to these statutes – to which MacLeod of Harris had put his name, under duress – the 1697 expedition was illegal in any case.

The retinue had an agreed food allowance, delivered regularly to their lodgings twice a day, of bread, butter, cheese, mutton, sea-birds and eggs – in early June, it seems, mostly guillemots' eggs, the allowance being 18 per man per day, plus 'a greater number of lesser eggs'.[54] The retinue's departure was probably intended to take place after the first harvest of the gugas, the young gannets which had put on fat in preparation for their long migration south. Although guests might be distributed evenly among island families (as on Berneray, south of Barra[55]), in some places there were 'public huts' for travellers and visitors.[56] Have the large, supposedly 'medieval' houses at Village Bay (such as 'Calum Mòr's House') survived because they were used as 'guest houses' in the summer?

One wonders whether the visitors behaved like the members of King Lear's retinue: 'disordered … deboshed and bold', full of 'epicurism and lust'.[57] Pennant described a chief's retainers as 'instruments of his oppression and freakish tyranny'.[58] Traditionally, they were energetic young men, accustomed to rowing galleys as well as handling weapons – including bows and arrows – wrestling, swimming, jumping and dancing.[59] They sound rather like the young St Kildans, who were also indefatigable oarsmen, as well as good swimmers and divers; they enjoyed ball games on the beach.[60] Members of the retinue did not just sit around talking and flirting with the island women; Moray makes it clear that the 'strangers' were involved in climbing with ropes, egg-collecting and bird-catching.[61] The trip must have been something of an 'activity holiday', a more elaborate, competitive version of the hunting and

FIGURE 39.
Stac Li; a rewarding
challenge for the
fowler.

fowling parties which went out every year to outlying islands in the sixteenth and seventeenth centuries. They caught young gannets on Sula Sgeir, a practice which continues to this day;[62] the tradition is at least 500 years old.[63] They hunted feral sheep and wildfowl on the Flannans, and seals on Haskeir[64] and the Monachs, where they used clubs and nets.[65] The hunters were very interested in the falconry potential of the hawks encountered on the islands;[66] they would have appreciated the 'extraordinary good' ones to be found at St Kilda, and they admired the islanders' skills in reaching the most formidably-sited nests.[67] In part, these trips were traditional Hebridean food-gathering expeditions; but they were also raids without enemies, involving male bonding, opportunities for competitive displays of skill and prestige, and the emergence and readjustment of male hierarchies. These expeditions were risky; they involved rock-climbing, difficult manoeuvres with boats and confrontations with changing conditions of sea and weather. Robert Moray described the men who hunted seals in the caves of western Hirta as mad: 'if the wind changeth during their being there, it is not possible to save man or boat'.[68] Performance of the correct rituals was essential, especially on wild, remote islands which were 'places of inherent sanctity', according to one of the men who went to the Flannans. Martin describes the Flannan expedition in some detail.[69] Before arrival, a novice had to be 'instructed perfectly in all the punctilios observed here' and he was given a partner who acted as his mentor. On landing, the hunters bared their heads and went sunwise, thanking God for their safety. They went to the ruined chapel, stripped to the waist and offered three different prayers. Among other things, they were not allowed to defecate near the boat, to kill a bird with a stone or after evening prayers, or take home any sheep suet. As usual among seafarers, some words were taboo and had to be replaced by others. This included the names of islands; the St Kildans referred to Boreray as 'the north country', for instance,[70] and Hirta itself was 'the high country'.[71] These rituals and taboos psyched individuals up for the demanding tasks which lay ahead, and established strong bonds among members of the group; concentrating on their observance took men's minds off the more fearsome risks to which they were exposed.[72]

Such hunting and fowling trips required leadership, in terms of planning, strategy and tactics. Someone had to be lead climber, to make the tricky leap from boat to rock stack, to be first to observe the disposition of the prey and determine the group's strategy accordingly. Local expeditions were led by the headman, variously referred to as the *maor*, the Ground Officer, or the *gingich*, the big man.[73] Headmen emerged naturally; they were distinguished for their physical skills, intelligence, experience and capacity to inspire trust and loyalty. Of course the lead could be taken by a man higher up the regional social hierarchy, such as the steward, co-ordinating members of his retinue and boat crew. In the case of St Kilda, there are clues which suggest that the 'steward' once claimed fowling rights on outlying stacks and islands. It was not only the *Tigh an Stallair* whose name associated it with a person of high status; Stac an Armin means 'the stack of the steward' or the 'sub thane'[74] and Levenish (Figure 40) traditionally 'belonged' to the galley's crew.[75] We can thus perhaps discern a pattern of visits and hunting trips led by the 'steward', going back to the period of Norse rule, if not before. Members of the retinue liked to

FIGURE 40.
Levenish in foul weather.

party. Island couples tended to get married on the occasion of the steward's visit; sometimes he brought a priest (in 1697 the minister married 15 couples[76]). There are hints that the visitors helped to make the celebrations go with a swing, courtesy of the whisky they brought with them; in 1797, Edward Daniel Clarke was told that he had just missed a wedding feast with 'the whole island dancing, and the whole island drunk'.[77] In the eighteenth century, before the arrival of official, organised Presbyterian disapproval, there was also a great deal of drinking and dancing at Christmas and New Year, with old women joining in; the St Kildans loved music.[78]

Who and what else was in the steward's galley? The following suggestions are based on reading between the lines of Martin's account, or using even later literature, and it may be unwise to project this information back into the later Middle Ages. Nevertheless, these sources are illuminating. At least one or two members of the retinue had been coming to Hirta for years, and knew the place and people well.[79] There were usually a few servants, such as young women to help with dairying, a tailor, or a boatwright;[80] sometimes they stayed over for a year, or even married into the island community. The steward's wife evidently came on the trip; Martin noted that she gave presents to the wife of the *maor*.[81] According to Martin, 'the most meagre in the parish are carried thither to be recruited with good cheer'.[82] Careful reading of the sources makes it clear that there was always a small group of 'passengers' in the steward's galley, who had various reasons for making the journey. In the mid eighteenth century Rev. Kenneth MacAulay mentioned that 'many' of his Harris parishioners had been visiting Hirta 'almost annually' since Martin's trip; one or two came for therapeutic reasons, to sample the properties of the Well of Virtues (in those days 'virtues' meant 'supernatural powers').[83] Like the new bull or the supply of fresh seed corn – which were also brought in by the steward from time to time – people who married into the Hirta community helped to diversify the gene pool, and provided the St Kildans with potentially useful relations by marriage on the Long Island. The *Hirteach* were, after all, parishioners of Harris. At times, the steward may have gone in for a little social engineering. According to Martin, the MacNeill of Barra used to supply widows and widowers on Mingulay and Berneray with new wives or husbands on request, as well as taking men too old to work into his own household.[84] In his recent book on Harris, Bill Lawson mentions a name on Taransay which marked the spot where a servant boy from St Kilda used to rest his pack,[85] and he twice refers to the presence of people originally from Hirta living at An t-Ob (Leverburgh); one of them served young gannets from St Kilda at his daughter's wedding.[86] These are sparse and relatively recent references, but they reflect a network of kinship connections and social relationships – perhaps all the more intense for being renewed infrequently? – which must surely go back at least to the Middle Ages.

Historical sources are not very forthcoming about what the steward brought to Hirta. The incoming cargo represented the chiefdom's investment in the island community. When necessary the steward brought a new boat, large enough to be co-owned by the island families, and to make the trip to Boreray and the stacks and return loaded. Sometimes the islanders were not afraid to take their own boat to the Long Island or even Dunvegan.[87] From the outside world they needed – though not necessarily every year – wood (although they had some driftwood), iron tools, querns, seed corn, the occasional new bull, salt (if available) and, by Martin's time, tobacco.

Scope for resistance?

The relationship between the chiefdom and the *Hirteach* was not evenly balanced or symmetrical. Although the chiefdom was essentially predatory, the island community's dependence on the chiefdom was ultimately more critical than the chiefdom's need for the products of this particular part of its realm. The island community needed the chiefdom *in the long term*. In the eighteenth century Kenneth MacAulay understood this: 'if the proprietor should have neglected his vassals … and if the only boat of the isle should have been destroyed … the inhabitants may have perished altogether … their instruments of agriculture would have been worn out … their fishing hooks lost …'.[88] The chiefdom and its regional sub-chiefdoms, on the other hand, needed St Kilda's exports and facilities *on a regular basis*, in order to maintain control over food and people; they had to *invest* in the island economy. Severance of the relationship was probably unthinkable, as the chiefdom demonstrated when it made good the population losses due to the smallpox epidemic of 1727. For each party, freedom of manoeuvre was limited. For the chief and the steward, finding a fresh source of supply, and a different venue for summer hunting expeditions, would have been more costly than maintaining and supporting existing arrangements. The islands were a sitting target. But distance and the wild seas of winter gave the islanders a measure of protection, cutting down the potential frequency of predatory expeditions. And when the retinue arrived in early summer, the St Kildans relied on native wit to try to minimise its exactions.

The steward wanted to get his hands on as much of their produce as his boat would hold, allowing its value against payment of rent and other charges and against the cost of the supplies which he brought. These were not routine transactions; they were often tense negotiations, in which customary law might be set against established or disputed precedents. The islanders' major line of defence was their solidarity. 'They are very cunning', said Martin, 'and there is scarce any circumventing of them in traffic and bartering; the voice of one is the voice of all' and 'there is not a parcel of men in the world more scrupulously nice and punctilious in maintaining their liberties and properties'.[89] Although the steward and the *maor* customarily exchanged gifts, there was also a ritual which highlighted the adversarial nature of the encounter. The *maor's* conduct of his side of the discussion was expected to provoke the steward into hitting him on the head not once, not twice, but at least three times with his 'cudgel'.[90] A few years before Martin's arrival, the steward had attempted to

FIGURE 41.
Mark Edmonds
inspects a hiding-place
in the screes of Mullach
Sgar.

extort a sheep from every family, citing precedent. The St Kildans refused, arguing that the precedent was a response to particular circumstances. When the steward tried to use force, the islanders armed themselves with daggers and fishing-rods, beat his brother about the head, and told him they would pay no new taxes. Their robust approach paid off. During Martin's visit, an argument broke out about the wooden stave-built tub which was used to measure corn. Over 80 years or more its rim had become very abraded, and the islanders strongly objected to the method adopted by the steward to compensate for the short weight. The steward attempted to set up an arbitration panel, and promised to accept its decision. But the people argued that only the MacLeod could assent to any change in the use of this venerable measuring-tub, and they resolved to send the *maor* to Dunvegan to plead their case.[91]

Evasiveness was another strategy. Martin recorded how the people of Berneray never went fishing when their laird or his steward was present, in case 'seeing their plenty of fish, they might take occasion to raise their rents'.[92] The St Kildans took a similar approach. As Kenneth MacAulay put it, 'the people have their own mysteries of state', and he argued that the imposition of 'a certain heavy tax' based on livestock numbers meant that 'a practice of lying soon becomes general and habitual'.[93] Perhaps one reason for the retinue's long stay on Hirta was to allow the steward to make an assessment of the grain yield, harvested or in prospect, before departing. Almost certainly the St Kildans had their intricately-made wooden tumbler-locks[94] long before 1697. In passing, Martin records a corn-drying kiln on Skye with a lockable door,[95] and wooden locks certainly existed in the western Highlands in the 1720s.[96] So it would have been possible to keep certain resources under lock and key.

These were serious matters. 'Mysteries of state' were evidently involved in the two cases of murder mentioned by Neil MacKenzie;[97] they must have taken place a long time before the 1830s. In one of them, a Skye man married into the island and settled there; he was a MacLeod ('and consequently a clansman of the proprietor'). However, he soon 'came to be suspected of giving information in regard to some things which had come to the factor's knowledge'. The following winter he was thrown into the sea. This may be a different version of a story about 'the sending of a stranger *maor* to collect the rent: 'they contrived to lead him to a precipice, and precipitate him out of the world', commented MacLean wittily.[98] The other case involved an ex-servant of the steward, a woman who had also married into the Hirta community. She too was suspected of giving information to her former master. One day, after her husband had diplomatically departed to Dun for the day, a loop of rope was put round her neck and she was strangled by 'all the men', so that 'all might be equally guilty, and thus less risk of anyone informing'. How very communitarian. One wonders how far the steward encouraged kinsmen and servants to marry into the island, in order to take future advantage of old loyalties. If he did, he was putting lives at risk. Neil MacKenzie tells us that among the St Kildans the ultimate punishment was banishment.[99] Where external threats to its solidarity were concerned, the community could be ruthless in the extreme.

Foreign policy

The annual visit of the steward, perhaps the most important event in the St Kildan calendar, was ultimately a fairly routine affair. Arrivals of vessels carrying other kinds of outsiders were much more problematic; the St Kildans had to learn the art of flexible response. From the beginning of the fifteenth century, there were numerous English 'doggers' and merchant vessels in the north-east Atlantic, fishing and trading with Icelanders.[100] 'English' fish-hooks, trapped inside fish, sometimes ended up in gannets' nests, or in their stomachs.[101] Martin mentions foreign vessels putting in at Village Bay, to shelter or take on fresh water.[102] It is very interesting that on late sixteenth-century sea charts St Kilda is depicted much more accurately than any other part of the Western Isles.[103] One can imagine skippers developing good relations with the islanders, calling in on a fairly regular basis, knowing what the St Kildans liked and needed, just as trawler and whaler captains did in the last decades of the community's history.[104] No doubt some visiting fishermen offered to pay for water and hospitality in kind, with tobacco, salt, or the odd piece of replaceable equipment (barrels, spars?); they must have carried some cash to cope with all kinds of eventualities on these unpredictable long-distance voyages. According to Neil MacKenzie the St Kildans were on good terms with visiting pirates, trading with them and taking in their washing![105]

In principle, the islanders were a hospitable people; as Martin said, 'their charity is as extensive as the occasions of it'.[106] Members of his party were accommodated in a house made ready for them, furnished with straw beds. In Martin's day the islanders were kind to shipwrecked sailors, particularly a French and Spanish crew whose ship was wrecked at Rockall in 1686.[107] But English fishermen had become notorious for their violent and lawless behaviour in Iceland (including the kidnapping of children and young people)[108] and the islanders had learnt from bitter experience to treat them warily. In 1696 the crew of one boat, despite carrying a man who spoke bad Gaelic, managed to anger the islanders by picking up ballast on the Sabbath, taking away cattle without offering more than 'a few Irish copper pieces' in payment, and attempting to persuade women to prostitute themselves.[109] On another occasion, visiting seamen had filled their breeks with eggs; the St Kildans gleefully recounted how they had managed to deprive them of both by dislodging a few rocks from above. As a consequence of such incidents, the *Hirteach* had made a rule that visiting seamen were welcome to hospitality, but their number must not exceed ten, and they must come unarmed.[110]

The sighting of large or unfamiliar ships was cause for considerable anxiety. The island was exposed and vulnerable. The St Kildans could hide but they could not run! One option was to conceal themselves and observe newcomers from a distance, gauging their numbers and likely intentions. The earliest record of this practice dates from the piratical visit of Coll MacDonald in 1615, when MacDonald is said to have sent men to persuade them to come out of their hiding-places, assuring them of his peaceful intentions, and offering snuff.[111] Another traumatic event occurred in 1746, with the arrival of three ships and 100 soldiers searching for Bonnie Prince Charlie.[112] It seems that the St Kildans still occasionally fled 'to the rocks' in the later nineteenth century, when it was said to be impossible for visitors to arrive unobserved, even if they came in the small hours, because they were always greeted by the barking of numerous dogs.[113] We know where the islanders took refuge; they had carefully constructed shelters, dry-walled with slab roofs, in the screes below Mullach Sgar (Figure 41). Sands, who instigated some archaeological excavations on Hirta in 1876, dug out a shelter which had two beds built into its walls, like the pre-Improvement houses.[114] These shelters were also investigated by work parties directed by archaeologists from the University of Glasgow in the late 1990s. An inspection of the lower parts of these screes reveals something seriously unnatural about their surface relief. Is it possible that there was once enough subterranean accommodation here to provide temporary refuge, at a pinch, for the entire community?

Coping with outsiders called for negotiating skills and the deployment of keen social and political intelligence. The visitors also had to satisfy the St Kildans' insatiable curiosity about the outside world. Such encounters frequently involved transactions between people who could only communicate at a rudimentary level, like the interpreter who spoke poor Gaelic and failed to convince the St Kildans that his shipmates were Christians.[115] Later, there were better educated, more thoughtful visitors, who came here purposefully, their curiosity about the islanders perhaps almost as intense as that of the islanders about them. However, interchanges with tourists were not necessarily more satisfactory than those with sailors and fishermen. Visitors, especially the more exotic ones, were a potential threat to good order on the island. The *Hirteach* 'are reputed jealous of their wives', remarked Martin nervously.[116] Robert Campbell, one of Henry Brougham's companions in 1799, tells how the men of Hirta returned from an expedition to discover that the women were getting on rather well with the visitors, and promptly locked them up (the women, that is) in one of the houses.[117] From the time of Brougham's trip onwards, there were periodic complaints about pick-pocketing, theft and begging.[118] Campbell had been pleased to feel a girl's arm around his waist, but was less than delighted when he discovered that his handkerchief had been stolen. Brougham and his companions took a dim view of all this, claiming that 'the criminal code is reduced to a very small compass'.[119]

As in parts of the Third World today, the behaviour and attitudes of nineteenth-century St Kildan 'natives' towards tourists triggered a range of unwelcome emotions – notably annoyance and disillusion, especially among romantics. But as rich and evidently leisured outsiders, tourists fell outside the moral universe of the islanders. And according to Neil MacKenzie, anything belonging to the laird was fair game.[120] As in the case of 'natives' encountered by explorers and sea captains the world over, the giving of presents, in some cases on request, was a major form of social cement, binding individuals and families together. Social prestige and generosity were inseparable, chiefs and people of social standing being expected to distribute food and gifts among their followers and clansfolk. English-speaking tourists came from a society much more deeply stratified by wealth and social prestige than any community in the Hebrides, and they were conditioned to hang onto money and property, keeping charitable gifts and disbursements within bounds. As far as the St Kildans were concerned, what looked to tourists like begging and theft were probably natural ways of soliciting gifts and presuming on understood relationships. The islanders in turn must often have been disappointed by the tight-fistedness of visitors, although pleased to receive their carefully-prepared packets of tobacco or snuff.[121]

A far-flung archipelago?

How far is it justifiable to project the St Kilda of Martin's day back into the early centuries of the MacLeod chiefdom, and further back into the Norse world, when 'The Stags' were an outlier of the Southern Isles? I would argue that in the period before well-organised states came into being, chiefdoms of the north-east Atlantic worked in much the same way. They were unstable in the short term; considered on a different time-scale, they had the capacity to endure and re-create themselves intermittently over long periods of time, having evolved a set of tried and tested patterns of behaviour. Accounts of Norse chiefdoms in Iceland, for instance, make them sound similar to Hebridean chiefdoms. This is Paul Durrenberger, commenting on the Icelandic chiefs of the saga era: 'the alternative to expansion was to lose influence, the ability to make good one's claims, one's followers, and one's power as a chieftain. The resources for expansion came from the householders' funds, from the production they appropriated ...'.[122]

That said, there must have been diversity, partly in response to different ecologies and regional traditions. Niall Sharples and Mike Parker Pearson have shown that the Norse occupation of South Uist, the 'isle of barley', dates from the ninth or tenth centuries.[123] They have suggested that in Norse times this island, with its potentially fertile machair plain, was the granary of the southern sector of the Long Island, though herring fishing, probably for a long-distance market, was also of considerable importance.[124] Hirta probably belonged to a different sphere of interaction. Its traditional links were with islands in the Sound of Harris – Pabbay, Berneray, Ensay, and Killegray; the mid seventeenth-century retinue was described as coming from 'the nearest islands'.[125] There is respectable evidence for Norse settlement here;[126] the MacLeods had a 'castle' on Pabbay which was occupied from perhaps the fourteenth to the sixteenth centuries.[127] These islands formed the 'bread-basket' of Harris,[128] even after parts of Pabbay and Berneray had been devastated by the severe sandstorms of the years around 1700. Looking at population figures for the mid eighteenth century, we can see that if it had not been for the impact of infantile tetanus, Hirta would probably have had much the same population as Pabbay and Berneray;[129] between a quarter and a third of the population of Harris lived on the islands in the Sound. We should think of these islands collectively, not as individual bits of land; in 1705 a boat was bought to serve as a ferry, linking all of them with Harris and Skye.[130] In an age of maritime confidence, these islands – including Hirta – would have formed the heartland of Harris, their peoples forming an intermarrying population of several hundred. Hirta not only contributed to the breadbasket (in the late sixteenth century the island paid '60 bolls victuall' (*c.* 3.8 tonnes) in rent[131]); its other products would have added a welcome diversity to the local network of redistribution.

History is virtually silent about the significance of *Hirtir* in the times when the Norsemen ruled the waves. But one cannot help feeling that from a Norse perspective, the archipelago would have offered tempting opportunities to a vigorous and predatory Viking leader from North Uist, Harris or one of the islands in the Sound. Recent archaeological work on South Uist has shown that Norse settlement in the Western Isles has to be taken seriously; placename evidence and fortuitous archaeological discoveries suggest that *Hirtir* participated to the full. There is a story about the MacDonalds and the MacLeods racing against each other to lay claim to Hirta; when the MacDonalds were just about to claim victory, one of the MacLeods stole the victory by cutting off his hand and hurling it onto the beach.[132] Apparently this tale post-dates the time of the Norsemen, and it was also told in relation to places other than St Kilda. Nevertheless, there would be little point in telling it about an island regarded as little more than a pirates' lair. I suspect that somewhere in the space between this story and the undated former head dykes at Village Bay lie the roots of the populous and organised community encountered by Martin Martin. But ultimately only archaeology will reveal further details of the saga which waits to be told.

CHAPTER FIVE

A Study in Cultural Competence

'The most knowingist people I have ever come across' –
Nairn stonemason, 1860, of the St Kildans

G. Seton (1980) p. 255.

FIGURE 42.
Ewen MacDonald.

It is a widespread perception that the key to St Kilda's history is encapsulated in one word: 'marginality'. Some people believe that the St Kildans should be celebrated as historical heroes – enduring a wretched existence for centuries, buffeted by Atlantic gales, marooned on an archipelago which was marginal not only in a geographical sense, but economically, socially and politically as well. This is a simplistic view.

Commentators use the word 'marginal' to describe several perceptions which are not mutually exclusive – that the land was not very productive; that the weather was often terrible; that the people led an unenviable existence; that self-evidently those living 'on the periphery' must have been culturally impoverished. Let me be clear; Hirta was no island paradise. Upper and middle class visitors in the eighteenth and nineteenth centuries were repelled by the St Kildan ambience. As Heathcote put it in 1900, 'I fancy that a little Keating's powder would add to the comfort of anyone sleeping in a native house, and they are not very particular as to where they throw the refuse parts of birds and fishes'.[1] However, it is not at all clear that the living standards and general health of the St Kildans were worse than those of contemporaries in other parts of Britain – miners, quarrymen, factory workers, sailors, fishermen or farm labourers, for example. Nor do they seem to have been worse off than other inhabitants of north-west Scotland, who faced similar environmental, economic and social conditions. A special correspondent of the *Glasgow Herald*, who visited St Kilda in 1926, had seen worse poverty in Lewis, Harris, and 'other parts of the Western Highlands' and argued that whilst 'an epidemic of a slight and common infection' on Hirta required the dispatch of a special medical team, the unnecessary deaths of hundreds of children in the slums of Glasgow passed 'almost unnoticed'. People fussed too much over the St Kildans, he felt: 'living on the island has become a trade in itself'.[2]

Dodgshon, writing about north-west Scotland, has suggested that 'the survival of communities on such sites cannot be rationalised by treating them as remote or isolated settlements surviving on the edge of a much larger and wider system *and as handicapped by that fact*, but by seeing them as sufficient unto themselves or as communities that functioned within a relatively localised network of relations. Such sites only became remote when the pressures of modernity forced them into the framework of a national economic system.'[3] The application of a label like 'marginal' encourages lazy thinking; it does not *characterise* the St Kildans and their history, but rather *stereotypes* them. Hordern and Purcell, writing about long-term Mediterranean history, have expressed themselves eloquently on this topic. 'The vocabulary of prosperity or desolation as applied to whole geographical regions should be seen as part of the rhetoric of political authority and central management', they write; 'the areas that we often dismiss as least hospitable, or perceive as residual fragments of a landscape that was once hostile to humanity, are amongst the most diverse and complex of complementary production opportunities'.[4] In these terms, St Kilda has to be regarded as a 'risk laden environment' – like many other parts of the world – and the real question is the one faced by most humans in most places: how were they to 'buffer' their economy, and protect themselves against risk?

The basics

Past commentators have been quite optimistic about the potential productivity of the St Kilda archipelago, even after we have allowed for the proprietorial viewpoint which is concerned with what a place *should* be worth. Let us start with the arable sector. A late sixteenth-century report described Hirta as *paying* '60 bolls victuall'[5] – exactly the same as the figure for Pabbay in the Sound of Harris. MacAulay gave a figure of 50 bolls per year for the mid eighteenth century.[6] The rent in the 1790s is listed as 43 and 50 bolls of barley.[7] If a boll weighed around 140 lbs or *c.* 60.35 kg[8] the island was expected to produce some 3.6 tonnes of grain as rent in the late sixteenth century, and about 2.6 tonnes a couple of centuries later – 20 to 30 kg per head, adjusted for contemporary population figures. Confusingly, the rent in barley in the 1720s is listed at only 16 and 18 bolls;[9] perhaps it was reduced in response to poor harvests.

Visitors were complimentary about Hirta's barley. Martin said that yields were 'ordinarily sixteen, eighteen or twentyfold' and that the barley was 'the largest produced in all the Western Isles'.[10] MacAulay noted that the St Kildans sowed early and were able to reap early as a consequence of the effect of solar radiation in the shelter of Village Bay.[11] For MacCulloch, the barley was 'by much the finest to be seen in the whole circuit of the isles'; for Atkinson it was 'excellent'.[12] This was a high input, high output gardening system; compost-making was the key to success. As MacAulay put it: 'the soil around the village though naturally poor, is rendered extremely fertile, by the singular industry of very judicious husbandmen'.[13] The compost-makers attempted to counteract the continuous leaching of soil nutrients by introducing marine products into the cycle, including fish and sea-bird offal; they had a standard, trusted recipe.[14] MacAulay records the islanders' serious concern about the long-term conservation of sea-weed, and how they reserved the 'choice sort' of compost for barley and used 'the ordinary kind' for oats.[15] Buchan claimed that 'the corn produced by this their compost is perfectly free of any kind of weeds' and pointed out, as did Martin and MacAulay, that 'it produces much sorrel, where the compost reaches'.[16] As a source of vital fresh 'greens', sorrel was very important in the Hirta diet. To this day, considerable spreads of sorrel survive among the long-abandoned 'lazy beds' at the west end of the island of Dun. Photographs show that it often grew on thatched roofs, sometimes in abundance. Sorrel did well on Hirta, flourishing wherever compost was applied[17] and around fulmar and puffin colonies, where it resists the high nitrogen content of guano.[18] The St Kildans ate a variety of wild plants, including sea-weeds;[19] Hebrideans knew the importance of eating scurvy-grass.[20] In the later Middle Ages, the *Hirteach* had a communally-organised system of allocating arable land and, presumably, making sure that the land was efficiently manured (see Chapter Four, page 66).

There are numerous favourable comments about the quality of the pasture. MacKenzie quoted a popular saying that Hirta grew as much grass as Harris.[21] MacAulay praised the 'many excellent plots of grass' and the 'peculiarly fine' pasture in Gleann Mór (Figure 43); the cattle fed 'most luxuriously during the summer season', producing 'more than ordinary quantities of milk' and extremely rich cream.[22] For Martin, the cattle produced 'fat and sweet' beef.[23] The agricultural expert MacDiarmid noted the excellence of the pasture-land ('as fine a sheep-run of its size as can be seen anywhere'). The cattle were 'all in wonderfully good condition – much better, in fact, than on many places on the mainland in this trying season'. Despite being 'badly managed' the sheep 'are said to be very fat in autumn when killed, which may well be believed from the nature of the pasture; and the St Kilda mutton that was presented to us for dinner would favourably compare in flavour and quality

FIGURE 43.
Gleann Mór.

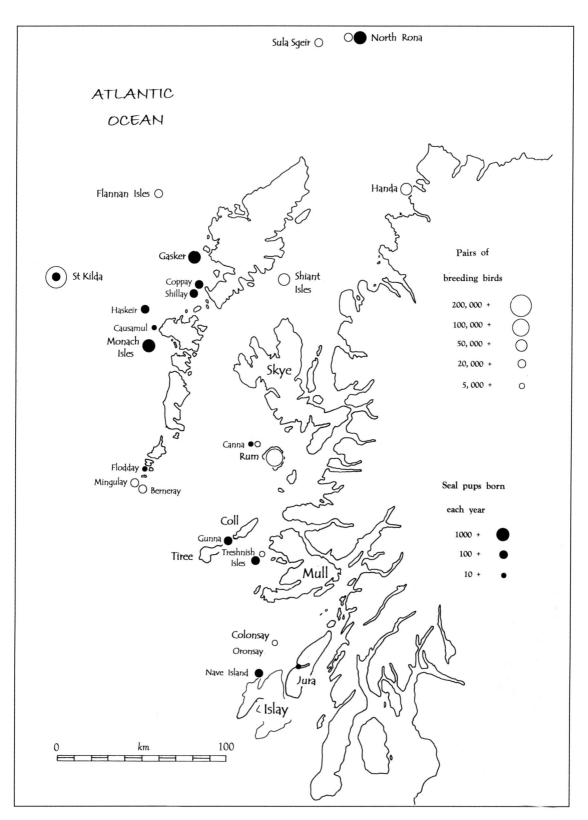

Sula Sgeir ○   ○● North Rona

ATLANTIC

OCEAN

Flannan Isles ○

Handa ●

Gasker ●

St Kilda ●

Coppay ●
Shillay ●

Shiant
Isles ○

Haskeir ●

Causamul ●

Monach ●
Isles

Skye

Pairs of

breeding birds

200, 000 + ◯

100, 000 + ◯

50, 000 + ○

20, 000 + ○

5, 000 + ○

Canna ●○
Rum

Flodday ●

Mingulay ○○
Berneray ○

Coll

Gunna ●

Tiree

Treshnish ○
Isles ●

Mull

Seal pups born

each year

1000 + ●

100 + ●

10 + ●

Colonsay ○
Oronsay

Nave Island ●

Jura

Islay

0   km   100

86

with the best fed blackfaced'. The sheep which MacDiarmid saw were apparently 'quite free from scab and other skin-diseases'.[24] Both Martin and MacAulay were impressed with the lambing percentages of the Soays.[25] Atkinson praised the quality of the cheese, which seems to have been usually made from a mixture of cows' and ewes' milk.[26] An interesting comment on animal husbandry was made by MacCulloch who argued that the islanders were 'the only Highlanders who have the command of animal food' – because livestock were not exported, preventing 'that acquisition of disposable wealth which would speedily find its way to the landlord in the form of rent'.[27] Cattle *were* exported, however, in the late nineteenth century, when Hirta's 'carrying capacity', or the entitlement granted by the estate, was 1200 sheep and 50 head of cattle.[28]

Then, famously, there were the sea-birds, dominated by the triad of puffins, fulmars and gannets. The literature contains a good deal of detailed information about techniques of egg-collecting and bird-catching, and quantities of birds and eggs harvested, most of which I will not repeat here. In the last decade of the nineteenth century, H. A. MacPherson, who was researching a book on the history of fowling, got the factor of St Kilda to ascertain the precise numbers of birds caught each year.[29] It seems that there were 16 'shares' (one for each house, evidently) each assigned 80 young gannets, 120 adult gannets, 560 fulmars, 600 puffins, 120 common guillemots, and 50 razorbills, making 1530 birds for each share – a grand total of 24,480. This implies an average annual consumption of somewhere between 300 and 350 birds per head. In general, they caught between two and five times as many fulmars as gannets.[30] Such catches was a drop in the ocean, so to speak; the archipelago was the best fowling station in Britain (Figure 44). Currently St Kilda is host to five-sixths of the gannets in the Hebrides (50,000 pairs), almost half the fulmars (63,000 pairs), and about three-fifths of the puffins (230,000 individuals) (Figure 45), and there are substantial populations of guillemots (Figure 46) and razorbills.[31] Puffins were easily taken and formed a regular food source on Hirta. The gannet has been a delicacy and a prized resource in Scotland since at least the Iron Age (see Chapter Three, page 58).[32] And until the late nineteenth century, the St Kilda archipelago was the *only* breeding-station for the fulmar in Britain.[33] Atkinson recorded that it was 'infinitely the most esteemed fowl the St Kildeans have'; the egg was 'superior to the egg of any other seabird'; the fat young birds were held 'in very high esteem'. The oil was 'much valued ... for the cure of rheumatism'[34] – a serious adult health problem on St Kilda.[35] Before the nineteenth century, the St Kildans also took the great auk, a large, flightless bird, as big as a goose and laying an almost ostrich-size egg; the bird could easily be clubbed on the ground.[36] On Hirta, its favourite haunt was, understandably, on the rocks at the mouth of Gleann Mór.[37] This intriguing bird, now extinct, was a popular target in prehistoric times in various parts of northern Britain.[38] By the mid seventeenth century it had been generally hunted out in Britain, though it may still have been present in a few spots, such as the Isle of Man, Rathlin and Lundy.[39]

FIGURE 44.
Map of north-west Scotland, showing seabird and seal resources (data from Boyd and Boyd 1990).

FIGURE 45.
A puffin amongst sorrel; vital 'meat and veg' for the St Kildans.

FIGURE 46.
A typical guillemot ledge on the colourful cliffs of north Hirta – the highest in Britain.

Each species set different problems for the fowlers, who had developed ingenious and flexible methods. For example, in the eighteenth century, methods of puffin-catching 'varied according to the nature of the place he is in. Upon rocks and stones they are caught with gins, from under these rocks they are fetcht out by terriers; when they are in holes under ground they are forced out by sharp pointed stones; when they sit on plain ground they are taken with rods and gins on the end of them …'.[40] In 1900 Norman Heathcote recorded that 'the natives talk to them all the time in puffin language, and while the bird is trying to make out what they are saying, he finds his neck has got entangled in the noose'.[41] The St Kildans did not restrict themselves to the species which could be caught most easily. They went after kittiwakes – which often involved a multiple-rope climb to get to the lowest parts of the cliffs.[42] And they caught guillemots, which generally breed on very narrow ledges (Figure 46) – a hunt which involved taking terrifying risks, as well as having the patience to rest up all night on the cliff-face. The fowler waited for dawn, when the birds returned to their ledges, and then used a piece of white cloth to attract one of them in, subsequently showing the white flash of its body as a decoy for others. Sometimes a stuffed bird was used as a decoy[43] (and the taxidermist's skill (Figure 21, page 36) came in useful in the tourist season[44]). And these were birds 'of no great value', a single gannet yielding as much meat as ten guillemots.[45] (Fresh guillemots' eggs, however, were great delicacies, and young kittiwakes were apparently a favourite 'starter' in north Britain in the eighteenth century.[46]) Of course the St Kildans knew a great deal about the habits of their prey, and had rules intended to ensure that these resources were sustainable. For instance, they carried out an early-season cull of gannets' eggs on Stac Li but not on Boreray; this was done specifically in order to stagger the harvest of young gannets ('if all were allowed to hatch at the same time, the loss of the product in one rock would at the same time prove the loss of all the rest'[47]). In the mid eighteenth century it was forbidden to kill adult fulmars or take their eggs, a measure intended to maintain the seasonal availability of fat young fulmars in August.[48]

Then there were the seals, the denizens of the sea-caves and skerries of western Hirta (Figure 47); they were hunted from at least the sixteenth century.[49] Moray, writing 20 years before Martin Martin, documents the hunting of 'great seals' with wooden poles in a narrow inlet on or near Soay. Seal-hunting was a dangerous and difficult business, but was felt to be worth the risks; in Martin's time the St Kildans thought that seals provided 'very good meat'.[50] Numbers fluctuated. Kearton, for instance, was told that seals

FIGURE 47.
The realm of the seals.

had become very scarce.[51] However, in the 1960s there was a resident popula-tion of several hundred grey seals.[52]

St Kilda and the
Wider World: Tales
of an Iconic Island

The St Kildans also caught fish with lines, in 'craig seats' off the rocks, or sometimes from boats – an opportunistic, small-scale method already noted in the sixteenth century;[53] it has been part of the Western Isles repertoire since at least the Iron Age.[54] Outsiders regularly suggested that Hirta would make a good commercial fishing-station.[55] The St Kildans were not persuaded, although in the late nineteenth century they dried or salted fish and sold them.[56] It is understandable that they preferred to intervene at a higher level in the ecological pyramid, letting the birds catch the fish and convert them into meat and eggs. A disaster at sea would usually have meant the loss of several men. And there *were* catastrophes. In the late eighteenth century several men returning from Boreray were lost when their boat capsized near the Village Bay landing-place;[57] and in March 1909, on a glorious day, three men were drowned off Dun.[58] Climbers were less vulnerable to sudden changes in the weather; death on the cliffs tended to involve only one or two individuals rather than entire boat-loads.

Neil MacKenzie listed the winter stores of a typical family. At the begin-ning of winter, a cow was killed, and thereafter 12 sheep, mostly wethers. There would be two or three barrels of young fulmars ('which are tender and fat as bacon') and a barrel or a barrel and a half of young gannets; there would also be six stones (*c.* 65 kg) of cheese and some fish and eggs, the milk of two cows, and 'a considerable quantity of barley, with some oats and potatoes'. MacKenzie concluded: 'I know of no place where people can have such a plen-tiful supply of food with so little exertion'.[59] In 1860, the laird claimed that 'the St Kilda people, compared with the other islesmen, have food in abun-dance and in variety. They eat a good deal of mutton, and have wild fowl without stint and of good quality, together with excellent fish, which they can catch with very little trouble without quitting the shore … they consume all the cereal produce of the island, and commonly a good deal more … from time immemorial down to the year 1804 the island annually exported 50 bolls (*c.* 32 tonnes) of grain, oats and bear … plenty of very fine sorrel, a capital corrective of the scorbutic tendency … dulse, carragean and a kind of wild spinage'.[60] In July 1840, the naturalist John MacGillivray sat down to 'the following bill of fare: fulmar, auk, guillemot, one of each, boiled; two puffins, roasted; barley-cakes, ewe-cheese, and milk; and by way of desert, raw dulse and roasted limpets'.[61] Malcolm MacNeill, reporting in 1885, said that each family had 800–1200 meat rations salted down for the winter in fulmars and gannets, as well as three to six 40 lb (18 kg) wedders.[62] Captain MacDonald of the *Vigilant*, writing in the late nineteenth century, considered that there was 'not a more comfortable set of people between Cantyre and Cape Wrath, or from the Butt of Lewis to Barra Head, than the St Kildans'.[63]

Several accounts portray the people as reasonably healthy. When he visited Hirta in 1697, Martin noted that 'both men and women are well proportioned, nothing differing from those of the isles and continent' and that from a medical point of view 'providence is very favourable to them'.[64] The men had a reputation for being twice as strong as the men of Harris, and Martin thought that several of the women, if properly dressed, 'would be reckoned among beauties of the first rank' (Figure 7, page 14). In assessing the significance of the health problems which he listed,[65] it is important to remember that the Hebrideans had recently endured 'King William's Lean Years'. In the 1690s, ferocious storms hit the west coast of Britain, creating massive sand dunes, swamping medieval churches and changing low-lying coastal landscapes on a permanent basis. Mary Harman suggests that Hirta was over-populated at this time.[66] So the St Kildans' state of health may have been indifferent when Martin arrived. Nevertheless, there was a contrast with Lewis, where, according to Martin: 'the late years of scarcity brought them very low, and many of the poor people have died by famine'.[67] For MacAulay, writing in the mid eighteenth century, the St Kildan men were 'stout hardy fellows' and 'remarkably strong'. The women were 'mostly handsome', much superior to those of the Western Isles; some of them, 'if properly dressed, and genteely educated, would … be reckoned extraordinary beauties in the gay world'.[68] After Hirta had been largely repopulated following the smallpox epidemic of 1727, it would have to be living conditions, rather than genetic inheritance, which differentiated the St Kildans from their Hebridean neighbours. According to MacCulloch: 'the men are well looking, and better dressed than many of their neighbours of the Long Island; bearing indeed the obvious marks of ease of circumstances both in their apparel and diet'.[69] In the late nineteenth century, a time when there was some concern about the St Kildans' welfare, uncomplimentary remarks were made about obesity; for MacDiarmid some of the women were 'more than ordinarily stout' (Figure 58, page 122).[70] Seton 'observed a good many examples of something more than plumpness' and noted that 'they are said to lose flesh when placed upon the comparatively low diet of the inhabitants of the Long Island'.[71] At much the same time, Sands, whose political antipathy to the laird should have encouraged him to paint a gloomy picture of the St Kildans' state of health, testified that 'both sexes look strong and healthy. They have ruddy cheeks, remarkably clear eyes, and teeth like new ivory [the whiteness of St Kildan teeth was frequently remarked upon]. Their limbs are hard as boxwood, and their whole frames capable of severe and long-continued exertion'.[72] For the last decades of the community's existence, we have the visual testimony of photographs. In the late nineteenth century there were some tough times. The St Kildans sent out 'mailboats' containing urgent requests for help.[73] There was a bad crop failure in 1882, with severe consequences over much of northern Scotland,[74] and another after the terrible weather of September 1885.[75] However, there seems nothing much wrong with the 'members of Parliament' who posed for MacLeod's now celebrated photograph the following summer (Figure 10, page 17). I have never seen anyone in the St Kilda photographs looking in the least emaciated.

Nor did 'in-breeding' have much effect on mental health. The St Kildans were well aware of potential problems here; as Martin put it, they were 'nice in examining the degrees of consanguinity before marriage'.[76] Dr Arthur Mitchell, amateur archaeologist and Commissioner for Lunacy, made an investigation in the mid nineteenth century – admittedly by proxy – and was able to show that none of the 17 children of five marriages between second cousins was 'in any way defective in body or mind' and there was only one (unmarried) female who was 'weak in intellect'.[77]

Cultural competence

Neil MacKenzie was disparaging about the amount of work done by the men of Hirta. But he was not being entirely fair. (It has to be said that MacKenzie's approach to his flock displayed at times a touch of the cynicism which perhaps comes naturally to someone who successfully manipulates the minds of others.) The minister's calculations took no account of what had to be done to maintain the economic infrastructure – time spent making or repairing ropes, nets, rods, baskets and all manner of fowling equipment and containers, as well as maintaining houses and cleits and their fittings and furnishings, and equipment which supported the arable and livestock components of the economy. The men were the tailors, dress-makers and shoemakers, and they also had to make and repair their looms.[78] The island boat, or boats, had to be looked after. The community's relationship with the outside world also involved work – feathers and other commodities had to be bagged up, and items made to sell to tourists. Critical comments were sometimes made about the men's habit of lounging around in their 'Parliament'.[79] But a man was more conspicuous when carrying out his 'parliamentary' duties, in the open air in daylight hours, than when quietly mending a spade at his hearth in the evening.

On a remote island, one might expect the material culture to be impoverished, in terms of diversity – rather like the flora. But this was not the case. The *Hirteach* had a remarkable repertoire of craft skills, and utilised available materials to the full. For instance, an important component of the cereal harvest – even in years of poor *grain* yield – was straw. In later years, straw must sometimes have been the main product of cereal cultivation. It was twisted into ropes of varying thickness, which, according to Neil MacKenzie, were 'wonderfully strong and durable'. They were used for climbing, for tethering animals, and securing thatch (Figure 48). And it was mostly ropes made of straw which were tied and woven together to make baskets for egg collection or the transport of peat, sacks for storing grain and feathers, gates for gathering-folds,[80] tubs for household storage, as well as chairs[81] and beds.[82] Straw ropes, festooned with feathers, were used to keep sheep off the bird slopes.[83] Ropes provide a good example of the flexibility and diversity of St Kildan material culture; as well as straw, they were made from plaited, salted cow-hides,[84] horse-hair,[85] heather[86] and willow.[87] Ropes of hemp were also available.[88]

FIGURE 48.
With its wooden door, and plants growing from the turves of a roof secured with ropes and stone weights, the cleit in this old photograph reminds us how these sheds once looked.

The gannet fulfilled a variety of non-alimentary functions. Gannets' stomachs were commonly used as containers,[89] notably on an occasion when the islanders helped themselves to the contents of a cask of wine washed up on the beach.[90] Disposable shoes were manufactured from gannets' neck-skins,[91] and gannet feather quills were used in puffin-catching.[92] This involved 'a running noose of horse-hair and gannet-quills ... cunningly plaited together'. 'The ... interwoven quills ... whilst preserving a sufficient amount of flexibility ... so stiffen the noose as to make it stand up in the form of an almost perfect circle'. In the mid nineteenth century the beaks of gannets were used as pegs on thatched roofs,[93] and their sternums were used as scoops[94] or as lamps.[95] Various other materials were also part of the craft repertoire. Like other Hebrideans, the St Kildans made their own simple pottery, with clay brought in from the Long Island; they made horn spoons; and they were opportunistic tinkers, able to fashion needles, fish-hooks and brooches out of nails, coins, and buttons.[96] It would have taken good craft skills to maintain musical instruments, and wooden locks and keys, in the St Kilda climate.

The cultural competence of the St Kildans was also displayed in their approach to climbing. Children were trained to climb on house walls, using ropes, from an early age; climbing ropes were always tested before use.[97] According to Moray,[98] it was customary for the *maor* to stipulate that 'the best climbers and the worst are mixed together'. He claimed that this was to ensure even coverage of the cliffs. But since climbers were often roped together, such a practice must sometimes have saved the lives of the careless, helped younger and more foolhardy climbers to develop better judgement, and prevented the simultaneous loss of two good practitioners. St Kildan climbing techniques were sophisticated,[99] and their climbing stories included the classic ethical dilemma where, in order to avert *two* deaths, a climber has to cut his partner's rope and send him hurtling to his doom.[100] It has recently been stated that

Samuel Taylor Coleridge's descent of Broad Stand, at Scafell in the English Lake District, in 1802 'is generally considered to be the first rock-climb'.[101] But long before Coleridge, unsung poets had developed tried and tested techniques for climbing cliffs, at St Kilda and elsewhere in northern Scotland.

Climbing fatalities would have been traumatic, particularly in such a small community, but they were not particularly frequent. An old woman told Neil MacKenzie that there had been only 11 climbing deaths over the period 1783–1843.[102] This can be compared with two such deaths in the period 1830–46, recorded in the registers started by MacKenzie himself, and two for the period 1856–76.[103] So there was one climbing fatality every seven years or so, on the average, in a community of around 100. From an individual's perspective, of course, this is not a trivial figure. It implies that a 60-year-old could recall the distress occasioned by seven or eight climbing deaths, on average. But from the long-term perspective of the community, and from a Darwinian point of view, such losses were bearable; some of the men killed would already have begotten children.

Outsiders criticised the islanders' approach to the conservation of natural resources, notably fuel supplies. Traditionally, both peat and turf were used as fuel.[104] Visibly, some areas – notably the land above the 1830s head dyke, and on Am Blaid – have been stripped bare of surface vegetation. Visitors expressed their concern about this, and bemoaned the fact that the islanders were destructively stripping turf when peat was still available.[105] MacKenzie noted that despite the presence of 'quite enough of moderately good peat to supply them with fuel', the St Kildans never actually cut enough to satisfy their fuel requirements, and 'for the rest of the year they use the peaty turf which covers the rocks, and in this way they have gradually destroyed a considerable extent of useful pasture'.[106]

It is worth considering whether the critics may have misunderstood something. Peats vary in their properties, according to their origins and the ratio between mineral and organic content.[107] Peat gives off more heat than turf, and the St Kildans may have preferred to reserve it for winter fuel, using turf for cooking and as roofing material (which was eventually used to make compost). Given the number of people in each house, the presence of cattle indoors in winter, and the likelihood that houses were quite well insulated, burning turf – or bulking out peat with turf – on a slow-burning central hearth may have been an economical form of heating in St Kilda's relatively mild temperatures. Possibly work at the peats was given low priority when there were labour shortages, or when more crucial tasks had been delayed by bad weather. Since turf would dry more quickly than peat, the islanders may sometimes have been forced to use it as winter fuel to supplement inadequate stocks of peat caused by labour deficits. According to MacCulloch, 'much of [the peat] is consumed in the manufacture of salt',[108] so some may have been reserved for this purpose. A good deal of peat was granulated[109] to form an essential component of the compost; it was good for absorbing urine. It may have been more important to secure high quality compost than to keep every bit of the pasture green. Outsiders, accustomed to abundant peat in other regions, may not have understood that the use and abuse of turf and peat supplies was a complex matter for the islanders. One woman observed to the agricultural expert MacDiarmid: 'we must have our food cooked'.[110]

Diversity, storage and redistribution

Around the Mediterranean, according to Hordern and Purcell, the three critical strategies for coping with risk have been economic diversity, storage, and redistribution.[111] Were these strategies applicable in the north-east Atlantic? The St Kildan economy was diversified both in terms of sources of food and in relation to the exports which they had to offer. Martin listed nine items – feathers, wool, butter, cheese, cows, horses, birds, oil, and barley.[112] Two centuries later, the list also contained up to nine exports – tweed, blanketing, feathers, cattle, tallow, oil, fish (dried or salted), cheese and wool.[113] The islanders were also receptive to new ways of making a living, as they demonstrated in the late nineteenth century, in relation to the manufacture and sale of tweed and blanketing and the exploitation of tourism.

Figuratively, as well as literally, they did not put all their eggs in one basket. The Island of a Thousand Sheds was well equipped for storage (Figures 48, 49). However, cleits are as yet not very archaeologically informative. Although most of those within and near the 1830s head dyke must surely have been constructed in the nineteenth century (and in a few cases, the early twentieth[114]) we do not know when the more distant cleits were built, nor when they went out of use. There are a few observable facts. Clearly many of the cleits on the western side of Oiseval were abandoned quite a long time ago, and in some cases robbed of stone. The 'boat-shaped structures' above the 1830s head dyke and towards An Lag are now thought to be dismantled cleits, but we know little else about them. Some of the cleits in the Am Blaid area are perched on 'pedestals' *above* the present turf-stripped land surface, suggesting that deep peat was stripped from this area *after* they were built.

Common sense and post-medieval literature, rather than archaeological reasoning, imply that some outlying cleits at least were in being well before the thirteenth century. For a start, the name 'cleit' comes from the Norse word *klettr*, a rock.[115] Its Gaelic equivalent *clach* ('stone') also appears in the literature; if this is a translation from the Norse, doesn't this imply that cleits go back to Norse times at least – or earlier if the Norsemen reached for the word *klettr* to translate the name of structures already here when they arrived? (They used different words in other places – *skeo* in Orkney and Shetland, including Fair Isle and Foula, and there were wooden slatted *hjallar* in Faeroe.[116]) Visitors often remark upon the line of cleits ('Cleit Street') leading up from An Lag to the Gap, and there is another beside the path leading down into Gleann Mór. Evidently these lines were once more widespread. The dismantled cleits of An Lag occur not only on the shoulder above the 1830s head dyke, but also higher up, in the heather on the lowest south-east slopes

FIGURE 49.
This abandoned cleit
has lost its turf roof,
but its stone door and
a well-constructed
'window', relieving
pressure on the lintel
above the entrance,
may still be seen.

of Conachair. They tend to be disposed in lines, at least one of which comes down onto the shoulder below, as shown on Mary Harman's plan [117] (and see Figure 17, page 24). There are also intriguing *clusters* of cleits, notably beside the path up onto the Mullach Bi ridge, and near the military quarry at Creagan Breac (Figure 25, page 45). Some of these display rare features which may be quite old, such as 'finial' stones at the ends of roofs, and stone closing-slabs at their entrances. (In the early eighteenth century there were regulations governing compensation payable for animals which died in cleits whose doors were not properly closed.[118]) In general it seems that most of the cleits on Hirta were used primarily as drying sheds, and also for storage. But a few must have been essentially depots or caches – where food, fuel and equipment were kept for people working in outlying places, or food could be stock-piled when fowlers and egg-collectors had acquired too much to take home on one trip. The 'depot' interpretation makes sense for the outlying islands. Interestingly, Dun has no cleits; perhaps it was considered 'home territory', from which catches were always brought back overland – and then, after it became an island, by boat. But there are about 40 cleits on Soay, 50 on Boreray and 80 on Stac an Armin.

Redistribution, the third of Hordern and Purcell's risk-buffering strategies, was also practised. Surplus produce was exported, via the steward, tacksman or factor, and some of its value was bartered for imported goods. And there was plenty of redistribution *within* the community, between families; this helped the disadvantaged, and supported newly-wed couples.

Gender, food and sex

On Hirta there were two important social entities within the community – 'families' and groups defined by gender – one for males and one for females. Martin reported that the arable land was 'very nicely parted into ten divisions, each distinguished by the name of some deceased man or woman';[119] 30 years earlier, Sir Robert Moray recorded that there were ten 'families'.[120] Each family must have contained around 20 people on average – a set of adult siblings, unmarried or with spouses, their children, and surviving members of older generations. It sounds as if the system was flexible, with kinship potentially reckoned bilaterally, through either male or female lines. Given the recorded size of the settlement (the *clachan*), each family would have occupied two or three houses. For some purposes – though this must have varied over time – these families acted as autonomous entities, though in a wider sense they were far from independent. Commentators sometimes noted variations in livestock numbers owned by different families. Martin said that the maximum family holding consisted of 8 cows, 80 sheep, and 2 or 3 horses,[121] and the early eighteenth-century *maor* is said to have had about 20 cows and 200–300 sheep.[122] MacAulay quotes cattle numbers as a measure of economic stratification; the highest 'class' owned 7 or 8 cows.[123] Perhaps livestock production *was* the area in which it made most sense for resources to be privately owned and competitively accumulated. But 'wealth' of this kind would have been temporary, and ultimately only its owner's sense of generosity and obligation could translate it into social capital. Such 'wealth' would have been whittled away by the obligations of families to supply animals or meat for exchange or consumption on various occasions, such as when relatives got married, and at wedding and

FIGURE 50.
North-east part of Gleann Mór, showing the old field system and structures of 'Amazon's House type (probably Pictish houses with later modifications. For a plan, see Figure 35).

funeral feasts. Accumulation and maintenance of 'capital' in the form of live-stock would also have been affected by changes in family fortunes and composition over time. Successful livestock rearing depended to some extent on the investment made by the community (and the laird). The community boat was used to take sheep to and from the outlying islands, as well as people to attend to them; right up to the evacuation, people meticulously contributed their share of the fodder for the village bull.[124]

For many daylight hours there were effectively *two* communities, one of men and one of women, cross-cutting the integrity of families. In principle at least, most tasks were either men's or women's work, though sources are fairly scanty and we cannot rule out changes over time, or flexibility in some situa-tions. Women were involved in dairying.[125] They apparently did quite a lot of the agricultural work, carrying manure to the fields,[126] harrowing,[127] and reaping,[128] though some sources suggest that the men mucked in (literally sometimes, filling baskets with manure and helping to spread it[129]), and men did the sowing.[130] Harvesting, often carried out under pressure during a brief break in the weather, probably involved all the family.[131] It was women who ground the grain into flour on rotary querns.[132] Women did the spinning,[133] men were the weavers;[134] the cloth they wove went to the women for waulking,[135] and then back to the men, who were tailors and shoemakers,[136] making clothing for their womenfolk as well as themselves. Work was usually done in groups; in some cases this was logistically unavoidable, as in the case of expeditions involving the island boat. The nature of men's and women's work (and also the assistance rendered by boys and girls) ensured that the sexes were separated for considerable periods of time. Dairying activities took women to Gleann Mór in the summer (Figure 50; Figure 43, page 85; Figure 19, page 25); in Martin's day some of them lived there for the duration,[137] but later they may have commuted on a daily basis.[138] Men sometimes stayed on stacks and other islands overnight or for several days, fowling, egg-collecting, and dealing with sheep, though in some circumstances, for example when catching and plucking puffins had to be done, women also went on trips to the outlying islands.[139]

The gendering of work was not simply a matter of logistics. Martin implies that there were separate 'assemblies' for men and women.[140] These were male and female communities in their own right, each with its own cultural tradi-tion, songs and stories, its own patterns of authority and deference, its own rules and customary attitudes. Socially and in terms of working efficiency, all this made good sense. If the respective 'assemblies' were made up mostly of male and female heads of families, the groups which took critical decisions would have been both small and representative; equity between families was built into the decision-making process. And potential tensions in this area would have been further diminished by the existence of numerous rules and regulations, the drawing of lots, and the authority of the *maor* and his female equivalent.

The skills and traditions of these different kinds of work, the rituals and the songs and the jokes, would have engendered solidarity in the men's and women's groups, involving fields of inclusion and exclusion which added a distinctive dimension to the politics of the island. And yet at the same time the sexes were deeply interdependent, as we have already seen in the case of cloth production and the manufacture of clothing. A man's skill as a rock-climbing fowler was deployed in an arena of masculine prowess and prestige, and the physical courage of the St Kildan cliff-climbers was akin to that of warriors (Figure 51). Martin made the connection: 'their frequent discourses of

FIGURE 51.
The rock-climbing
skills of the St Kildans.

99

climbing, together with the fatal end of several in the exercise of it, is the same to them, as that of fighting and killing is with soldiers ...'.[141] The shrewd Kenneth MacAulay understood about the adrenalin rush: 'those pleasures and advantages which are dearly bought, or pursued amid imminent dangers, are tasted and enjoyed with greater relish'.[142] (In MacAulay's day, mountain travellers were beginning to recognise and describe this syndrome.[143]) A successful fowler was admired and appreciated by women; 'he is the prettiest man who ventures upon the most inaccessible', said George MacKenzie, writing in the 1680s.[144] Martin put it beautifully: 'they single out the fattest of their fowls, plucking them bare, which they carry home to their wives, or sweethearts, as a great present, and it is always accepted very kindly from them, and could not indeed well be otherwise, without great ingratitude, seeing these men ordinarily expose themselves to great danger, if not to the hazard of their lives, to procure those presents for them'.[145] One of the best-known St Kilda legends concerns the famous 'Mistress Stone', also mentioned by Martin; on the seaward edge of this stone, poised above a precipitous drop, a suitor would demonstrate his agility and fearlessness by carrying out a tricky gymnastic exercise, success ensuring that he was 'ever after accounted worthy of the finest woman in the world'.[146] (Martin was offered the opportunity to display his own machismo on the Mistress Stone; he had the good sense to refuse – for

FIGURE 52. Distributing a catch of fulmars, on the rocks near the Feather Store, in 1886. Although it is the men who pose for the photograph, the involvement of the women in the process is evident.

which posterity should remain eternally thankful.) The love songs of Hirta, mostly composed by women, emphasise that the ideal young man had to be a successful bird-catcher. As one of them says, in successive verses of an eighteenth-century duet: 'thou gavest me first the honied fulmar … thou gavest me the gannet and the auk … thou gavest me the puffin and the black-headed guillemot … may … the Holy Spirit be behind thy rope …'.[147] In the same poem, the young man is excited by the sound of the gannets returning to the islands, and the beginning of the fowling season; his expressed feelings for the girl are decidedly more romantic and less self-interested than hers for him. There are elegies, mostly about men who have fallen into the sea, often in the dangerous overnight guillemot hunt. In the best-documented example, about a young man lost on Soay, the girl regrets the loss of her share of the eggs and of the birds which flutter and sport in the clouds, while her true love's body is battered by the waves.[148] It was unbearably ironic that such bodies were sometimes kept afloat and made more visible by the strings of dead seabirds attached to them.[149]

A well-known late nineteenth-century photograph shows the seabird catch being distributed on the rocks near the Feather Store (Figure 52). The men are standing roughly in a circle, amongst the bundles of birds. One has to look carefully at a version of this photo whose original edges have not been masked off for publication to realise that it depicts just as many women as men. They sit among the rocks in ones and twos on the fringe of the action; but there can be no doubt of their keen interest in the proceedings. I am reminded of the attitudes of women in a rather similar community on the island of Great Blasket, in the west of Ireland.[150] When they discovered that some of the men were behaving like 'tricksters and rascals', claiming to be afraid to go down the climbing ropes to collect the eggs of guillemots and razor-bills, they refused to let their husbands volunteer for more than their fair share of the work, and insisted – successfully – that the skipper should not take anyone along who was not prepared to take his turn on the end of the rope. And there is a fine description of the arrival of a shoal of mackerel close inshore, where the women could watch their men fishing. They got totally involved in the excitement; the shore rang with their raucous, sometimes incoherent cries.

Optimal foragers?

There is something quite Darwinian about all this. It makes one wonder how far the linkages between food, sex and death might be analysed and understood in terms of a rough version of Optimal Foraging Theory.[151] Is it possible, in other words, that the strategies adopted by men and women for obtaining and sharing food were optimally efficient in terms of the opportunities and risks presented by their environment? In biological and evolutionary terms, might they have increased men's and women's reproductive fitness – in terms of nutritional levels and sexual opportunities? In theory, one might quantify this, carrying out a cost/benefit analysis in terms of the proteins and carbohydrates to be won by hunting each bird species, or by growing cereal crops or hunting seals. On St Kilda, the women saw to the production of the carbohydrates supplying the calorific values which sustained the men in obtaining the proteins and lipids which were essential for pregnancy, lactation and the raising of healthy children.[152] For the women, the risks of childbirth posed enough of a threat to their prospects of intensive child-rearing without the added dangers of fowling and handling boats. As for the men, success in hunting evidently improved their chances with women. The specialist knowledge and expertise applied by men and women respectively in obtaining food and other resources – which were then shared – enhanced the prospects of reproductive success for both sexes.

This way of thinking might be developed. One might predict that unmarried women and widows would need good information about the hunting prowess of unattached males. Although men's hunting often depended on mutual collaboration, there were ways of attributing catches to particular individuals. We have noted the use of fat young gannets as suitors' gifts, and how such presents were acknowledged in love songs. Martin saw about 800 gannets taken from dry storage in cleits on Stac an Armin and landed on Hirta, where they were piled into one great heap. He noticed how meticulously individual gannets were assigned to different men, which surprised him ('they being all of a tribe'); but then he found out that each bird 'carried a distinguishing mark on the foot, peculiar to the owner'.[153] Presumably recently killed birds, as well as baskets of eggs, could be marked in similar ways; we know that such marks *were* applied to the ears of sheep.[154] For women needing to know who were the good hunters, the proof of the pudding was more or less literally in the eating, although when they acted as porters, carrying home the catch,[155] they would have got a good sense of the weight of their obligation. They would not need to be present when their men swapped interminable anecdotes about past hunting exploits, or when they put on climbing displays for tourists (they often chose the Gap for this, in order to avoid disturbing the main nesting areas[156]). The St Kildan men were quite fearless (as they had to be) and enjoyed showing off their skills, which included climbing 'up the corner of a rock with their backs to it, making use only of their heels and elbows',[157] and swinging on the end of a rope like a human pendulum in order to get onto an otherwise inaccessible ledge.[158] George Atkinson noticed the unspoken understanding between climbing partners, how they assisted each other 'so slightly by the little touches and checks of the rope'.[159] Visiting spectators were immensely impressed by the St Kildans' performances; they climbed with speed and agility, displaying a light touch which reminded their audience of dancers or acrobats.[160] George Seton felt that they made 'the most startling feats of a Blondin or a Leotard appear utterly insignificant'.[161] Martin noted their exploits on Stac Biorach in the Sound of Soay[162] (which was then called Stac Dona, the Stack of Doom; the two stacks evidently swapped names after the eighteenth-century repopulation episode[163]). Stac Biorach (Figure 53) is 'much of the form and height of a steeple'. It is about 73 m in height, and was later climbed by Richard Barrington, the first man up the Eiger; a recent article in a climbing magazine suggests that the grade of VS (Very Severe) is 'not beyond belief'.[164] There was one place where the lead climber had to lever himself up quickly and decisively, using just his thumb, before securing the rope for his fellow climbers (in another version, a risky leap had to be made[165]). This feat was rewarded with a bonus of just four extra birds! But as Martin said, 'it is reckoned no small piece of gallantry, to climb this rock' and the successful leader 'has the advantage by it, of being recorded among their greatest heroes'. As a sporting challenge, Stac Biorach had the advantage that failure often meant nothing worse than falling into the sea and being hauled in by the standby boat.[166] In 1831 two young men climbed this stack 'for a little tobacco'.[167] Another activity which allowed men to show off was catching, or attempting to catch, the notoriously elusive Soay sheep on Soay itself; this required courage as well as athleticism, since it involved tearing up and down very steep slopes and facing the aggression of cornered rams[168] (Figure 20, page 25).

A Darwinian approach predicts that women would have chosen their men carefully, and that some of them might have benefited by being not altogether faithful. In this connection it is interesting to recall Martin's comment that 'they are reputed jealous of their wives'.[169] One of Henry Brougham's companions in 1799 claimed that this jealousy sometimes led to violence, and that 'adultery, fornication and pocket picking seem here ... to be regarded rather as proofs of genius, than as crimes'.[170] However, he was only on the island for 36 hours. According to MacDonald, 'incontinence, or unchastity, is seldom heard of, except ... when strangers come among them'.[171] The arrival of exotic visitors may sometimes have had a destabilising effect. But we have to be careful here; the truth about sexual behaviour is notoriously difficult to establish. Those who commented on St Kildan sexual morality often turn out either not to have been in a position to know, or committed to a particular moral stance – or both!

There were good reasons for families to take primary responsibility for feeding themselves. But it would have made little sense for them to compete in trying to accumulate wealth which could not be maintained and perpetuated in the medium and longer term. Social prestige, a much more useful form of 'wealth' in this society, would have stemmed from generosity – from the power to *share* food or fuel, preferably at feasts or on ceremonial occasions. At wakes it was said that 'the more sheep and cows they kill, and the more barley they use, the more honour do they intend to confer on their deceased friend. Those who have lost many relatives have been much reduced by this foolish custom'.[172] If a death occurred in late winter or early spring, the islanders had the good sense to postpone the wake until the livestock had put on more fat.[173] MacKenzie noted how on special occasions it was the men who took charge of the cooking, wrapping the meat in a hide and baking it in hot ashes, 'an operation which required much judgement and careful attention'; some men were celebrated for their skill as cooks and undertook these tasks 'with a

FIGURE 53.
Stac Biorach, in the Sound of Soay (known as Stac Dona before 1730). Judged by modern climbers as perhaps Very Severe, this stack was a challenge to St Kildan climbers, who sometimes ascended it for small quantities of tobacco.

due sense of the honour and responsibility'. On such occasions people were expected to stay until all the food had been consumed, though on some occasions, with the permission of the host, they could take some home with them.[174]

Optimal Foraging Theory tends to predict that while the women work steadily away producing a regular supply of basic 'low risk, low return' food, often plant-based – and caring for their children at the same time – their work will be complemented by the 'high risk, high return' strategies of the men, who may hunt without much success for some time but then one day bring home a bonanza of meat. ('High risk' refers here to uncertainty of return rather than physical danger). This kind of 'high risk' food will be *shared*, and one would certainly expect this on St Kilda, given that quite a lot of the fowling was collectively co-ordinated and depended on investment by the community. Fowling provided a field of competition for men, in terms of prestige and access to women, but the economy was not *driven* by social and sexual competition. In this environment the axioms of Optimal Foraging Theory must be treated with caution, for men did some gathering (collecting eggs) and women hunted. Women were in fact extremely effective puffin-catchers. MacAulay describes them going out 'like the maids of antient Sparta' early of a summer morning with their 'extraordinary dogs', to bring back fresh meat for the day.[175] When men hunted on Hirta, their womenfolk carried home the spoils.[176] It is not clear to what extent women climbed, and in what circumstances. According to Campbell, 'the women also dare to climb the butting cliff, from whose giddy heights many of these luckless maidens have been washed by the sea, and hurled into eternity',[177] and female climbers sometimes figure in poems written in the late eighteenth and early nineteenth centuries. Is it possible that in the late eighteenth century the rapacity of the laird, and/or his factor, which is mentioned by more than one commentator, was putting extra pressure on the St Kildans? Or do these images mostly reflect contemporary tastes in an erotically-charged version of Sublime horror? Much later, Sands mentions women endangering themselves on the cliffs in efforts to gather grass for their cattle.[178]

There is something rather impressive about the way in which families, the men's and women's groups, and the community interacted to produce a reasonably harmonious society with an effective economic system. They were not unique; other Hebridean communities were probably similar in many respects. Nor did the islanders work through their problems in total isolation; the chiefdom, as both investor and predator, played a significant role, as did the random interventions of outsiders. As far as I know, Optimal Foraging Theory has at present little to say about situations in which the hunters are themselves the subjects of predation by those higher up the social hierarchy. The St Kildans altruistically looked after elderly widows and the poorest members of the community,[179] and their generous treatment of shipwrecked sailors[180] can hardly have increased their own inclusive fitness. In terms of 'selection pressures', the perpetuation of particular genes and combinations of genes must have been affected much more by deaths in accidents or childbed, and by the incidence of infantile tetanus. Optimal Foraging Theory provides useful insights, but it should not be taken too literally. St Kildan lifeways and Darwinian principles strike a chord – but only up to a point.

CHAPTER SIX

The Social Psychology of
the St Kildans

It does not matter to the Gael that a changed practice will reap him
a bigger material reward. That is not recompense for having to that
extent placed himself outside his group. If the material reward is
real, he will be envied by his fellows ... If the reward is illusory, he
will be ridiculed, and that is not good either in a society where there
is no privacy.

Frank Fraser Darling, West Highland Survey *(1955) p. 304.*

FIGURE 54.
Sharing a joke at
Village Bay.

Martin Martin[1] described the St Kildans as 'almost the only people in the
world who feel the sweetness of true liberty', in an atmosphere of 'mutual love
and cordial friendship' free from 'anxious covetousness, envy, deceit and
dissimulation'. But ironically it is his own account which reveals that the
people of Hirta inhabited a strictly regulated world, with frequent drawing of
lots, locked doors, and financial penalties for various crimes or misde-
meanours. A high value was placed on social conformity, a mindset no doubt
reinforced by the nature of the tight huddle of houses in which the people
lived.

Martin described the numerous regulations and mechanisms intended to
ensure that each family had fair or equal access to resources, took its share of
the costs and burdens associated with community membership, was rewarded
for its contribution to the commonwealth and penalised for anti-social behaviour. The island boat, for instance (Figure 55), was 'very curiously divided into
apartments proportional to their land and rocks'; when it was beached in
summer, each 'partner' had to supply 'a large turf to cover his space of the
boat' to protect it from the sun.[2] Judging by a later account, the woollen sail
would have been constructed like a patchwork quilt, each square supplied by
a different family.[3] When the boat visited outlying islands, the providers of
fire-making equipment and the family who supplied the cooking-pot were
both paid for their trouble, and these duties were evidently rotated.[4] The co-
ownership of the boat sometimes annoyed visitors, who complained that to
visit the outer isles they had to 'pay and put up with an overcrowded load of
bad boatmen'.[5] The three long climbing-ropes made of horse-hair were
communal property, and were 'not to be used without the general consent';

FIGURE 55.
Men of St Kilda in
1886, with their boat
(which was collective
property) on the rocks
near the Store. The
jetty had not yet been
constructed.

the islanders drew lots to establish who was to use the ropes, where they were used, and when.[6] Drawing lots was common practice; it was done, for example, to set up a roster for the use of the communal corn-drying kiln.[7] Drawing lots determined rights to craig-seats used for line-fishing from the rocks, and particular fowling zones on the coast; periodic reallocations took place under the direction of the *maor*. This is a twentieth-century description of the practice: 'you would put a penny under a stone, or another wee stone or a bit of stick. The other guy would be away and he wouldn't see what was going on. He would come back and say, pointing to one of the stones, "he has got that part of the Cambir" or Oiseval or Dun'.[8] This procedure should have ensured that the bird and egg harvest was spread fairly evenly around the coast. Food resources varied in quantity and predictability, and varying degrees of risk were attached to different harvesting areas. Decisions made on a random basis diminished the scope for recriminations; exposure to good and bad luck was entrusted to Fate (or the will of God). Aspects of this strict system of self-regulation survived into the community's final years. In the 1980s, Lachlan MacDonald, who was 24 at the time of the evacuation, recalled how the crofters shared responsibility for feeding the bull in winter, avoiding quarrels by using an agreed rope measure to regulate the size of the bundles of hay which each had to provide.[9]

It was a communal responsibility to look after 'the poor' – mostly widows and widowers living alone, and the physically or mentally handicapped – shipwrecked sailors, as well as guests.[10] When the steward and his retinue were on the island, the duty of providing their precisely-stipulated daily rations was, needless to say, a shared one.[11] Communitarian attitudes were noticeable when anyone was ill: 'they think it only their duty to collect in the sickroom till it is full and there squat for hours'.[12] In the late nineteenth century, a police inspector turned up to take an alleged sheep-stealer into custody; but after the islanders formed a protective cordon around the suspect, the forces of law had to beat a retreat.[13] In dealing with outsiders, solidarity was sometimes essential.

A great deal depended on people's respect for the office of *maor* and for the *maor* himself, and his sagacity and political judgement. Traditionally he was chosen by the community. By Martin's time he was supposed to be 'appointed' by the steward,[14] though it beggars belief that the steward could have successfully countermanded the choice already made by the islanders. The *maor* had to be tough-minded, since he had to answer to both the laird's representative and the community, two parties whose interests were potentially in conflict. As in most well-regulated commoners' organisations,[15] the *maor* was recompensed for his extra responsibilities, each family making an annual payment of barley.[16] A system of fines was in place to punish crimes and breaches of the rules; it was administered by the *maor* with the support of the steward. This too is a frequent feature of well-regulated communities. People could be fined up to two shillings for assault, or four and sixpence if blood was drawn; these crimes were to be reported to the steward.[17] Compensation was payable for sheep which became trapped in cleits and died there, or fell over the cliffs while being rounded up; the regulations were complicated.[18] Many payments would have been in kind. There was an agreed system of values for livestock, and the price of a sheep varied from season to season.[19] The islanders were involved in many different kinds of transactions, involving a range of payments, services and commodities; they had to negotiate not only with the steward but also with other members of his party, with resident missionaries such as Alexander Buchan in the early eighteenth century, with visiting fishermen, and amongst themselves. They were well aware of the monetary system used in the wider world, and often preferred to use it rather than try to reduce everything to its value in livestock units. Judging by the experience of Alexander Buchan, who arrived seven years after Martin's visit, they were quite capable of turning the price system imposed by the steward to their own advantage. A letter written by Rev. Daniel Campbell, dated March 1706, noted Buchan's problems: 'he buyes everie thing at a dear rate: they give him nothing for nought, no not a drop milk to his tender young one ... he adds yt he payes twenty pennies for every pint to his two babbies. But now yt he has not a farthing to buy onie more, and yt he cannot get a drink of whey wtout giving thrice ye worth of it of tobacco for it ... yt he must hire one to fetch him peats.[20] In 1717 it was said that 'they [the minister's family] are obliged to hire the natives to grind their meall in quirns, cast and lead their peats, herd their few cattle, thatch their oun house and do other services, wherethrough the three hundred merks [Buchan's salary] is every year exhausted long before the Stewart come to the island, and they are put to the borrowing, which exposes them to disdain and reproach'.[21] Buchan was charged Edinburgh prices for milk.[22]

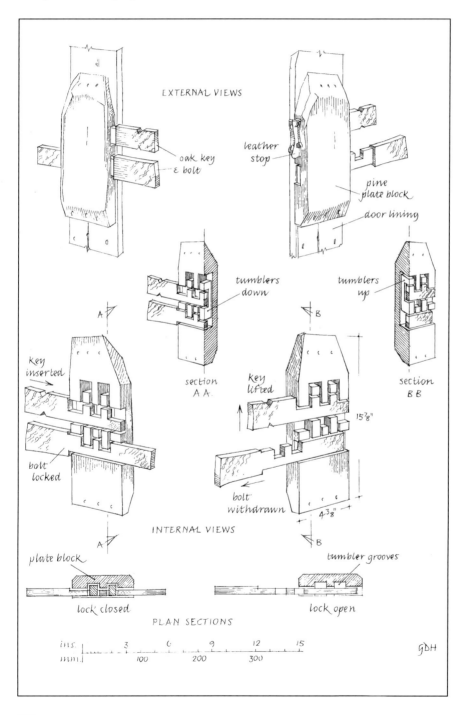

FIGURE 56.
The anatomy of a tumbler lock.

Freedom under lock and key

Another apparently paradoxical feature in a community allegedly 'free from anxious covetousness' was the widespread use of locks and keys.[23] Historians of technology and folklife experts have long been fascinated by the St Kildans' intricate and ingenious wooden tumbler-locks, some of which are preserved in museums (Figure 56).[24] Such devices were not confined to Hirta; they were widespread in northern Scotland and the Faeroe Islands.[25] The St Kildans made the locks themselves;[26] local manufacture was the usual practice in the region.[27] These security devices would also have to be *maintained* locally too; in the humid atmosphere of the north-east Atlantic, they would have been prone to warping and sticking. The first reference to locks on Hirta occurs in 1799.[28] Neither the change made in the 1830s, from the close-packed dwellings of the *clachan* to houses standing on individual crofts, nor the subsequent transition from black-houses to modern houses in the early 1860s, made any difference to the St Kildans' habit of locking their doors.[29] In the late nineteenth century, when they were serious about their commitment to Christian morality, they not only fitted the new 'brass-knobbed' locks, but transferred the old wooden ones to their cow-houses.[30] On at least one occasion most of them locked their doors while they were in church,[31] although this may have been because tourists were around at the time.

I do not believe that the St Kildans were very worried about the theft of household furnishings – such as they were – or feared that they would be unable to recover them if they were stolen. A more likely explanation for locks and keys is that there was more cash on the island than one might at first imagine.[32] According to MacAulay 'silver and gold ... they neither have nor desire';[33] Martin claimed that 'the inhabitants make no distinction betwixt a guinea and a sixpence'.[34] But in fact there is plenty of evidence that the islanders were familiar with money and with the concept of cash as a medium of exchange – as they showed in their dealings with Alexander Buchan. Given the variety of coins which must have found their way onto the island, via foreign seamen, the St Kildans must have developed a flexible and necessarily idiosyncratic way of using cash amongst themselves – which may account for the contradictory statements made by some of the commentators. Coins, of course, were small enough to hide within houses; they were the only form of 'wealth' which a family might reasonably hope to conceal. In 1861 the catechist Duncan Kennedy told the man who had come to take the census that every family had some money laid by.[35] In negotiations between families, it would clearly be advantageous to play financial cards close to the chest. We do not know much about the transactions surrounding marriage, though Buchan tells us that 'the richer sort give their help at this time to the poorer, to enrich their stock, viz. by giving the married parties some of their cattle; others seed to sow their land, etc'.[36] One can imagine the games of bluff and counter-bluff involved in some of the negotiations. A hoard of coins would have represented a kind of 'holdout' from communitarian pressures, a means whereby a family might retain a small and no doubt valuable measure of independence. Presumably this was the area of island life where secrecy was most prevalent and practicable.

For this reason alone, one can understand the locking of doors. But there is a more serious explanation for this practice. The theft of privately-owned resources in the form of coins could have triggered appalling tensions *in the community*, threatening to generate a Kafkaesque situation. As I have written elsewhere: 'since a hoard's existence was supposed to be secret, its owner could not be seen too frequently checking its hiding place, and thus drawing attention to it. To announce the occurrence of a theft might well be problematic. The amount stolen could hardly be openly discussed (and the thief might in any case have split it into several components). The identity of the thief would be difficult to discover, and there would have been almost limitless potential for various accurate and inaccurate accusations, accusations of false accusation, and so on. Could the victim of the theft afford to be seen scouring other people's houses, openly or surreptitiously trying to recover his or her property?'[37] One can imagine the damage done by an unresolved dispute, and its escalation into a running feud. Evidently it is not only good fences which make good neighbours. Locked doors helped to prevent open feuding. In the final analysis, the community as a whole had a greater interest in the employment of locks and keys than did any of its constituent families.

However, there is another possible explanation for the locking of doors – the fear of witchcraft. This is a subject on which the Hirta literature is virtually silent. The practice of witchcraft was widespread in the region. Martin mentions belief in the evil eye and the use of charms,[38] and much information on the topic was collected in more recent times.[39] It is inconceivable that witchcraft and divination were not commonplace on Hirta, for both malicious and innocent purposes, and in order to foretell and influence the future. This was not the sort of thing which visitors were likely to be told about; resident ministers must often have turned a blind eye on the occasions when they happened upon it. MacCulloch was surely wrong to claim that the power of an evil eye was 'the only existing popular superstition'.[40] 'Second sight' was an accepted phenomenon on Hirta.[41] Witches often needed to get their hands on, or at least sight of, something belonging or relating to their intended victims. A lot of witchcraft, actual or alleged, centred around dairying activities, including tricky processes like butter-making – which may account for the locking of cow-houses. Tensions and frustrations in a small community would have encouraged both malevolent witchcraft and accusations of witchcraft, perhaps especially among women, whose power to control their own lives was arguably weaker than that of the men. In social terms, witchcraft plays out like theft. Accusations and counter-accusations could have massively damaged the social fabric of the community. Rivalries between families had the potential to become so destructive that door-locking would have been of great benefit to the community as a whole. Of course, as explanations for locking doors, the anti-theft and the anti-witchcraft hypotheses are not mutually exclusive.

It is hard, I think, to over-estimate the potential for social tension. In a population of 200, each individual has to handle up to 199 interpersonal relationships. The *total* number of such relationships, if one includes everyone from the youngest baby to the oldest inhabitant, is 19,900. In terms of social harmony in a small island community, there is a lot to go wrong. The consequences of discord were potentially even more serious for St Kildans; when men are roped together on a cliff-face, swimming into a seal-cave carrying a torch and a club, or trying to make a tricky landing on a towering rock stack, anger, bitterness or hatred might have fatal consequences. However, this was not a 'reality' TV show, nor yet *Lord of the Flies*; numerous tried and tested social institutions and customs were in place to counteract such tensions.

A view of the cosmos

Mention of witchcraft introduces the subject of the St Kildans' views of the world, and how individuals thought they might improve the conditions of their existence, or achieve their objectives. In theory, this depends on the time period in question. We know nothing of the nature and influence of early Christianity on Hirta, be it 'Hiberno-British' or Norse, and little about the 'Popish practices' supposedly superseded by 1697. In these times, priests or ministers were rarely present. From the 1820s, the determined propagation of the Christian doctrines which eventually led the islanders to join the Free Church must have pushed older rituals and beliefs to the margins. To outside appearance at least, this created a community intimidating for its monolithic religious and Sabbatarian observance and the strength of its adherence to the tenets of its faith.[42]

Christian teachers would have struggled to contain 'pagan' beliefs and practices, as well as those based on earlier forms of Christian faith and ritual. In Martin's time, a matter not resolved by the drawing of lots might be settled by swearing upon a crucifix; these two practices, he said, 'do mightily contribute to their peace and quiet, keeping every one within his proper bounds'.[43] In every age, the St Kildans had to consider how far it was possible to perform magico-religious rituals to avert disaster, or change things for the better, or whether in some areas of life they should simply accept the intervention of 'fate', or 'the will of God'. According to Martin, they were fatalists, believing that all events were predetermined by God.[44] The Rev. Kenneth MacAulay pointed out that 'at St Kilda, fate and providence are much the same thing'. He also noted, however, that the *Hirteach* accepted the notion of free will. So how did they reconcile the concepts of free agency, predestination and divine prescience? MacAulay felt that the islanders, untroubled by these metaphysical conundrums, displayed an instinctive philosophical wisdom.[45] When they were cliff-climbing, the Free Church St Kildans liked to carry bibles,[46] and they regularly 'made worship' when they were on the outer islands or taking shelter in sea-caves.[47] As far as practical knowledge and action were concerned, neither pagan beliefs nor early Christianity made a clear distinction between the natural and the supernatural.

In Martin's time, the people of Hirta were 'neither inclined to Enthusiasm nor to Popery'. Significant roles in marriage and oath-taking were taken by 'a brazen crucifix'.[48] Martin noted that 'they begin their labours always in the name of God'; they had 'a set form of prayer at the hoisting of their sails'.[49] In the early twentieth century, people offered prayers before lifting their fishing-lines, and when they fed their cattle.[50] The islanders had a good practical knowledge of the cosmos. They told the time from the position of the sun in relation to skyline features, and failing that, from the tides; they were apparently 'very exact' in observing the phases of the moon.[51] Martin noted their use of applied ornithology: '[the St Kildans] take their measures from the flight of those fowls, when the heavens are not clear, as from a sure compass … every tribe of fowls bends their course to their respective quarters'.[52]

For Hebrideans, going sunwise, *deasil*, was important;[53] the St Kildans carried the dead sunwise round the *clachan* before taking them to the grave-yard.[54] Supernatural powers were everywhere; as Martin put it: 'they have a notion, that spirits are embodied, and fancy them to be locally in rocks, hills, or wherever they list, in an instant'.[55] Particular places in the landscape were highly significant; offerings of shells, pebbles, rags, pins, needles and rusty nails were made at *Tobar nam Buadh*, the 'Well of Virtues', near the seaward end of Gleann Mór.[56] There were several 'altars', including one on Mullach Geal,[57] and another near the highest point of Soay.[58] These may have originated in earlier Christian times, with the *turais*, pilgrimage circuits through a Christianised landscape dotted with wells, cairns and altars.[59] It was especially important to perform the right rituals in 'liminal' contexts – that is to say, at thresholds and transitions; when starting a task, upon arrival in a new place, at the beginning and end of the day, and at important stages in life. Supernatural beings were often associated with liminal zones – where water comes out of the earth, where land meets sky, where the hills rise from the plain. On Hirta the zone immediately west of the Village Bay settlement, evoking the passage from the

FIGURE 57. Effie MacCrimmon, as recorded by Captain Thomas; a rare photograph of someone who was a little girl at the time of the French Revolution.

enclosed land to Gleann Mór and the hills, evidently had this liminal character. Here there was 'a little green plain' – the *Liani nin Ore*, The Plain of Spells, where 'cattle were sained with salt, water and fire whenever they were moved from one grazing area to another'.[60] In one possible location for the Plain of Spells there is a circular rock basin which may have been used in these rituals.[61] Not far away, near the entrance to the modern quarry, is the *Clach a'Bhainne*, the Milking Stone ('where they used to pour milk for the *gruagach* or 'brownie' … after the first spring milking, when they heard the fairies beneath rattling their spoons').[62] (The Milking Stone was also held sacred by RAF bulldozer drivers in 1957; they left it on a little earthen pedestal.) Somewhere in this zone was an area which must on no account be cultivated ('on the grounds that it was sacred to a divinity whose name was forgotten').[63] I have already noted the distinction made in ancient Scandinavian cosmologies between the inhabited world and the outer realm of trolls and monsters. So was this a zone of fear, associated with leaving the security of the in-bye land, and the familiar, domestic landscape? Or was liminality here to do with women's anxieties about upcoming dairying tasks, and the welfare of their cattle in Gleann Mór?

A world beneath the waves

Just off the south coast of Soay is a spread of frequently submerged rocks with the curious name of *Sgeir Mac Righ Lochlainn*, the Skerry of the Son of the King of Norway. In the nineteenth century, Effie (Euphemia) MacCrimmon (Figure 57) told a tale of an unfortunate Norwegian prince who was shipwrecked here, got ashore and was ambushed and drowned by the islanders while taking a drink from a burn.[64] In Hebridean terms, any story in which a Norseman comes off badly would have been gratifying, although this one does jar with the St Kildan tradition of offering hospitality to shipwrecked sailors. But there was more to this tale than met the ear. *Lochlann* did not only mean Norway; it was also a name for the Otherworld beneath the waves. Corryvreckan, the name of the famous whirlpools between Jura and Scarba and between Rathlin Island and the Irish mainland, also related to the drowning of the son of the King of 'Norway', whose name was Brecan. But in stories told at many a Hebridean hearth, not to mention in Ireland and the Northern Isles,[65] the children of the King of Norway, or Lochlann, were seals, and they featured in those compelling legends about liaisons between seals and humans which are nowadays best known from folk songs. David Thomson's book, *The People of the Sea*, tells a story from South Uist about the origins of the MacCodrum clan. A man hunting cormorants disturbs a number of people on a skerry, who promptly put on seal-skins from a heap and make their escape by diving into the sea. One skin is left unclaimed; our hero conceals it. It turns out to belong to a beautiful young woman. She remonstrates with him, pointing out that she is the daughter of the King of Lochlann and wants to put on her clothes and join her people. However, he takes her home, gives her human clothes, and they have a large family together. She is homesick, but the hero manages to frustrate her by regularly changing the sealskin's hiding place. When she eventually finds it she swims away, but not before promising that there will always be plenty of fish for the family around a certain smooth rock: 'you will see me rising up in the sea and I shall call to you, but do not go out to me in case you should be drowned'. The promise of abundant fish is duly fulfilled, the sons and daughters eventually marry: 'and that is how the Clan MacCodrum came to this earth'.[66] Some of these stories feature seal men rather than seal women. There are also tales of people who believe that they are the progeny of seals, that seals are human beings under enchantment, and that drowned persons take the form of seal-men and seal-women, who assume human form during the night-time; sometimes hunters are reproached by seals for having harmed them in the past.[67] Mermaid stories make use of similar motifs. In Irish traditional belief there was a land under the waves, *Tír fó Thuinn.*[68] This was described as an 'underwater paradise of mermaids', who often possessed 'magic garments with a hood, with which they cover their heads when they return to the land underneath the waves'.

It is not difficult to see why such tales have an enduring appeal. Of all the wild creatures encountered in the north-east Atlantic, seals are the ones with which we feel most empathy. They have large, expressive eyes and smooth skin; they appear to display great curiosity about people; they like to play and sing, and may be attracted by music. They are mammals, and they sometimes cry like babies. Killing seals was often a dangerous and difficult task, demanding the exercise of an exceptional degree of (accurate) violence; it involved facing 'the ferocity and little stratagems of these unwieldy creatures when assaulted'.[69] Alasdair Alpin MacGregor, who detested cruelty to animals, says that hunted seals were frequently skinned *alive*;[70] one or two must sometimes have thrashed their way into the sea after the operation had commenced. The idea of a seal getting its skin back and making its escape must have been rooted in adrenalin-charged experiences like this. But these stories also reflect much deeper levels of human engagement with the natural world. They usually end by 'explaining' a long-term relationship between seals and people; the humans in the tale may acquire a taboo on eating seal-meat, or young seals, perhaps in exchange for a promise that good luck will attend their fishing. Essentially, the moral is that seals should be treated with respect. There are echoes here of totemism, of men dealing with the emotions aroused by the seal-hunt, seeking a greater spiritual meaning for their relationships with prey animals, making sense of acts of necessary violence towards sentient creatures and seeking good fortune in the hunt by so doing. In the Hebrides, people had been hunting seals ever since the Mesolithic, several thousand years ago.[71]

These stories also evoke the ultimate fascination with liminality – the belief in the fluidity and permeability of the boundaries between this world and the Otherworld, or between humans, animals, and supernatural beings. Consideration of the nature of seals would have reinforced this way of thinking. Seals and humans are complementary opposites in relation to land and sea. One is uncomfortable in the very medium in which the other is 'in its element'. Yet humans can learn to swim and become skilled in handling boats; seals 'haul out', and spend time out of the water. The skerries where they bask are often liminal – sometimes above the waves, sometimes beneath them. Seals and humans make serious attempts to inhabit each others' worlds. One of Thomson's story-tellers said of seals that 'it is given to them that their sea-longing shall be land-longing and their land-longing shall be sea-longing'.[72] Seals know distant seas, and the world beneath the waves; yet they also 'long' for the land, and display affinities with humans. If the Otherworld lies beneath the sea, seals are its perfect emissaries.

So the islanders themselves may once have imagined an otherworld, whose gateway was a spread of rocks off the south coast of Soay – the Skerry of the Son of the King of Norway.[73] Naturally, this skerry often lurks beneath the waves. Last time I was there, in a powered boat on a beautiful July evening, with puffins fluttering busily around us, there was no sign of it. I reminded the skipper of its existence. 'Yes I know', he said cheerfully, 'but I'm not sure I can remember where it is'. We both adopted a not entirely convincing air of insouciance ...

These stories were widespread in Britain and Ireland, and we cannot know whether, or for how long, the St Kildans might have perceived *Sgeir Mac Righ Lochlainn* as an Otherworld gateway. For all we know, the name might have been attached to the skerry for the first time by an eighteenth-century story-teller. Similar uncertainties are attached to the Hill of Blessings (*Cnoc a'Bheannaichta*) and the legendary or supernatural females commemorated in place-names, such as the Female Warrior (better known as the 'Amazon') associated with an ancient structure in Gleann Mór, or the Old Woman remembered at the *Geò na Seanag* and the *Uamh Cailleach Bheag Ruaival*.[74] Some place-names are in any case difficult to interpret in the forms in which they have come down to us.[75] But these dimly-understood survivals are important, reminding us that land-marks and sea-marks once carried names evoking a wealth of stories and legends, some of them harking back to ancient ideas about the nature of the cosmos.

Mind games

Like all humans, the St Kildans had to find ways of coping with anxiety. In many situations, the performance of ritual, pagan or Christian, may have provided a measure of reassurance. Like many hunter-gatherers, the islanders were probably quite calm and philosophical in times of foul weather, or when food was scarce – displaying a mixture of self-confidence, optimism and fatalism which would have served them much better than worry. T. H. Mason once remarked to an Aran islander, fishing with his legs dangling over the edge of a mighty cliff: 'if you caught a conger eel now, he would pull you in', to which he received the classic reply: 'he would so, sir'.[76] The fatalism which seems at first sight an abrogation of responsibility plays a key psychological role, allowing individuals to classify certain risks as beyond their control, freeing them to concentrate on the calm exercise of their practical skills in dangerous situations. In a similar vein, modern mountaineers acknowledge what they call the 'objective' danger which they face in the necessary crossing of areas prone to avalanches.

In the dense cluster of crowded, smoky little houses and narrow passageways which formed the Hirta *clachan*, people would have known each other all too well – secrets and foibles, flaws and snores. One might imagine that serious social tensions would be caused by 'cabin fever' – especially during the winter period of bad weather and isolation. How would people have coped with the virtual absence of personal privacy? How would the individual have found space for self-expression among the conformist pressures of this small community, in an atmosphere which must sometimes have been almost literally suffocating?

To a large extent, these are issues only for an urbanised, western mindset, and to keep a sense of proportion we might consider how unimpressed the St Kildans would have been by our own socialisation of the young, and our lip-service to the notion of social inclusion. On Hirta, people cannot have been in much doubt as to how they were expected to behave over the courses of their lives. The separate groupings of males and females would have gone some way towards addressing the more oppressive aspects of a small community. They would have provided a measure of social and behavioural space for the individual. For example, such groups could concern themselves, subtly or more directly, with the business of courtship, marriage, and parenting from the viewpoint of one sex, providing an opportunity for councils (and counsels) of war in the battle of the sexes. To an extent the gender groups were a respite from pressures within families, and a counterweight to them. There may well have been social practices which have not really found their way into the literature. With reference to courtship, for example, it is intriguing to read, just once, of the existence of a special house where young people spent the night, in a sort of institutionalised sleep-over.[77]

Community theatricals

Anyone who has lived in a small community knows how its members tend to play 'roles', partly based on their own personalities, past histories and social status, and partly 'scripted' by the expectations of others. There are also occasions when elaborate dramatic performances are called for, as for example when an Inuit man comes home and has to tell a self-deprecating, downbeat story about his hunting trip even when his sled is visibly weighed down with game.[78] But it is the more regular, formal, community rituals – especially those which have an element of competition – which provide serious scope for self-expression, for creating an impression, making a role one's own. On Hirta, one of the most elaborate performative rituals must have been the 'cavalcade'.

In 1697 the St Kildans had 'up to eighteen' horses. At Michaelmas, at the end of September, they held their 'anniversary cavalcade' – each man riding a horse, bareback and restrained by only a short length of straw rope, from the beach to the houses.[79] To us the 'cavalcade' would have looked ludicrous, I think, for it also involved *races* between horses 'very low in stature';[80] in Norse times, the festivities probably involved horse-fighting too. According to Martin, such cavalcades also took place on Coll and Tiree, and throughout the Western Isles. In Lewis and on North Uist, women took part; there was a race for prizes, and the horses were controlled only by 'two small ropes made of bent ... The men have their sweethearts behind them on horseback, and give and receive mutual presents ... the women receiving knives and purses, the men fine garters and wild carrots'.[81] Some of these equestrian shows must have been highly impressive. On Eriskay, on the very beach where Bonny Prince Charlie was soon to make his fateful landfall, Martin saw about 60 horsemen, silhouetted against the western sun. The festivity described by Martin is the Michaelmas '*oda*' which was held, for obvious reasons, at a time of plenty; it survived into the nineteenth century.[82] The St Kildans baked a large triangular cake, which was eaten in the evening ('and it must be all eaten that night'). This must have been a night of mutual visiting, like modern New Year's Eve; on Barra and Eriskay the cake was consumed by 'strangers' as well as by the household which baked it.[83]

Only one other St Kilda festival is described in any detail. This is the *Nuallan na Calluinn*, (the Calends' Yelling): 'On the evening before New Year's Day it is usual for the cowherd and the young people to meet together, and one of them is covered with a cow's hide. The rest of the company are provided with staves, to the end of which bits of raw hide are tied. The person covered with the hide runs thrice round the dwelling-house, *deseil* – i.e. according to the course of the sun; the rest pursue, beating the hide with their staves, and crying, "*A cholluin, so cholluin, so cholluin a bhuilg bhorcionn, buail an craicion*" – that is, "Let us raise the noise louder and louder; let us beat the hide". They then come to the door of each dwelling-house, and one of them repeats some verses composed for the purpose. When admission is granted, one of them pronounces within the threshold the *beannachadth-urlair*, or verses upon the whole family ... "May God bless the house and all that belongs to it, cattle, stones and timber! In plenty of meat, of bed and body clothes, and health of men, may it ever abound!". Then each burns in the fire a little of the bit of hide which is tied to the end of the staff. It is applied to the nose of every person and domestic animal that belongs to the house. This, they imagine, will tend much to secure them from diseases and other misfortunes during the ensuing year'.[84] Neil MacKenzie says: 'it was customary for the one half of the houses to prepare for the *Calluinn*, year about in rotation, and the other half to go with this *Nuallan* [yelling] from house to house of those whose turn it was to make ready. After collecting the bread, the cakes were compared one with another. The biggest (*bannock*) was deemed to be the best, as it indicated the greatest skill in baking, and also the liberality of the goodwife of the house. Some of these *bannocks* or barley cakes were as broad as the stone of the quern, or about the size of a shield, and frequently contained above seven pounds of meal. The cheese and bread were then equally divided among all the men, and carried home to be used.' This festivity was widespread.[85] In Morvern, in the western Highlands, for example, it had the same essential components – the beating of sticks on a hide, the sunwise progression, and loud noise (helped in this case by a piper); the day after, New Year's Day, involved serious eating, drinking, dancing and a vigorous game of shinty.[86]

The description of the New Year ceremony confirms the solemnity of the complex annual rituals of the Hirta community; there is no sense of cultural impoverishment here. Despite its location 40 miles (*c.* 65 km) out in the Atlantic Ocean, this was a community which took itself as seriously as any of its Hebridean neighbours. These pagan-sounding 'calendar customs' took their place beside Christian festivals such as the feast-days of St Brendan and St Columba, which were celebrated in May and June – significantly, at another time of plenty, when large quantities of milk were distributed and consumed.[87]

Although the St Kildans marked off the days by cutting notches in a stick, and kept up this custom even when there was a calendar on the island,[88] it is unlikely that they traditionally thought of time as we do, as a straight line extending into the future, like a ruler of infinite length on which the individual's lifespan is marked by a number of sub-divisions, and what is past is past. Their concept of time would probably have been cyclical, with each year of an individual's lifespan conceptualised more like a circuit on a running track. Almost everything came round with the cycle of the seasons – times of hardship and times of plenty, times for sowing and reaping, the return of seabirds, the arrival of the steward's birlinn. Even 'biological' events would have been quite seasonal. There was a season when death was likely to visit the old and weak – as with Soay sheep, according to recent studies – and there would probably also have been seasons for match-making and marriage. People needed reassurance that there was more shape and pattern to life than the formless transactions and commonplaces of work and gossip, quarrels and friendships, enmities and intrigues. Some of these festivities were competitive theatrical spectacles, where young men and women could make an impression upon each other within a traditional, well-understood ritual format, under the gaze of the whole community. The *oda* involved excitement, competition, display; it took place at a time of year when families were best able to entertain others, and to make a play for continuing respect by a show of (sometimes competitive?) hospitality. This was the ideal opportunity for winning credit in the community, for making social plays and ploys. Festivities encouraged the subtle re-arrangement of the social order. Implicitly they provided an opportunity for the Hirta community as a whole to take stock of its strength and social well-being on a longer time-scale, to review its own future.

Calendrical rituals were more than simply 'events' punctuating the more humdrum passages of the year, keeping time in an abstract sense. They are much more than items to be 'collected' away under the heading of 'folk customs'. Culture is not a filing cabinet. Our knowledge of St Kilda festivals may be thin, but their existence reminds us that we must always try to think holistically about past communities.

CHAPTER SEVEN

A Man with a Mission

'Yet we may express a hope, that while the people of St Kilda are taught to cultivate their soil to the best advantage, their minds will not be neglected'

Sir David Brewer (ed) The Edinburgh Encyclopedia *(1830), p. 452*

FIGURE 58.
'Several of the women
are ... more than
ordinarily stout'.

Among the people who might claim to have changed the course of St Kilda's history, one man stands out above the rest – the Rev. Neil MacKenzie, minister on the island during the 1830s and early 1840s. MacKenzie wrought profound changes in the cultural landscape of Hirta and in the mindscapes of its inhabitants. Though he would doubtless have been appalled by such comparisons, it is hard not to feel that he had his own 'John the Baptist' in the form of the Rev. John MacDonald – 'the Apostle of the North', as he was known. MacDonald was a Caithness man, a catechist's son. In 1813 he took up a living at Urquhart in the Black Isle (Easter Ross), then still a Gaelic-speaking district. The manse had fine views across the Firth of Cromarty. During MacDonald's lifetime, the landscape of the Black Isle saw immense changes, brought about by the introduction of improved methods of farming. In 1793, the publication date of the Old Statistical Account, when MacDonald was just 14 years old, farms were small and little land had been enclosed.[1] But according to the Urquhart entry in the New Statistical Account of 1840 – which MacDonald wrote himself – 'hundreds of acres' of waste ground in the parish had been improved and enclosed to form the chequerboard pattern of the present day; the outbuildings at the manse had been modernised too.[2] Agricultural improvement was supposed to be matched in the spiritual field, and MacDonald felt able to report 'progress in religious knowledge and in moral conduct'.

It was John MacDonald who introduced a new version of Christianity to St Kilda. When he started his controversial preaching tours, tension had been mounting within the Presbyterian church for some years. The fault line was between the 'Moderate' or 'Establishment' wing, consisting of ministers who saw no problem in being appointed by lairds, and were often fairly relaxed about the need to set a Christian example – and the 'Evangelicals' or 'Dissenters' (sometimes known as the 'High Flyers'). Evangelicals practised a fervent, emotionally committed Christianity, and argued that ministers should be appointed by bodies of local elders, since their primary loyalty should be to their congregations. 'The Apostle of the North' was an Evangelical, whose detractors referred to him as 'the wild man of Ferintosh'.[3] He encountered a good deal of opposition, but the force of his missionary zeal could hardly be denied or ignored; he was described as 'the greatest Gaelic preacher of his day'.[4]

He was 43 years old when he and his assistant undertook their first mission to St Kilda in 1822, at the request of the Society for the Propagation of Christian Knowledge. The voyage out from the Long Island was hard; it took nine and a half hours, and the wind direction forced them to land in Glen Bay and hike over the hill to the village. It was mid-September, harvest time, and MacDonald went out into the fields and talked to the people. In the evenings he managed to gather them into 'the only barn', which was 'a sort of common property' and doubled as a schoolroom (there was a teacher on the island at the time). This was probably the Feather Store, since apparently all the inhabitants (apart from the children?) were present. MacDonald preached on 'the nature, the evil and the extent of sin'. On the first day some of the St Kildans reacted 'as if the view presented was new and alarming' and within a few days they had progressed from being 'evidently impressed' to being moved to tears.[5] In nearly two weeks on the island, MacDonald preached 13 times ('besides other services') and conversed with the people about 'the momentous concerns of eternity'. The islanders were even more lachrymose on the occasion of his final sermon, and again when they heard he was leaving, to preach in other venues (notably Tottenham Court Road, London, where he held forth to over 3,000 people).

MacDonald took a detailed census of the community. He was critical of the islanders. Having been on Hirta for less than a fortnight (during harvest-time!),

FIGURE 59.
The manse. It was not always painted white. The original front garden has been truncated by the military.

he claimed that 'they cannot be exempted from the charge of almost habitual indolence'.[6] And the missionary deplored the system of communal open fields, with land allocated by lot; he thought it 'militated greatly against real improvement'. He also found the people 'extremely dirty' though they did wash and make more of a sartorial effort on the Sabbath.[7] Medieval-style swearing – 'by the Book!' 'by Mary!', 'by the soul!', 'by the Sacred Name!' – was also rather too prevalent.[8] On his next visit, he found that the teacher had made considerable progress; the people were hungry for religious education, and 57 people had enrolled in the class. Paradoxically, people whose culture was closely adapted to island life were highly receptive to influence from outside.

The islanders presented MacDonald with 'a good fat wedder' and the women kept him supplied with gifts of fresh milk. In their generosity lay a potential problem. Missionaries (and ministers) had to try to be even-handed in their relationships with different people; destructive social tensions could develop if they appeared to favour particular individuals. The imposition of serious Christianity set out a new field of endeavour, in which ordinary islanders, in their roles as respected and knowledgeable 'elders', had the opportunity to exercise spiritual influence and leadership. But it also created a new arena for competition. The new religion had a censorious, authoritarian face in certain respects, and there was plenty of scope for disputing the high moral ground – or simply vying for the attention and praise of the man of God.

On his second visit, the Apostle devised a programme involving a two-hour lecture in the early morning and a two-hour sermon in the evening; he persuaded the islanders not to bake or fetch potatoes or vegetables on the Sabbath. He had raised £800 to construct a church and a manse. On the occasion of his third visit, in 1827, these buildings were nearing completion. They were erected by a team of masons from Dunvegan,[9] having been designed in the office of Robert Stevenson, the celebrated engineer who built the lighthouse on the Bell Rock, among others.[10] And the workmanlike solidity of the manse does rather call to mind a lighthouse keeper's accommodation, especially now that it is painted white (Figure 59). The church seated 106, and it was designed so that the minister could enter it directly from the manse without braving the weather, walking along a short corridor past his storeroom and the small dairy before appearing in front of his flock.

Consolidation

MacDonald's final visit was in 1829, and this time he introduced the incoming minister, the Rev. Neil MacKenzie, a Gaelic speaker in his early thirties who had been brought up in Glen Sannox, on the Isle of Arran. A graduate of Glasgow University, who had 'volunteered to go to any place for which no one else could be got',[11] MacKenzie had recently married Elizabeth Crawford, a builder's daughter from Paisley who did not speak Gaelic. In July 1830 he brought her to Hirta; she was in an advanced state of pregnancy.[12] Her husband was settling in for a long haul. Feeling that the ethical standards of the St Kildans still left a good deal to be desired, he set up a vigorous programme of religious education. It took time, but in 1838 he at last felt able to arrange for some of them to be admitted to full membership of the Church.[13] This was a very special occasion for MacKenzie. He left Glasgow in the steamship *Vulcan* on the 25th of July, accompanied by two of the most highly respected and influential churchmen of the day, the Reverend Dr. David Dickson from the SPCK in Edinburgh, and the Rev. Dr Norman MacLeod from St Columba's church in Glasgow. He brought with him equipment and furnishings for the projected new houses, which had yet to be constructed; godliness had preceded cleanliness. One of the passengers, Lachlan MacLean,[14] has left an interesting account of the voyage, during which the passengers ate strawberries and cream, encountered a black barman at Lochmaddy ('who spoke and sang in Gaelic') and took pot shots at the gannets around Stac Li (bringing guns to Hirta was not unusual; MacGillivray, who was here in 1840, describes 'securing' a dozen puffins at a single shot, and blasting many more off a rocky shelf into the sea[15]). When they got to St Kilda, several of the tourists went for a bathe. The islanders were not yet fully accustomed to steamships, and the arrival of the *Vulcan* in Village Bay, with smoking funnel and brass band playing, created 'terror and amazement', according to Neil MacKenzie's daughter.[16]

Dr MacLeod preached a sermon without delay, reducing quite a number of people to tears. The following morning, after breakfast, 16 would-be communicants were examined by Dr Dickson, with Dr MacLeod acting as interpreter. Later, MacLeod preached in the church, in a service which took up much of the afternoon; Dickson presented communion vessels, and a font. Holy Communion was administered in English (by Dr Dickson) and then in Gaelic (by Neil MacKenzie). Then Dickson preached an English sermon on the *Vulcan*, sitting on a camp-stool on deck; MacLeod preached to the St Kildans again. It was a beautiful evening, a crescent moon appearing in the sky just as the sun was going down. On that day, there was no way of avoiding these passionate men of God. They weighed anchor at one in the morning, in order to catch the tide in the Sound of Harris. For Rev. Norman MacLeod, the whole trip had been a wonderful, unforgettable experience. 'I have not passed a sweeter day on earth', he wrote a week later. He was moved by the 'fearful and sublime' scenery. And he was deeply impressed by the physical courage of the inhabitants, and the contrast between the conditions in which they lived ('their huts are not better than those of the Kaffirs') and their 'marvellous' moral and spiritual condition.[17]

MacKenzie had instituted a demanding ritual calendar. According to Malcolm MacQueen, an emigrant to Australia who was 15 years old when MacKenzie left Hirta,[18] towards the end of his ministry there were three Sabbath services in Gaelic and one in English, and at one stage a two and a half hour Bible class held at two o'clock in the afternoon. There were also church services on Wednesdays, and a range of meetings and classes on Thursdays and Fridays; the minister was 'very vigorous in looking up absentees'. MacKenzie was also teaching children and adults to read and write, as well as instructing them in the English language; he recruited suitable members of the community as teaching assistants.[19] The new 'academy' described by MacLean was nine feet by eight (92.7 x 2.4 m), with a canvas-covered window and a tiny square 'chimney' made of wood;[20] Mary Harman has suggested that the remains of one of its gable ends can still be seen, incorporated into a wall in the Glebe.[21] The present schoolroom (Figure 75, page 164) was not built until 1898.

In its early days, re-education was a deeply chastening experience for the islanders, but ultimately the process must have increased their self-assurance, not to say their self-righteousness. According to Wilson there were about 20 communicants, and 20 more under instruction; 'several of the older men ... are very fluent in prayer, and never fail to conduct a kind of public worship during the few occasions on which the minister is absent'.[22] A whole new field of social competition had been created. Now there was a range of roles, statuses and levels of Christian education to which individuals might aspire, and a group of elders endowed with a more intimidating authority than they held in the less formal, more task-oriented 'parliament'. This sometimes created tension. Doctrinal disputes and accusations of backsliding were ideal instruments for the pursuit of rivalries and power struggles. In due course the post of minister's housekeeper was to provide an ideal platform for a female control freak.[23] The diary of George Murray the schoolmaster recounts how he became involved, along with the minister, in a running dispute during the autumn and winter of 1886–7; at various times the islanders came to blows, spread malicious gossip, accused each other of lying and thieving, moved into cleits for the night, moved house altogether, and threatened to dethrone the precentor for being seen to laugh on the Sabbath.[24] 'Satan seems to have a few strongholds on the island', commented Murray. This kind of competitive Christianity was a divisive form of community control compared to the other mechanisms developed by trial and error over the years.

Another significant change involved the field of choral singing. Like many Hebrideans, the islanders liked to sing; they sang a great deal, often in unison and when working together in groups. In principle, Presbyterians were supposed to discourage the secular tradition of music and dancing – though MacKenzie was actually rather interested in the islanders' old songs, and wrote some of them down. The St Kildans came to like what the minister put in their place. As Wilson noted: 'the singing of psalms and hymns is even a favourite spiritual recreation of the people, and is resorted to frequently and voluntarily in their own houses ... these spiritual songs may even be said to be of ordinary use almost as the *popular poetry* of the day, and have in a great measure superseded all ordinary vocal music of a worldly character'.[25] Some of those who heard the St Kildans singing were mesmerised. Commentators are sometimes highly critical of the taboos surrounding observance of the Sabbath Day, and their practical effects. But the St Kildans were quite accustomed to the discipline of belonging to a highly regulated community; more

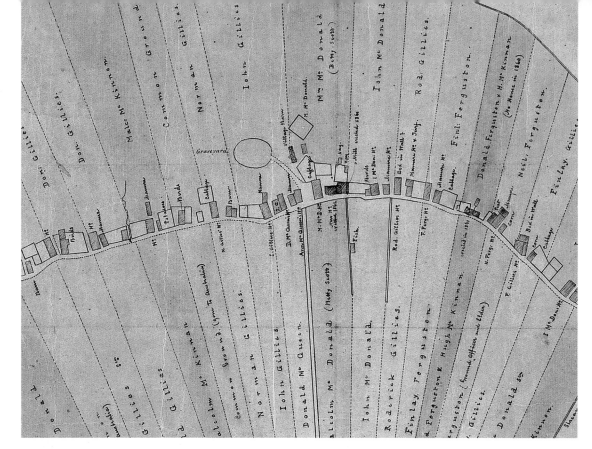

rigorous Sabbath observance was probably a small price to pay for the emotional outlet and sense of salvation provided by the new faith, and the prospect of a place at the Lord's table.

FIGURE 60.
Sharbau's map of the village, 1860.

Transforming the landscape

Neil MacKenzie also set himself the task of reforming agriculture and improving housing conditions. The event which triggered the revolution seems to have been the second visit of the St Kilda enthusiast Sir Thomas Acland in 1834, on a handsome yacht. Sir Thomas donated the sum of £20 to encourage the people to build new houses. The community agreed, and decided also that each house should stand on its own croft. The laird consented to the plan, and a surveyor from the Isle of Skye was brought in. However, his plan was rejected by the St Kildans, who eventually devised their own, and then apportioned the crofts by lot. MacKenzie, who had seen almost all his relatives back home in Glen Sannox evicted and forced to emigrate to Canada in the very year in which he took up his St Kilda ministry,[26] would have been keen to establish a less socially destructive version of land reform.

Sometime between 1838 and 1842, the St Kildans demolished the huddle of houses in which they were living and set about building new ones; they re-used the old roof timbers. The later interpolation of the 'modern' houses makes it now quite difficult to visualise the village which they created – a string of new blackhouses with thatched roofs, set end-on to a paved causeway incorporating a series of well-constructed stone-lined drains. However, the beautiful coloured map (Figure 60) made by Sharbau, Captain Thomas's assistant, is helpful, particularly since Thomas labelled it to indicate what was kept in cleits and other structures. As well as peat, birds and corn, the crofters were also storing manure; each house now had a compost pit, lined with stone.[27] Although cattle were still over-wintered in the houses, MacKenzie managed to persuade the people to muck out the byres more frequently and keep their floors cleaner. No longer did he need to suppress a shudder when he entered the homes of his flock in late wintertime, wading through dead seabird residues and 'every abomination you can think of ',[28] before clambering over a pile of manure. As Captain Thomas' plans show (Figure 61), each new blackhouse had a window (with glass), and there was a partition, the *talan*, between the byre and the living room. Occasionally a sleeping-space was set in the thickness of a wall, a throwback to earlier arrangements. MacKenzie raised money from various sources, calling in favours from some of his former pupils in Glasgow[29] to furnish the new houses, and purchase window frames and glass, as well as bedsteads, dressers, chairs, stools and crockery. The laird provided £20 to pay for the carriage of the equipment.[30] This looks like 'matched funding'; one wonders whether MacKenzie used Acland's donation to persuade him to cough up.[31] The fittings and furnishings unloaded from the *Vulcan* in 1838 acknowledged St Kilda's egalitarian principles; there were 21 glass windows, stools, tables and dressers, 24 chairs, and 47 bed-steads, as well as a quantity of china.[32] (Apparently the first tea arrived around this time; the naturalist George Atkinson had a 'most acceptable' cup of tea at the manse in 1831.[33] There is a revealing story about Ewen Gillies tasting the new beverage and telling the factor (who had imported the tea): 'if I am killed you will be blamed'.[34])

The islanders set about reorganising the in-bye land, setting out a fan-shaped array of crofts with straight boundary-banks, within a massive stone head dyke (still in annual use for rounding up Soay sheep). It isn't at all obvious today, but at the coast it became a high sea-wall, successfully designed to shelter the crops from the wind and the worst of the salt-laden spray.[35] Early photographs show something of its original size;[36] before bulldozers got to work in the late twentieth century, its line was visible running along the top of the pebble beach. The total length of the wall surrounding the in-bye land was about 2000 m. MacKenzie got the islanders to clear and drain the arable land, straightening and deepening two small burns. They disturbed or removed quite a lot of archaeology in the process, including a few *cnocan sithichean* – fairy mounds – which sound like prehistoric burial cairns; sometimes they contained stone slab-built cists and broken pottery, and occasionally bones.[37] At the upper ends of some crofts, they demolished a considerable proportion of the thick walls of the ancient Tobar Childa field system. They cleared out the springs which supplied their water, and put protective stone cowls around them; they dug a saw-pit for cutting up driftwood. It was conveniently sited, not far from the distinctive 'coffin cleit' (no.

*St Kilda and the
Wider World: Tales
of an Iconic Island*

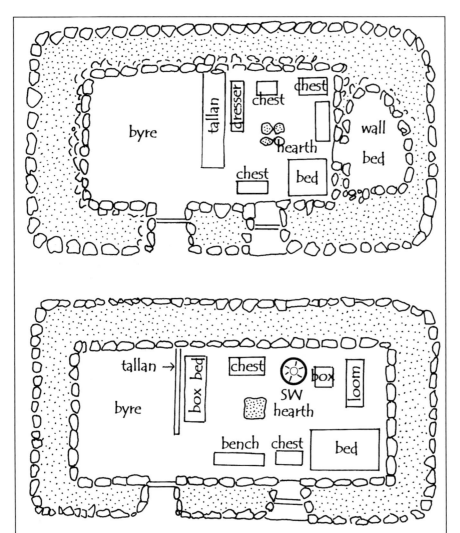

FIGURE 61.
Captain
F. W. L. Thomas' plans
of Hirta blackhouses
and their internal
fittings around 1860
(redrawn). Upper:
blackhouse, featuring a
traditional wall bed;
lower: Betty Scott's
house, now known as
Blackhouse K (SW =
spinning wheel).

2), a wood store which was extra long, and open at both ends.[38] It was near the church (Figure 4, page 3). Finally, a wall was built around the graveyard (Figure 62). MacKenzie was trying to promote more scientific agriculture, and he insisted that the islanders use the 'English' spade rather then the *caschrom*.[39]

It was tough going. For the minister, the project involved muscular Christianity in its most literal sense. Motivating the men was a constant concern; unless he got stuck into the work himself, and participated fully, they tended to slacken off. As he acknowledged, it was not as if they were actually lazy, or out of condition. But being essentially hunter-gatherers, they were not really accustomed to sustained manual labour; it was the women who did most of the agricultural work. (Having worked on an archaeological excavation on a tiny Aegean island, with a gang composed of farmers and fishermen, I can sympathise with MacKenzie. The farmers picked and shovelled all day, working at a steady pace; the fishermen spent much of their time gazing out to sea ...) It was an affront to MacKenzie's Protestant soul that the men did not need to put in long hours (although the women worked a good deal harder). Presumably it was MacKenzie's attitude that led MacLean to assert that the tattered appearance of the men's clothes across the upper parts of their backs was caused by 'lounging the half of their time with their backs against the houses, talking of this and that one's feats among the rocks'.[40] Calculating how many days' work was involved in supplying their wants, MacKenzie claimed that 'if they wrought as long hours and as steadily as other people have to do, they could finish all their work in about a third of their time' and he noted that 'they do not care to do any more than is strictly necessary'. But considering the risks involved in fowling, and the factor's trading monopoly, what would the men have gained by increasing their productivity?

The minister's achievement was phenomenal. Of course, he had his responsibilities as a family man. The damp manse, originally two-bedroomed but extended in the late 1830s[41] – housed a large brood of children described by a visitor[42] as rosy-cheeked, 'with clean hands and well-washed faces, tidy dark green tartan frocks or trowsers ... and little bare feet, the whole under the superintendence of a by no means tidy, but good enough looking, St Kilda lass'. Part of Mrs MacKenzie's mission was to show the women how to sew, so that they might make for themselves the calico mutches, the frilly white head-dresses which expressed their married status, and to learn to wash them 'upon scientific principles'.[43] Sometimes, in response to climbing accidents, the minister had to discover some medical expertise, setting broken limbs[44] or dressing a head-wound 'from which the brain was protruding' after a fowler was hit by a falling rock (a common hazard).[45] It is likely that the minister also delivered his wife's babies; all but three of their children survived infancy, no doubt owing to their avoidance of unhygienic, dangerous St Kildan midwifery practices.[46] MacKenzie had plenty of intellectual curiosity. He was interested in the archaeology of Hirta, making a record which was eventually published by his son.[47] His diary contains numerous observations on birds – the timing of their arrivals and departures, their egg-laying and breeding habits, and visits made by migrants such as geese and swans.[48] MacKenzie had a gun, and he was frustrated at not being able to 'secure' a rare roller.[49] Keeping up with what was happening in the outside world was something of a problem. The minister had a good method of dealing with a year's supply of old newspapers; every week, he read the one published exactly a year ago. It was mortifying to discover that several months after Queen Victoria had ascended the throne he had still been praying for the health of the king!

After these land reforms, the St Kildans' agricultural shortcomings and problems could no longer be attributed to the evils of a communal farming system. Visibly, they were now *tenants*, responsible as individuals for paying rent on their crofts. They were now dealing with a 'factor' rather than a 'tacksman'. However, their crofts were not really precocious versions of the ones created in the region at the end of the nineteenth century, because the

FIGURE 62.
The graveyard. The handful of inscribed memorials includes Alexander Ferguson's marble 'open book' memorial to his parents (near the centre).

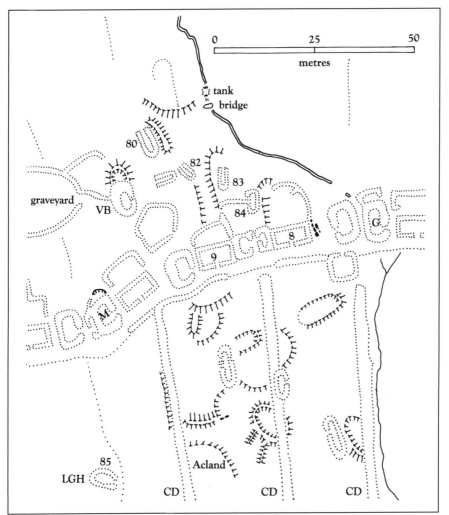

FIGURE 63.
Left and opposite
The pre-Improvement *clachan*. Left, traces of houses and house-platforms not destroyed by Improvement in the 1830s. Letters and numbers refer to blackhouses, houses and cleits mentioned in the text.
CD:Consumption Dyke; LGH = Lady Grange's House; VB = Village Barn. The position from which Sir Thomas Acland made his sketch is also indicated. Opposite, the general character of the *clachan* as reconstructed. Only houses for which there is archaeological evidence are indicated – a mixture of probables and possibles.

estate still operated the truck system. Rents and grazing charges were not simple cash payments, they were a charge against the 'agreed' value of St Kilda's exports. And changing the system of land tenure did nothing to counter the serious and growing nineteenth-century problems of low yields and crop failure. Fortunately, however, agriculture was only one component of the multi-stranded St Kildan economy.

From clachan to planned village

Where was the *clachan* which was replaced by the present layout? MacLean's account seems clear enough; there were 26 houses which looked 'like a cluster of bee-skeps, 200 yards (*c.* 180 m) westwards in the centre of the glen'.[50] This suggests that they were located halfway along MacKenzie's 'street' – on the low, stony and relatively dry spur extending south from the foot of Conachair, where they would not intrude upon deeper-soiled farming land. However,

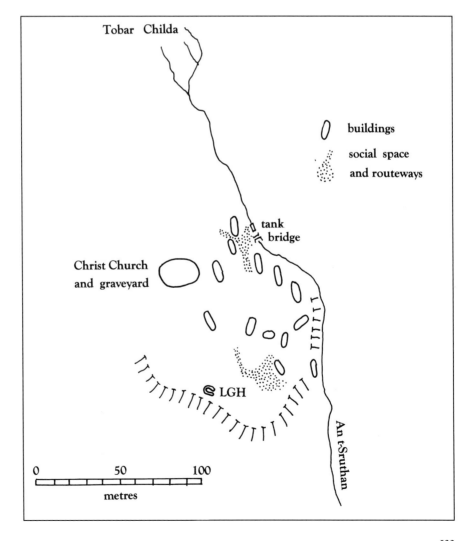

several twentieth-century commentators had other ideas about the location of the pre-Improvement 'village'. In 1957 the naturalists Williamson and Boyd became interested in a small number of distinctive corbelled stone structures, the best known of which is 'Calum Mór's House'.[51] One might call them 'super-cleits'; they are larger than cleits, more oval in plan, and have small chambers set in their thick walls or within corbelled annexes. Williamson and Boyd thought these primitive-looking buildings were probably medieval houses. They are not really clustered, although seven out of ten *are* within 120 m or so of the Tobar Childa spring, which, according to MacAulay was 'near the heart of the village'.[52] Williamson and Boyd also thought they had identified the road to the old settlement, the 'tolerable causeway ... which they call the Street', in MacAulay's words.[53] It made its approach from the east. The naturalists concluded that the 'old village' must have been near Tobar Childa, and just below the foot of Conachair.

This view is widespread in recent St Kilda literature.[54] However, it has now been superseded. During my 1994 visit I reinterpreted the 'roads' or 'tracks' which approach the foot of Conachair from the east as abandoned and robbed-out head dykes (see Chapter Three). And not long after this, the discovery of George Atkinson's portrait of the pre-Improvement *clachan*, done in 1831,[55] made it pretty clear that it was located on the centre of the Conachair spur rather than near Tobar Childa – as Robin Turner, senior archaeologist for the National Trust for Scotland, pointed out.[56]

Thinking about it, in September 2002, I found it hard to believe that a group of 20 or 30 stone-walled houses could have been destroyed as recently as the 1830s without leaving any trace whatsoever. Obviously, evidence would have been totally eradicated along the narrow zone occupied by the houses and the street. But what about areas to the north and south? Keeping in mind the small, rather ovoid houses illustrated by Atkinson, I started to explore the rather crowded zone to the east of the graveyard, where there is a group of five cleits on the croft associated with House 9, as well as a structure marked 'Village Barn' on Sharbau's 1860 plan.[57] It soon became clear that this area contains several odd archaeological features (Figure 63). For instance, one or two structures are perched on pre-existing banks; the small 'garden' put out of commission by the construction of cleit 80 is enclosed on the east by a stretch of wall considerably thicker than the walling around the rest of its perimeter. The 'Village Barn' was obviously preceded by a structure whose truncated, rounded end is visible on its north side; it looks as if the same is true for Blackhouse M. Also there seems to have been a track approaching from the north-west, which becomes a hollow way as it heads south between cleits 82 and 83.

To the south of the Street, I noticed several features marked without comment on the plan in Stell and Harman's *Buildings of St Kilda*. They look like the remains of small houses, or platforms for houses; one or two have 'dished' interiors and/or traces of walling along their edges, and they are mostly aligned roughly north-south, as Atkinson's illustration suggests they should be. But what most intrigued me was the land surface a little further south. It too was 'dished', and one could imagine a trampled, muddy area just outside and below the 'village', flooded periodically by water flowing down the slope, and poached by cattle hanging around after milking; it would have been a natural meeting-place. A couple of days later, lying awake at night, I realised where I had seen this image before – in Sir Thomas Acland's drawing of 'the principal square of St Kilda', done in 1812. The artist's position was evidently below the 'village', looking north. Archaeological ground detail matches the features recorded by Acland very well (Figure 64, with a recent view for comparison, Figure 65) – a house to the right, a screening wall to the left, a couple of upright stones between them, and the muddy public space in the foreground.

The stony promontory on which these features occur is also where 'Lady Grange's House', alias cleit 85, is located. This is the building in which Rachel Erskine (or Chieseley) is supposed to have lived during her banishment to Hirta in the 1730s. With its broad profile and turf top – on which a skua sometimes perches, exuding a tangible air of menace – the structure looks from a distance rather like a giant Christmas pudding. According to Mathieson it was rebuilt as a cleit, after most of it had fallen down;[58] this seems to be confirmed by marked differences between the north and the south walls, in terms of thickness and straightness. Mathieson said that the building's original roof was laid on timber beams – which would suggest that it was a conventional thatched house. In 1838 MacLean was shown Lady Grange's lodging by the grandson of the man who had 'attended' her, and made her a straw seat.[59] He quotes the dimensions as 20 ft by 10 ft, which fits the ground area of cleit 85 very well. Some commentators doubt that this structure really *was* Lady Grange's house,[60] but there is no reason to believe that there was any break in the islanders' oral traditions in the period since the 1730s. MacCulloch said that Lady Grange's prison was to be seen 'among the houses'.[61] And perhaps a house on the exposed south-west side of the *clachan* would have been the ideal place to lodge an aristocratic guest who has been described as 'a woman of insanely violent temper, eccentric, drunken and ill-balanced'.[62]

Another reason for believing that the old *clachan* was in this zone is the distribution of fragments of rotary querns, the hand-mills which women used almost every day to make flour, and occasionally for an ethnographic demonstration for the benefit of tourists. No quern fragments have been found in the Tobar Childa area. But two have turned up in nineteenth-century structures just along the street from the area of the *clachan*; there is one built into the window embrasure of the annexe to Blackhouse C,[63] and another on the wall of Blackhouse G. Excavations by Norman Emery at House 8 produced pieces of at least three querns.[64] In 2003 I discovered that the fabric of cleit 84 contains no fewer than three pieces of rotary quern (one of them in the doorway). It is possible that these pieces were spread around during the reuse of stones from demolished *clachan* structures, although, as Ann Clarke has

St Kilda and the
Wider World: Tales
of an Iconic Island

FIGURE 64.
Sir Thomas Acland's
sketch of the south end
of the *clachan* in 1812.

FIGURE 65.
The south end of the
former *clachan* in 2003.
The two prominent
stones, with a wall to
their left and a house
to their right (both
now visible as low
earthworks) may be
seen on Acland's sketch
(Figure 64, above).

recently pointed out to me, some of the querns might date from the Iron Age, and not from recent centuries.

So it is possible to deduce the whereabouts of about a dozen structures from the pre-Improvement *clachan*, about half the number recorded in the early nineteenth century; they housed a population of around 100. Traces of other houses must have been removed by demolition and cultivation. It is easy to imagine another dozen or so fitting into the space available, plus ancillary buildings, the *clachan* forming a tight huddle of houses, many touching one another on this slightly elevated stony knoll.[65] Most of the doorways faced east.[66] The people lived close to the site of Christ Church, which still had a thatched roof in 1697[67] but was in ruins during the last decades of the *clachan's* existence.[68] This situation fits the description of coffins being carried 'in the course of the sun round the gardens with which the group of houses which form the village are surrounded'.[69] When bodies had been carried out of the north end of the *clachan*, a sunwise turn would have taken the bearers to a single slab bridging the An t-Sruthan burn to the east of cleit 80. Just north of this little bridge is a small rectangular setting of eight upright stones, two groups of three facing each other across the tiny burn, with one set transversely at each end. This may have been a tank, used for tasks requiring some depth of water, such as washing or cold-dyeing wool. On Hirta, dyeing cloth was a female occupation.[70] One can only assume that the 'bridge' was mostly for the use of toddlers and small children, since it is easy for adults to step across the burn here (at any rate before arthritis has set in). It is tempting to assume that these features went with the *clachan*, and that this was an activity area and social space for women, girls and young children, the men tending to gather in the 'principal square' at the south end of the settlement. Acland's picture depicts men and women – probably both natives and tourists – but he does include three or four apparently male figures lounging against a wall (Figure 64). In this scenario, women would gather on the side of the *clachan* facing the road to Gleann Mór – very much a female zone in the summer – whilst the men looked out over the sea, towards the boat station. But this neat 'structuralist' model is problematic, given that Martin located the women's assemblies in the middle of the village,[71] and Atkinson, who visited Hirta in 1831, said that the men sat on the wall of a large house in the middle of the settlement.[72] In Kearton's time they sometimes gathered on the rocks near the Feather Store.[73]

One cannot help wondering how far this radical re-organisation of their life-space would have changed the St Kildans' behaviour and perception of the world, especially after the introduction of more modern houses in the early 1860s, with their larger windows looking directly over the bay. If the most famous photograph of the 'Parliament' is any guide (it was taken in 1886), the men now met outside House 9, in a space which still preserves a secluded atmosphere (Figure 10, page 17). This is created by Blackhouse K, which protrudes some way across the street to the west, as do Blackhouses H and G to the east; to the south the area is screened off by an unusually high wall along the edge of the street. This sense of seclusion would have been even greater when the buildings were roofed. Of course, this was a logical place to meet, since it is halfway along the street, and also a good vantage point. But it is also at the heart of the old *clachan*, and the choice of location may represent a conscious attempt to preserve some continuity with the past. Communitarian values were hard to eradicate. On Sharbau's map, three areas are marked 'common ground (gone to Australia)' – a reference to the recent emigration of 36 islanders in 1852. The areas involved are a) behind the Factor's House (and east of the Ilishgil); b) the westernmost croft; and c) the croft which includes Houses 12 and 13. In all these areas turf was removed, leaving a distinctive pattern of rectangular cuttings, and stone was quarried too; so it is impossible to see any early structures. It is highly significant that after the emigration, these untenanted crofts were immediately taken back into common use;[74] there is photographic evidence that by 1886 the turf-cutting had largely destroyed their agrarian value.[75] This looks like a re-assertion of community values, perhaps a conscious attempt to prevent the factor from claiming rent for these deserted crofts or bringing in new tenants for them (though probably he had no intention of doing so).

Disruption

Neil MacKenzie left Hirta in 1843. He had to admit that the past two years had told heavily on his health and mental vigour; he needed a time of rest and mental refreshment, and wanted to leave the island for a while, perhaps for ever. He felt that his work on Hirta was finished, and that he would be more usefully engaged elsewhere. Moreover, he wanted to attend the upcoming General Assembly in Edinburgh, where an agonising issue was coming up; he had thought and prayed about it, without reaching any conclusion.[76] A great national event was about to touch the most remote community in Scotland.

It is debatable how far MacKenzie had been fully in control of his mission on Hirta. He may have wanted to play the role of a shepherd, guiding his flock towards the light; but he was also riding a tiger. His preaching could unleash powerful emotions. In 1840 both grain and potato crops were very poor, and the autumn rains and gales prevented people from bringing in fuel. 'Everything seems to conspire against us this season', wrote MacKenzie in October. The scarcity of food and fuel was worse in February, when the minister noted that 'our religious meetings have been regularly attended all season'.[77] For MacKenzie this was not cause for complacency. In spite of his educational efforts, which had borne fruit in the summer of 1838, he felt that the islanders' religious conversion was only skin-deep. The people were apparently becoming 'more cold and formal'. There was a serious difference between 'mere formalists and hypocrites', as MacKenzie put it, and those who truly feared the Lord. And then, on Wednesday 28th September 1841, preaching to a largely female congregation (most of the men being on another island) MacKenzie started to get through on an emotional level. Members of the congregation started weeping and crying out. That winter, religious fervour spread like wildfire. MacKenzie noted the panting and heavy breathing, 'the movement of the hands like that of one drowning'. Women fainted; others rolled in the dust on the church floor. After experiences like these, the minister was often utterly exhausted; but he was also clever (manipulative?) enough to vary his methods to suit particular individuals. To satisfy the cravings of his flock he had to lay on another weekly meeting, on Thursday evenings.[78] The St Kildans were desperate for the forgiveness of their sins; one wonders what was weighing on their minds. Was it the anger of the Lord, recently expressed in the terrible weather and their consequent privations? Perhaps MacKenzie's re-housing project had created social tensions, resulting in more witchcraft – or a growing fear of it. And sometime around 1840, perhaps in the very year of religious revival, three men captured a great auk on Stac an Armin. They could not have known that this was probably the last one to visit the British Isles. But in any case they tied it up in their bothy. Soon afterwards a storm blew up, and delayed their departure. The men decided that their captive was a witch, and had raised the storm deliberately. So they battered the bird to death.[79] Belief in witchcraft and in an all-seeing God were by no means incompatible.

The islanders were going through the same sort of experience as many other people in the region. These were terrible times in the Highlands and Islands. Destitute, driven from their land, helpless to prevent the break-up of their communities, and politically impotent, people turned to the only project which empowered them. In a revitalised if emotionally manipulative form of Christianity, they glimpsed personal salvation within a collective enterprise. In the quest for a seat at the Lord's table, they could enter a realm of authoritative spiritual knowledge which challenged the ruthless, profit-driven materialism of principalities and powers. They sought *spiritual* empowerment as a *community*, expressing themselves in religious fervour and music stirring enough to raise hairs on the back of the neck.

Many of the ministers who created this religious revival were practical men, who campaigned for Gaelic language education in the Highlands and Islands. They often took to the road. They witnessed the privations of the people, spoke out publicly in towns and cities, raised money, and fought political campaigns. Norman MacLeod was appalled by the situation in South Uist: 'starvation on many faces – the children with their melancholy looks, big looking knees, shrivelled legs, hollow eyes, swollen-like bellies – God help them, I never did witness such wretchedness! ... many, very many, could not go to the shore from weakness, far less carry home the shellfish. Some were confined to bed, many suffering from severe dysentery from living exclusively on shellfish, or some wild mustard and spinach etc, and other herbs ...'.[80]

Reformers and educationists had a major problem. Ministers of the Church were usually appointed by the lairds (although in the case of St Kilda, patronage had been transferred to the SPCK in 1821[81]). Some of them were relaxed, even complacent – not exactly at the cutting edge of the faith. Congregations who had glimpsed the promised land needed the regular inspiration of a minister of Evangelical persuasion; bodies of elders whose authority stemmed from serious Bible study were no longer willing to have the laird's placeman imposed upon them. Eventually the issue went all the way up to the House of Lords, where in 1839 Lord Brougham (who had visited St Kilda as a carefree and facetious young man) delivered a landmark judgment – against the Evangelicals. One of Brougham's comments particularly infuriated them: 'the solemnly declared judgement of a Christian congregation would have as little value as the kick of a [champion's] horse'.[82] The Evangelicals now realised that they must break away. Their chosen day was May 18th, 1843, at the opening of the General Assembly in Edinburgh, held beneath the oval dome of the Neo-classical church of St Andrew in the New Town. In a carefully choreographed move, almost two-fifths of the ministers walked out, marching with firm purpose down the road to their own assembly at Tanfield Hall. The Apostle of the North preached the first sermon. This episode, which initiated the Free Church, became known as the Disruption.

The lairds reacted sharply and repressively, as the dissidents had known they would. Ministers who 'went out' were evicted from their manses, and locked out of their churches (despite the fact that the money to build them had often been provided by public subscription, and indeed by people who now wanted to join the Free Church). A good many farmers and crofters who joined the Free Church were expelled from their tenancies; the Marquis of Bute sacked his head gardener, 'a remarkable man of God'. Free Church ministers had to take to the roads, supported by the voluntary contributions of their supporters. They preached in barns and stables, cart-sheds and saw-pits, tents and wooden churches, and sometimes from places where they were legally immune from prosecution, such as boats and carefully-chosen shoreline locations. A remarkable 'floating church', a ship which could accommodate 750 worshippers, was built on the Clyde, and taken to Strontian, on Loch Sunart, a location carefully selected to serve the geographically dispersed adherents of the Free Church. John MacDonald had to move out of his manse and take up residence in a small cottage nearby. When he preached on his home patch in Ferintosh, 10,000 people came to listen. At first, lairds often refused to provide sites for the erection of new churches, schools and manses. But money for the Free Church poured in; within four years, over 700 new churches had been constructed.[83]

So what happened on St Kilda? The preaching of MacDonald and MacKenzie had laid solid foundations for the islanders to join the Free Church. When the mission yacht *Breadalbane* came to Hirta in early August 1846[84] they expressed their unanimous wish to do so. By this time Neil MacKenzie was gone. His agony had been resolved; he had 'disappointed his

FIGURE 66.
Kilchrenan church, Argyll. Neil MacKenzie is buried in the north-west corner of the graveyard.

FIGURE 67.
Kilchrenan manse, seen
from across Loch Awe.

former friends'[85] and remained within the Established church. He was in a very difficult situation. He might have chosen to stand up for his Evangelical convictions, and continue in the service of the community which had embraced them so eagerly. But to do that would be to condemn his wife and bairns to life in one of the blackhouses, leaving the manse with its busy, cheerful kitchen, as well as his Glebe and garden, with its carrots and onions and mustard (and unsuccessful beans and peas[86]). (The front garden of the manse is now largely under concrete; it was much bigger than suggested by the token wall put up by the military after they had converted the manse into the sergeants' mess.) Could they stand the closer physical proximity of the St Kildans? MacKenzie would have to teach, preach and conduct services in a house or a barn, or in the open air. Every day, he would be compelled to contemplate the locked and empty church and manse, troubling reminders of better times.

When he left, MacKenzie must have wondered whether he had betrayed his flock and everything that he had worked for over the past 14 years. But as we have seen, he was physically and mentally exhausted; he had given himself unsparingly to the St Kilda project. Probably he had become frustrated and impatient, working with an increasingly assertive and self-confident body of elders. (The elder Donald Ferguson told one of MacKenzie's successors, the uncharismatic John MacKay, in public at the end of a service, that he had better improve the quality of his sermons or start looking for another job.[87]) As the wind roared around the manse during the winters of religious fervour in the early 1840s, did the minister come to feel that he had unleashed the forces of a dangerous extremism? His remarks about the kindness of the laird and the relationship between the estate and the island community suggest that his radicalism did not extend beyond his style of preaching.[88] When push came to shove, he was an Establishment man; perhaps with the onset of middle age, he had come to long for a more conventional, straightforward parish, in which his spiritual authority would be more unquestioningly accepted. But he did return to St Kilda in 1845 and again in 1847[89] and the islanders were delighted to see him; in 1847 his 'parting exhortations' took two hours.[90] He obviously felt ambivalent about leaving.

St Kilda and the
Wider World: Tales
of an Iconic Island

Aftermath

Predictably, the laird – Sir John MacPherson MacLeod, an old India hand –
did have the church and the manse locked up, and refused to provide a site
for a new church.[91] For a period of ten years there was a tussle between the
Free and the Established churches, with the islanders and the estate in dispute
about church services and education (especially religious education).[92] A new
teacher called MacEwen arrived; with the laird's backing, he proposed to hold
services and classes in the church. The church elders had evidently been coping
well, in the Free Church mode. They resented MacEwen's arrival, and for six
months most of them held their own service in a private house. Norman
MacRaild the factor turned up, and tried to bully the people into attending
services at the church, on pain of eviction or expulsion; they wondered if they
had been wise to go over to the Free Church. But the laird over-ruled his
factor, and MacEwen left soon afterwards. The elders now had a decisive voice
in the appointment of the teacher; but this was because he was unwaged (the
salary of £25 being only payable to a Presbyterian) and thus in practice had to
be an islander. The St Kildans, their resolve stiffened by the sermons of ministers who came over once a year on the *Breadalbane*, held fast to their Free
Church faith.

In the late summer of 1852, a momentous decision was taken. Eight families, a total of 36 people, agreed to emigrate to Australia.[93] One or two of the
better-off families apparently sold up in order to pay for their passage; for
poorer people there were various loan schemes. The estate made the arrangements on the tenants' behalf, and paid the fares and clothing costs of those
unable to do so. It seems that the factor may have exceeded his authority,
incorrectly interpreting the wishes of the laird, who was closely connected with
the Highland and Island Emigration Society. Thirty years later, Rev. John
MacKay told the Napier Commission that it was MacRaild who wanted to get
rid of the more poverty-stricken islanders, bribing them with meal and
persuading them to sign an agreement.[94] But when the time came, the laird
made a dash to Glasgow, and then accompanied the would-be emigrants to
Liverpool docks (where the St Kildans, staggered by the crowds, thought they
were getting a foretaste of 'the last assemblage of nations at the day of judgement'[95]). MacLeod made them various offers to persuade them to return
home. Perhaps he had only just found out about the project; perhaps he felt
that MacRaild had gone too far. Or had he realised the serious demographic
consequences which would follow the emigration of so many people?

The St Kildans chose to make a political point about the religious intoler-
ance of the estate and the stand-off which had followed the departure of Neil
MacKenzie; they told Sir John MacPherson MacLeod bluntly that their fellow
islanders would soon be following them to Australia (which was what the
British Treasury expected to happen[96]). They asked that the manse and church
be given to the people. The laird, anxious to prevent a further exodus,
purchased what must have been the leasehold of the church and manse from

the Established Church for the Free Church.[97] (All this suggests that Hirta was hardly making a loss for the estate at this time.) In 1853 the church and manse were unlocked, and the new catechist, Duncan Kennedy, could look forward to proper accommodation. But pressure was building up for the establishment of an ordained minister. Eventually an endowment was raised, and in 1865 John MacKay commenced his 24-year ministry on the island.[98] Aided by numerous well-wishers from across the sea, the *Hirteach* had won their battle for religious freedom. It was a significant victory. The St Kildans were beginning to gain a greater understanding of the wider world and were starting to exploit the interest and concern of outsiders in order to out-manoeuvre the laird and his factor.

As for MacKenzie, he spent most of the last 27 years of his life as the Presbyterian minister of Kilchrenan, on the banks of Loch Awe, not far east of Oban in Argyll. (It is an odd coincidence that the old name of the parish was actually Kildachrenan.[99]) His loyalties were now firmly with the mainstream Presbyterian Church, and so were those of his children. Of the sturdy little bairns who had spent their childhood on Hirta, two eventually became Presbyterian ministers, and one of his daughters married one; MacKenzie's youngest son became Provost of Fort William, and lived in the house which is now the Highland Museum.[100]

Kilchrenan has a good deal of hilly, badly-drained land, much of it unenclosed and not significantly improved. The late eighteenth-century church (Figure 66) is beautiful in its simplicity, with pleasing, solid proportions and white-painted walls. Neil MacKenzie was buried at the north-west corner of the graveyard, his body having been conveyed to Kilchrenan from Glasgow by road and water in December 1879, 'with full Victorian splendour'.[101] The manse at Kilchrenan (Figure 67) stood beside the beautiful Loch Awe 'in a sweet and sequestered spot, upon the summit of a slope close by the lake, embosomed in wood';[102] it had elaborate gardens of the kind which MacKenzie and his wife could only have fantasised about in their years on Hirta. Every time the minister left the house, he had to go past the Free church at the top of his drive; the local minister had 'gone out' at the Disruption.[103] The scene does not seem to have changed much since Victorian times; it is still possible today to look across the calm waters of Loch Awe and see the former manse set among the woods. Neil MacKenzie must have been thankful for a quieter, more comfortable life. But as the wind ruffled the surface of the loch outside his study window, how often he must have recalled that other manse at the water's edge – the cries of the seals on the breeze, the gannets plunging in Village Bay, the almost unbearable roar of the Atlantic gales. How often too he must have pondered on the outcome of his youthful ambitions for Hirta, and wondered whether things might have turned out differently. And then, perhaps, he put his memories aside, and returned to the task of writing yet another sermon.

CHAPTER EIGHT

From MacLeod's Prison
to Fool's Paradise

Tea, white bread, and fancy biscuits now bulk largely in the diet of
the people. This is no food on which to raise a race of Vikings.

George Gibson (1925) p. 371.

FIGURE 68.
Mother and child.

In the 1840s and 1850s, the *Hirteach* won their battle with the laird over the
issue of freedom of worship. And the year 1860 saw another step in the process
of out-manoeuvring the estate. The story starts in January 1857, with the death
in the south of France of Charles Kelsall, a gentleman who lived at Hythe,
near Southampton, and had made money in the West Indies. In his will,
Kelsall had left £700 for the Improvement of the Highlands of Scotland. It
was the Edinburgh-based Highland and Agricultural Society of Scotland,
served by its able and energetic secretary John Hall Maxwell, which took on
the task of administering this money, which came to be known as the Kelsall
Fund. The Society had prioritised St Kilda, and in May 1859, Maxwell wrote
to the laird, Sir John MacPherson MacLeod, who lived in Bayswater. MacLeod
did not favour supplying the islanders with food, clothing or money; he
suggested attending to the infrastructure – improving the houses and their
furnishings, perhaps sending a boat – and addressing the issue of religious and
secular education.[1] The gist of a conversation held with his factor, Norman
MacRaild, in November 1859, was recorded in writing; they agreed that food
and clothing were 'enjoyed' by the St Kildans 'perhaps in a higher degree than
is usually to be met with in the class to which they belong'.[2] In August,
MacLeod informed Maxwell of the abundance and variety of the food enjoyed
by the people of St Kilda (see Chapter Five, page 90) and condescendingly
advised him to read Martin and MacAulay.[3]

A more useful contact for Maxwell was a naval captain, Captain (later Rear-
Admiral) Henry Otter. At this time St Kilda was a handy port of call for the
naval task force which was charting the seas around the Outer Hebrides. For
Captain Henry Otter and Captain F. W. L. Thomas, two of the officers who
put their names to the chart (which was published in 1865), landing on Hirta
must have been more interesting than plumbing the depths of the ocean.
Thomas was interested in the archaeology and traditional lifeways of the

Hebrides. Otter was a practical man, who wanted to help the St Kilda community; he once marketed a load of fish on the islanders' behalf, and gave them the proceeds, which came to £16.[4] Thomas had already called at Hirta on more than one occasion; it was he who put most of the labels on the map of the Village Bay crofts which was surveyed and drawn up by his assistant, Sharbau, in July 1860.

In the summer of 1860, serious changes were under way. In June, Captain Otter was already writing to John Hall Maxwell from the survey ship *Porcupine*, berthed in Portree, suggesting that the St Kildans needed an improved docking facility, fitted with a crane, and better houses with proper chimneys; they would need to send masons from Portree with blasting experience.[5] In July, Otter took Maxwell on the *Porcupine* on a fact-finding mission, accompanied by the Duke of Atholl, President of the Highland and Agricultural Society; they stayed overnight, the Duke lodging with Betty (or Betsy) Scott, an English-speaking mainlander who had married a St Kildan.[6] By August, workmen were on the island; it was intended that they would leave behind their 'forge, anvil, hammers, jumpers etc' for future use.[7] In this month Captain Thomas arrived, bringing his photographic equipment. He took some evocative pictures of the islanders; his portrait of the aged Euphemia MacCrimmon (more familiarly known as Effie) gives us a rare photograph of someone who was a little girl at the time of the French Revolution (Figure 57, page 114)!

The captain was accompanied by his wife. It is likely that the young Mrs Thomas discussed improving the islanders' home-made and rather primitive looms in order to exploit the commercial possibilities of weaving (apparently the *Hirteach* were already producing 'very good worsted').[8] It is said – though there is some dispute about it – that the first person to promote Harris tweed in the wider world was Lady Dunmore, proprietor of the Harris estate, after she was widowed in 1843; tweed made excellent clothing for her wealthy and aristocratic friends when they were in action on their recently-developed sporting estates. In 1859 or a little later, Captain Thomas's wife opened an agency at her home in Edinburgh for the sale of tweeds and knitwear.[9] Furthermore, one of Thomas' photographs[10] depicts a young woman (Mrs Thomas?) in front of a large house (their house in Harris?) with an upright loom set up beside it. There must be a strong suspicion that it was Mrs Thomas who introduced more modern cloth-making technology to Hirta at around this time. It was a considerable success; by 1877 – that is, before the steamers started calling regularly – St Kilda tweeds were already 'a good deal sought after'.[11]

Disaster and relief

And then came a terrible storm, which affected many parts of Scotland and northern England. Captain Otter happened to be at Hirta at the time, on the 43 metre *Porcupine*. On the evening of 2 October he got round under the lee of the north side of Hirta, to take shelter from a south-south-west gale. Just after midnight the barometer reading started to fall; it dropped six inches (15 cm) in less than three hours. Just before half past three, the ship was struck by a violent hurricane; the wind had switched abruptly to the north-west. The *Porcupine's* situation looked desperate; the ship lost the tiller ropes, the lights went out of action, the large paddle-box 'was lifted up and down as if made of paper'. The hurricane lasted for two hours, but the gale continued until around noon, when Otter was able to get into Village Bay.[12] The extent of the disaster in human terms then became apparent. All the roofs had lost their thatch, and the houses were knee-deep in water; the islanders' largest and best boat had been dashed to pieces on the new breakwater. In the gardens, the barley had been cut but not yet brought under cover, and the oats were still standing; the harvest was completely lost. Immediately Otter gave the islanders some meal and a barrel of ship's biscuit, and also some sails and boat covers to make temporary roofs for the protection of those in most desperate need.[13] There was no time to be lost. On 5 October Otter was in Lochmaddy, carrying an appeal for help to the laird from Duncan Kennedy, the Hirta catechist: 'I know you derive little benefit from the island, but surely there are many charitable people who would come forward ...'.[14] Otter contacted Maxwell, who quickly got in touch with newspapers and launched a public appeal. There was a magnificent response; by 23 October, over £420 had been collected, and at the beginning of November Otter was back on Hirta, bringing £255 worth of supplies. The navy sent 37 small casks of meal and 27 bags of biscuits.[15] The main supplies included plenty of oatmeal, as well as potatoes, barleymeal, peasemeal, bean meal and flour; there was seed corn (oats, barley and rye), bran for the cattle, and two tons of Peruvian guano. There was seed for sowing turnips, cabbages, 'German greens', carrots, and parsnips, as well as straw for renewing the thatch, and roofing timbers. There was 112 lbs (51 kg) of horse-hair for climbing ropes, 6,000 assorted fish hooks, two-dozen lead sinkers, and carpenters' tools; also 16 lbs (7 kg) of tea, 84 lbs (38 kg) of sugar, and one gross of tobacco pipes. Eighteen households were catered for; there were 18 tea kettles, 18 tea-pots, 18 tin plates, and six dozen tea-spoons. Six dozen handled mugs and six dozen breakfast cups and saucers completed the tea-drinking assemblage, though there were also wooden plates, horn spoons, and what seems like a good supply of pots, pans and crockery, with plenty of soap too.[16]

Maxwell's publicity campaign started a debate about aid for St Kilda. On 27 October Alexander MacDonald of Lochmaddy wrote to Maxwell suggesting that the houses should be better lighted and ventilated, with cast iron framed windows which could be opened; he also advocated building extensions to the houses, extra bedrooms which would also serve as weaving sheds, fitted out with improved looms. The St Kildans should be taught to make better cloth, and a 'depot' should be set up in Glasgow to sell it.[17] MacDonald also suggested that the islanders were in need of agricultural expertise. On this point Otter would certainly have agreed with him; in August he had written: 'their corn crops are most miserable, notwithstanding all the trouble and compost … in many places from 1/3 to ½ is weed, the wild marigold, by degrees I hope we may be able to instil into them that they are not the wisest people in the world, and reconcile them to take advice from strangers'.[18] Otter and Maxwell, like many of their contemporaries, felt that 'the gratuitous distribution of so much valuable property' would undermine the people's moral fibre; Otter proposed to take advantage of the situation by calling a meeting in the church, and making the heads of households sign an agreement that they would work to pay for the goods which he brought – by constructing new houses, as well as a building for 'an American hand grinding mill', and a wall for securing their boats when hauled up 'and any other little job I can find for them to do'.[19] When he arrived at Hirta, the sea was as calm as a millpond. Fearing a change in the weather, the captain made the people unload with all speed, and then took charge of the distribution of the food. The St Kildans were delighted with their new possessions; after a short break for prayer, they signed Otter's agreement, and made sure a letter of thanks to their benefactors was written.[20]

Otter and Maxwell had to act quickly and decisively; they were conscious that the weather was likely to deteriorate. There was really no time to consult with the laird (who now lived at Iver Lodge in Buckinghamshire). Otter had been concerned about MacLeod's reaction; he assumed that the laird would be pleased that there was now enough money to build new houses on Hirta.[21] But he was wrong. MacLeod did not find out about the great storm until a letter from Otter reached him on 12 October. 'Captain Otter's benevolence is worthy of admiration' conceded MacLeod in a letter dated 14 October[22] – evidently through gritted teeth. The laird was completely wrong-footed, and felt embarrassed and annoyed. There had been no need for a public appeal, he insisted; charitable gifts would only debase the character of the St Kildans, and the appeal was objectionable because it presented the public with 'a highly exaggerated view of the case'.[23] The wellbeing of the islanders was *his* responsibility, and the estate had the matter in hand. His factor, MacRaild, had been on the island only five days before the storm; the people could not be in great distress because the potato crop was good, he had heard (this wasn't true; on 7 November Otter noted that the potatoes were much reduced by disease, and those which had been recovered were very soft).[24] When Otter met MacRaild a few weeks later, the factor was indignant about the adverse publicity, calling the St Kildans 'all manner of names', and pointing out that he had left four bolls (c. 255 kg) of meal on the island (but as Otter noted, 'the four bolls would not have gone far with 70 people'[25]).

In early November, MacLeod was insisting that feeding the St Kildans should have been *his* responsibility.[26] But his practical response to the emergency had been completely ineffectual. So was his handling of the publicity.[27] His first instinct (on 12 October) had been to try to get the Kelsall Fund to pay for at least some of the food required,[28] offering to pay the bill himself if the fund directors would not agree. But he put in his food order too late, and it was evidently ignored, since money raised by the public appeal had already solved the problem.[29] On 5 November MacLeod offered to pay for a new boat.[30] Maxwell suggested that the laird's cheque, sent belatedly to pay for the food, should be redirected towards building the proposed new houses. MacLeod was furious; on 19 November he wrote to Maxwell insisting that he considered the supplies to have been ordered and paid for by himself. At the same time he refused to 'make a show of paying for supplies' when he had really paid for something else! He insisted that he would pay for new houses on his property himself, using the labour of the St Kildans.[31] The houses were erected in 1861 and 1862, at his expense, with modern roofs made of zinc.[32] (They were not very waterproof,[33] and must have been incredibly noisy when it rained. Later, they had to be refurbished with roofing-felt painted with pitch.[34]) Otter and Maxwell were left to deploy the Kelsall Fund on the building intended to house the public mill – which was erected at least in part, but apparently never used[35] – and on a new 30-foot boat, which was ordered by Otter and named *Dargavel*, after the place where Maxwell was brought up; it was probably delivered in the summer of 1861.[36]

The attitudes of the main players in this saga are revealing. In March 1861 the St Kildans told Otter that MacLeod 'would have done nothing' if others had not come forward.[37] They had now been alerted to the possibility of gaining the sympathy of a wider public and thus outflanking the laird and his factor. As we have seen, in the aftermath of the relief mission MacRaild the factor was furious with the islanders; he fully understood the significance of what had happened. The laird's comment expressed his feelings very well.[38] 'I trust', he wrote acidly, 'that [Maxwell] and Captain Otter will be so kind as to afford me the benefit of the influence which recent events have given them over the minds of that secluded little community'. In the late spring of 1862 Captain Otter again took up the cudgels on behalf of the islanders; once again, MacLeod had to defend himself. In an indignant letter to Maxwell, written on 1 May, he denied that the islanders were starving; according to MacRaild, they had got the barley harvest in before he left, and the condition of the potatoes was no worse than anywhere else in the Western Isles; as for the state of the sheep, did Otter expect the laird to provide the St Kildans with plenty of fresh and fat mutton throughout the year? The islanders had refused to buy meal from the factor, which according to him was offered at cost price and on 12 months' credit; apparently they expected a visit from Otter bringing a supply for which they would not have to pay.[39] At the end of May, MacRaild was back on St Kilda, writing to his employer to tell him how well the people looked; they had had to buy some meal and paid for it in cash – having failed to get 'anything gratuitous by going to Harris'.[40]

Evidently the islanders saw the *Dargavel* as a means of gaining access to the outside world and thus reducing their dependence on the factor. But their hopes were dashed by a tragic accident. Having managed one voyage in 1862,[41] in early April 1863 they tried again. The *Dargavel* left with a following wind, loaded with cloth, salted fish and other trade goods, as well as some money in notes; they were intending to make contact with Captain Otter.[42] The wind

St Kilda and the
Wider World: Tales
of an Iconic Island

changed, and a southerly gale blew up. Nothing more was heard of the boat. Some time later, items of clothing were washed ashore at Mealista, on the west coast of Harris; the pattern of the weave identified the clothes as St Kildan.[43] Seven men were lost, three of them married with children, as well as Betty Scott, an 'intelligent and superior' woman in her mid-forties, who came originally from Sutherland.[44] She had been Neil MacKenzie's housekeeper, and was married to Malcolm MacDonald.[45] At the time of her death she was the island's midwife;[46] it was a dreadful irony that she and Malcolm had apparently lost 12 of their 14 children in infancy, presumably from infantile tetanus.[47] Betty's linguistic and social skills may explain her presence on the *Dargavel*. With her good English, she had been of critical importance to the community's relationship with the two naval officers. She appeared in Captain Thomas' photographs, and allowed him to make a measured plan of her house (Figure 61, page 130) – now known as Blackhouse K – furniture and fittings included (which he later published).[48] In one of his letters, Sir John MacPherson MacLeod implied that there was more than friendship between Betty and Captain Otter[49] and MacDiarmid noted smugly: 'she ... proved unfaithful [to her St Kildan husband], but fate overtook her ... and it is said she found a watery grave'.[50] When Captain Otter said 'the touch of their skin is like velvet',[51] was he speaking from more than fleeting experience?

From *Dargavel* to *Dunara Castle*

In 1871 St Kilda was 'bought back' by MacLeod of Dunvegan for £3000.[52] The new laird was soon to suffer further public embarrassment. The thorn in his flesh was a young man named John Sands. Sands first visited St Kilda in 1875, spending seven weeks there.[53] He came partly out of curiosity about the people, partly to improve his Gaelic. He therefore tried to spend as much time with the St Kildans as possible, though he had the Factor's House to himself and did his own cooking, hiring a neighbour to fetch milk and water and do some cleaning. He brought his flute and a set of bagpipes; he liked drawing sketches of people, and also landscapes. Sands found that the St Kildans were still keen to get a boat big enough for them to get to Harris and trade independently; when he returned he started raising money and got one built. Getting it from the yard in Ardrishaig through the Crinan Canal and then to St Kilda proved complicated, but he eventually arrived on 21 June 1876, accepting a tow from MacKenzie the factor for the final stage. There are various accounts of the debate stimulated by the arrival of the new boat.[54] To Sands' annoyance, the factor mischievously challenged the islanders to trade for themselves if they could manage it, offering to match any higher prices they might obtain. Sands urged them to seek their independence; but John MacKay, the minister, feared that the islanders might over-play their hand, putting at risk not just their economy but also their lives – a concern which put him in good standing with the estate. The factor, no doubt anxious to clarify the situation, tried to persuade them to sign an agreement binding them to continue getting supplies from the estate as usual. Following the inter-vention of MacKay, the islanders signed it; according to Seton,[55] the minister persuaded the factor to insert a clause permitting independent trading. The laird wrote his factor a very supportive letter afterwards, praising his judge-ment and that of MacKay and the islanders.[56] However, the affair damaged the relationship between Sands and the minister.

John Sands spent an interesting summer. In July he carried out an excava-tion at the Iron Age souterrain (Figure 69), later claiming to be the first person to publicly recognise the stone implements for what they were. In September he started to get anxious; there was no sign of the factor with the autumn supplies. There was some glorious autumn weather,[57] but the estate did not manage to get a boat.[58] Sands resigned himself to a long winter. And then, on 17 January, in roaring seas, a ship's boat came into Village Bay, just after the start of a church service. The nine men on board were unwilling to grab the ropes thrown to them, preferring to save themselves by swimming. The boat was dashed to pieces on the rocks. The men were Austrians, crew members of the *Peti Dabrovacki*, whose ballast had shifted in a storm on the way to New York. The St Kildans took them in, and treated them with great kindness; in return, the sailors helped the women with the daily grind on the hand-mills. Conscious that they were a serious drain on the islanders' already low supplies of food, they wanted to leave as soon as possible. They lit a huge bonfire, hoping it would be seen on the Long Island. Then Sands made a little boat out of a log. The sailors helped him to rig and ballast it; into its hold they put two bottles containing letters. With a hot wire, they burnt the words 'Open this' onto its deck. This was actually the second of the celebrated St Kilda 'mailboats'; Sands had made and dispatched the first one back in December, to let his friends know he was alive, and the world that the factor had not supplied the island the previous autumn.[59] This one was picked up in Norway.[60] Mailboat no. 2 was retrieved at Poolewe, in Wester Ross, three weeks after dispatch. But it was actually another message in a bottle, attached to a lifebelt rigged with an improvised sail, which did the trick; only nine days later, it was in the hands of a Lloyd's agent at Stromness, in Orkney. In the meantime, the Austrians had become desperately impatient. Captain Chersonaz offered the St Kildans £10 for a passage out; characteristically, the islanders drew lots to decide on the crew. But while they waited for better weather, HMS *Jackal* arrived, in response to the mailboat message. On 22 February, Sands and the Austrian sailors were taken off.

On 13 February a worried laird had written to his factor. He feared that when Sands got back 'he will have plenty to say against us'. He asked why the autumn boat had not been sent, and suggested that a boat with food supplies should leave as soon as possible.[61] His fears were justified. The islanders felt that their problems would be solved if a steamer could be persuaded to call twice a year, and they had appointed Sands *fir ionad*, their representative in the outside world. On 27 February, the *Jackal* reached Greenock. Sands swung into action. On 1 March, he had a letter printed in the *Scotsman*, the first blow

FIGURE 69.
The souterrain, an underground store dating from the Iron Age. It probably belonged to a high status residence, demolished long ago.

in his vigorous campaign on behalf of the St Kildans. There was a public meeting in Edinburgh, and a committee was set up. Sands met with considerable opposition, although people from all over Britain wrote letters offering sympathy and support.[62] He now discovered the existence of the Kelsall Fund. He was shocked, because the St Kildans were also in the dark about it,[63] and had been told that various things paid for by the fund were supplied by the laird! The suspicion must be that MacRaild (who had been factor until 1873[64]) had been economical with the truth, and had told the islanders that the fund was exhausted. But in any case Fletcher Menzies, secretary of the Highland and Agricultural Society and administrator of the fund, told Sands that it was his policy not to tell the St Kildans about it 'lest they might have depended upon it and been spoiled'.[65] Menzies turned out to be an ally in the cause, though rather an ambivalent one. The fuss which Sands kicked up evidently caused the factor to make an unusually early trip to Hirta, in late March. Menzies eventually spent some of the Kelsall Fund, as well as £100 donated by a grateful Austro-Hungarian government to repay the St Kildans for their kindness; in May, HMS *Flirt* was dispatched, loaded with supplies for the islanders. It carried John MacDiarmid, an advisor on agriculture. He was only able to stay for 36 hours, most of which was taken up by the Sabbath. Some of the islanders were reluctant even to talk about farming on that day, and much of his published report must have been derived from documents in the files of the Highland and Agricultural Society.

The public debate had aroused considerable interest; from early May Martin Orme started to advertise the *Dunara Castle's* first excursion to St Kilda, departing Glasgow on Thursday 27 June.[66] The St Kilda run was an 'add-on' to a busy round trip, lasting a week, which took in the smaller ports of Skye and then An-t Ob (Leverburgh). When the steamer arrived at Hirta, on

Tuesday 2 July, the passengers encountered the laird's sister Emily, who had been there a fortnight, staying in the Feather Store;[67] doubtless her visit was in response to the public relations disaster earlier in the year. She got a return passage on the *Dunara Castle*.[68] The passengers were mostly well-off, influential people – clergy, lawyers, doctors, civil engineers, artists, and merchants.[69] They carried plenty of sporting guns (Major Colquhoun achieved the distinction of shooting a 'rarely seen' eiderduck), and, as usual, a demonstration of climbing and wild-fowling was laid on.[70] This was the start of regular tourist traffic, and some useful opportunities for the islanders to trade for cash. Passengers on the *Dunara Castle* bought stockings and knitwear, and had a whip-round to show their appreciation of the demonstration of climbing skills; eggs and stuffed birds were also available for sale, Seton obtaining a stuffed fulmar whose capture he had witnessed (taxidermy evidently being available 'while you wait').[71]

Soon Sands published a book, *Out of this World; Or, Life in St Kilda*, which went into a second edition the following year, 1878. *Out of this World* is an absorbing portrait of the island just before the onset of organised tourism. Sands was an intelligent observer, a Gaelic speaker of sorts, who had spent ten months at St Kilda. Partly on personality grounds, it seems, and partly because of his aggressive political agenda, he was not everyone's cup of tea. As the proofs of the second edition of his book were circulating, George Seton was writing *St Kilda*, which was designed partly as the antidote to *Out of this World*. This not very original book is essentially a scissors-and-paste affair, embellished with some rather laboured droll wit, but it does contain useful information about people and events in the nineteenth century. Seton compensated for the brevity of his visit by making use of current literature and being *au fait* with the sentiments of the chattering classes. Using ridicule, traditional right-wing rhetoric and sarcasm, he sought to discredit Sands, calling him 'the theoretical philanthropist' and mocking his claim to divine inspiration.[72]

The sympathies of John Sands

Sands had evidently grown very fond of the St Kildans. In fact he had fallen in love with a girl from the island, and tried to get back to Hirta in the early summer of 1877, with a view to marrying her.[73] He found the islanders' 'diligence and endurance' astonishing, noting how they stayed up half the night spinning and weaving, or plucking feathers. He was impressed by the massive loads of bird carcasses or peats which the women had to shoulder; some could carry about 200 lb (100 kg).[74] He noted the St Kildans' good manners and their courtesy to each other as well as to visitors. And he admired their generosity: 'in the evening, about twenty women in a party paid me a visit, each bringing a burden of turf in her plaid, which they piled up in a corner of the room, as a gift. After standing for a few minutes with pleasant smiles on their sunny faces, they departed with a kindly '*Feasgar math libh*' [good evening to you]. The women often came to see him, always in a group, and the men's group visited even more often.[75] After he sprained his ankle, his room was full of 'sympathetic male friends and ministering angels' bringing presents of salt mutton, potatoes, turf and fulmar oil. In their usual fashion, the St Kildans took turns to bring him supplies – fresh mutton in the autumn, salt mutton in winter, with potatoes and oatmeal; they would accept no payment.[76] When he left, the women gave him leaving presents – ewe's milk cheeses and pairs of stockings. To feed the Austrians, the St Kildans ground their precious seed corn into meal, and offered them enough meat at each meal as would feed three men; one islander took his carefully folded new jacket out of a box and gave it to the ship's mate.[77]

After ten months on Hirta, John Sands knew what he was talking about. He drew sharp comparisons between the generosity of the St Kildans and the way they were treated by the estate. Sands' central argument was that 'the trade of St Kilda is a two-edged monopoly. A large profit is exacted on the exports as well as the imports'.[78] The St Kildans were paid 3d a pound for feathers which fetched four times as much in Glasgow[79] and there were similar mark-ups for tweed, blanketing, ling, and cheese.[80] Lozenges (important to counterbalance the amount of salt in the St Kildan diet) cost over twice as much as they did elsewhere. At 6d a pound, the St Kildans could not afford to buy as much sugar as they wanted; soap at 6d a pound was also too expensive, and the tea was 'rubbish'.[81] Reading this, one of the *Scotsman*'s correspondents congratulated the paper on its continuing exposure of the infamous truck system.[82] Some of Scotland's lairds and factors had become notorious for taking back in rent much of what they had paid out for produce or as wages, and/or running 'company stores' charging monopoly prices. The St Kildans were in 'MacLeod's prison'.[83] Sands argued that if the estate's monopoly was ended, the islanders could probably afford to pay for a twice-yearly steamer service which would handle their imports and exports.[84] The estate's supply boat had not brought all the meal ordered, and the non-arrival of the autumn boat meant that young cattle were not taken off the island, so the people were forced to scrabble around on the cliffs to get grass for their fodder.[85] Several old men had declared that fresh seed corn had not been sent for 60 years (though this was not true).[86] Sands enjoyed sharing with readers of the *Scotsman* the contents of letters written by MacLeod to the St Kildans.[87] One threatened that if he came under too much pressure to change the existing setup he would let the island to someone else ('a middleman, I suppose – of whose tender mercies the St Kildans have had some experience' commented Sands). Another gave permission for the use of Sands' boat – but with impossible conditions.

Sands' campaign attracted criticism. Some people took a dislike to him, and cast aspersions on his character. Sands was a practising Christian; the only reading matter he took to Hirta was his Gaelic Bible. But he hated the austerity of the St Kilda Sabbath, and he felt that the islanders' contribution of £20 to the Free Church Sustentation Fund was an excessive drain on the economy (it wasn't). The minister, John MacKay, was a middle-aged bachelor, who at first invited Sands to stay at the manse; preferring 'freedom and the bagpipes', he declined. In the first edition of his book, published in the autumn of 1876, Sands gave MacKay a glowing reference: 'the Free Kirk has few soldiers she has more reason to feel proud of '.[88] But as the book went to press, Sands was on his second visit, during which he witnessed the minister's part in scuppering the success of his independent trading project. Unsurprisingly, the complimentary remarks were omitted from the second

The Minister

Natives of St Kilda

Donull Og.

FIGURE 70.
The sketches of John
Sands. Note the
unflattering portrait of
Rev. John MacKay.

155

edition of *Out of this World*, published in 1878. This edition contains a portrait of the minister, drawn without asking his permission.[89] The drawing (Figure 70) is a very sharp caricature. Discussing Free Church ministers, Sands wrote: 'the worst home ruler would be a well-meaning but feeble-minded, irresolute, yet domineering fanatic, whose servant would lead him by the nose ...'. Disingenuously, he adds 'this latter character is, of course, entirely suppositious'. On 13 April 1877, MacKay wrote to Fletcher Menzies telling him not to have anything to do with Sands.[90] A few days later he wrote again, saying that he did not want his opinion broadcast. MacKay was well aware that the St Kildans liked Sands and appreciated his efforts on their behalf. In a later letter to Menzies, he wrote: 'Mr Sands is quite right in giving a full and an accurate account of the state of the island'.[91] He added revealingly, speaking of his flock: 'ignorant people will do and say anything, for the sake of their bellies'. (One is tempted to comment 'as opposed to educated people?')

The defence put up by MacLeod and his factor, MacKenzie, was mostly a smoke-screen and an exercise in shooting the messenger. MacLeod enquired haughtily about the source of Sands' information about prices, although he did not actually contest the figures.[92] He claimed that the estate was simply trying to cover transport costs and allow for market fluctuations.[93] Writing from Cadogan Place in London, MacLeod repeated his predecessors' defence: the islanders were better off than 'any of their class anywhere', and the estate had matters in hand. He asserted that 'the care of the people should not be taken out of the hands of their proper proprietor unless there is some security that the change is not one of merely experimental sentimentality'. More revealingly, he added 'as it is the practice these days of the British public to take up the cause of oppressed communities, I suppose I must not permit myself to deprecate uncalled for interference between me and my tenants'.[94] MacLeod knew he was not going to win a public debate. Some of the later letters from Dunvegan were more emollient, especially when it became apparent that the relief mission of HMS *Flirt* was going ahead in any case. In April, there was a rather mean-spirited argument about the quantities of seed corn requested by the St Kildans. MacLeod, writing from the South Kensington Museum, wrote to Fletcher Menzies protesting about the wastefulness of the St Kildan habit of sowing their grain thickly;[95] Sands had already pointed out that this was intended for protection against high winds.[96]

Some of Sands' concerns were matters of public policy. He argued that people who paid taxes on tobacco and whisky were entitled to some kind of postal service, and noted that the benefits of the Education Act had not been extended to the island; he also wanted an inquiry into the causes of St Kilda's high infant mortality.[97] One of *The Scotsman*'s correspondents wanted to see the land 'pensioned, and given to the peasants on the communistic principle'.[98] There was also a proposal that the islanders should be paid to emigrate.[99] Lady Baillie, who paid a brief visit in 1874, noted in a letter to Menzies that the St Kildans were too inbred, and consequently weak-minded, unhealthy-looking, half-civilised, and greedy;[100] occupation of the island should be undertaken only in the summer, when feathers might be collected. Sands had in fact discussed evacuation with the islanders. The young and middle-aged were receptive to the idea, but would not abandon the older people, who were naturally reluctant to leave. His own view was that emigration would indeed be preferable to living 'under the thumb of their present arrogant and unsympathetic proprietor'.[101]

What was the truth about the St Kildan economy? The Dunvegan estate papers show that MacLeod's purchase had been quite a good investment decision. In 1877, the year of the controversy, the estate made a profit of £105, 42 per cent, on the goods which the factor 'purchased' from the St Kildans (although in the truck system the islanders were paid not in cash, but in credit against the value of goods supplied by the estate). In descending percentage order, profits were made from tweed (80 per cent) fish, feathers, cattle, tallow, cheese, wool, and blanketing (26 per cent).[102] Around the time of Sands' visit, the 'mark up' on goods sold *to* the islanders averaged 16.4 per cent, and the average profit made on goods obtained *from* them was 51.2 per cent. St Kilda was producing an average of £138 profit annually. Roughly speaking, rents and grazing fees paid by the islanders covered management expenses (boat hire, factor's fee, infrastructure maintenance, transport costs, auctioneer's commissions, and so on). MacLeod's profit from St Kilda (£1537 over the 1874–1884 period) was effectively created by the sale of its exports. Most years in the early 1880s the factor could count on making perhaps £70 on tweed, £20 on feathers, and maybe £10–20 on cattle and £10 on oil, with smaller amounts from fish, tallow, and cheese; usually one of these commodities would make a larger, 'windfall' profit. Thanks mostly to the St Kildans' willingness to improve the quantity and quality of their woven tweed and blanketing in the 1860s, and the assiduity of their feather-plucking, it looked as if MacLeod's £3000 investment would be repaid over 20–25 years, effectively during his lifetime (he died in 1895).

It would not have been sensible to let the islanders starve, and they were not literally starving. In that sense the robust estate view was justified, although perhaps not most tactfully expressed from an address in the leafier purlieus of west London. Broadly, and in relative terms, the islanders seemed to be doing quite well, as contemporary commentators noted. But there *were* serious dietary problems in late winter and spring. Probably the *Hirteach*, like young gannets and fulmars, were used to 'living off their fat'; Sands tells us that he lost about 30 lbs (13.6 kg) during the winter of 1876–77.[103] But a diet of rehydrated salted fulmar and thin gruel[104] was pretty indigestible without the balance of oatmeal porridge. Morale was not improved when supplies of tobacco ran out, and they had to smoke dried moss.[105] More seriously, living on reduced rations over the winter and early spring, consuming mutton derived from emaciated sheep, and so on, lowered people's resistance to disease. Sands was well aware of this; he heard one man say 'the young may see the spring, but the old will die'.[106] If the cereal or potato harvest failed, only the estate could make up the shortfall. And it is clear that the agricultural

*St Kilda and the
Wider World: Tales
of an Iconic Island*

side of the economy was going downhill in the later nineteenth century – mostly for reasons of soil exhaustion? Responding to the agricultural expert John MacDiarmid, who was careful to question *several* of them, the older men said they could remember crop returns twice or nearly three times those obtained in the late 1870s.[107] This made it all the more imperative that supply boats should run reliably and that the factor should be accurately informed about the quality of the harvest and the state of supplies in general.

Making sure that the islanders were fed was MacLeod's responsibility, as he acknowledged. Although the cost of hiring a boat (*c.* £15–20) was not itself prohibitive, the cost of a *free* emergency spring resupply would easily wipe out the annual profit (the bill paid by the Highland and Agricultural Society for supplies loaded onto the *Flirt* came to over £172; £123 6s (nearly 72 per cent) of this went on seed corn, potatoes, flour and oatmeal). If the factor charged the islanders for £120 worth of basic supplies, sent out on a special trip, a mark-up of 20 per cent would only just cover the cost of the boat. The factor had a strong incentive to mutter 'they'll manage'. But naturally this was unacceptable to outsiders like John Sands – who witnessed the situation at first hand – and grim for the islanders themselves. In springtime, then, the St Kildans must have been rather like the weavers of Shetland – another region notorious for the impact of the truck system – who were described in an official report as 'people on the verge of starvation yet magnificently dressed'.[108]

Much depended on the competence, honesty, understanding and flexibility of the factor. And 'honesty' becomes a problematic concept when it is recalled that the role of the 'factor' had developed from that of the 'tacksman'; it was the traditional practice for the factor or sub-chief to take his cut of the resources 'lifted' for the laird or chief, and it is not clear that it was always the latter who got the larger share. The man on the spot was very much the man in control, especially where distant islands were concerned. Norman MacRaild, the factor dismissed by MacLeod in 1873 after 31 years, claimed never to have gone beyond his instructions, and to be shocked to be told that he was disliked by the islanders.[109] In August 1877 he had to defend himself against an accusation that he had charged the islanders for meal which had been sent as a gift.[110] John MacKenzie, MacRaild's successor, seems to have displayed more understanding of the islanders' point of view.[111] But one may readily imagine how much the St Kildans welcomed the intervention of sympathetic outsiders, and eventually a broader public perception of their 'plight'; it might help them to bypass the factor's economic monopoly.

Sands' campaign on behalf of the islanders had been absolutely critical in securing regular steamer services packed with tourists – a market for their products which was not locked into the truck system, and thus gave the islanders more cash. The custom of sending 'mailboats' in cases of emergency, which he introduced, was to catch on. In September 1885, for instance, the 13-year-old Alexander Ferguson, later to build a remarkable career as a Glasgow businessman and St Kilda emissary in the outside world, wrote to his teacher in Harris: 'a great storm came on and all the corn and barley was swept away by the storm, and one of the boats was swept away by the sea; the men of St Kilda is nearly dead with the hunger. They send two boats from St Kilda to go to Harries, not the fishing boats, but little pieces of wood like the one I send'.[112] This mailboat was picked up on the beach at Aird Uig in Lewis, very close to the address to which it was sent; a separate message, sent by Rev. MacKay, arrived on Taransay four days later.[113]

An intelligent and talented man, Sands has not really received the credit he deserves for his intervention at St Kilda. He spent the rest of his life as a free-lance journalist and artist, writing humorous poems and contributing to *Punch*. He maintained his interest in archaeology and folklife, as well as his preference for small islands, living on Vaila, Papa Stour and Foula in Shetland, and on Tiree; he also spent some time on in the Faeroe Islands. On Foula he also fought passionately against the truck system, drawing biting political cartoons, one of which depicted Foula as a beautiful maiden, being throttled by a boa-constrictor labelled 'landlordism' and other reptiles labelled 'missionary', 'truck' and 'laird'.[114]

Demographic difficulties

When Sands mounted his campaign, the point of no return had already been passed, in demographic terms. As a result of studies carried out mostly in the 1980s we can now see that the emigration to Australia in 1852 was the critical event which made demographic failure inevitable in the absence of a 1730s style plan to recolonise the island.[115] The registers conscientiously compiled by Rev. Neil MacKenzie, together with the unofficial censuses taken by Dr John MacDonald in 1822 and Wilson in 1842, and national censuses from 1851 onwards, have provided useful information, from which 'population pyramids' have been constructed (Figure 71). Before the 1852 emigration, the pyramids are nicely balanced – even numbers of men and women, and not too many old folks. However, in 1861, 1871 and 1881 the three bands for people under the age of 44 contain appreciably more females than males. George Seton noted that in 1861 there had been eight unmarried men and nine unmarried women between the ages of 20 and 46;[116] ten years later, the figures for these categories were respectively three and fourteen. Sands counted two unmarried men and thirteen unmarried women.[117] No wonder he was popular with the girls.

Infantile tetanus, with its distressing symptoms and inevitably fatal outcome, carried off more boys than girls. This did not go unnoticed at the time. In an analysis of the causes of death which Neil MacKenzie had entered in his register during the 1830s and early 1840s, Seton pointed out that infantile tetanus had killed 23 male babies but only 9 female ones. For the later period of 1855–76, the corresponding figures were 13:2, or 26:15 if all infantile deaths within three weeks of birth were included. Over the two periods combined, 52 boys and 24 girls died in infancy. (Back in the mid eighteenth century, MacAulay had recorded an ill-balanced population, 38 males and 50

*St Kilda and the
Wider World: Tales
of an Iconic Island*

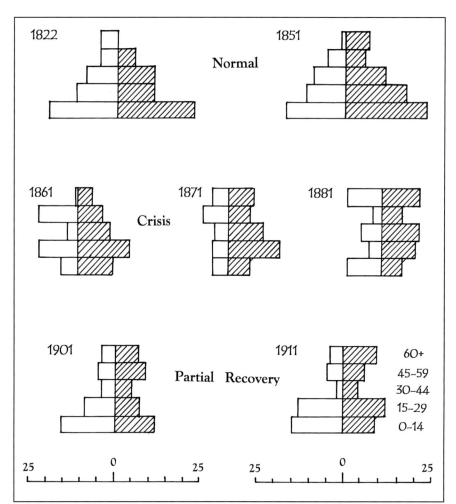

FIGURE 71.
Numbers of males and
females in different age
groups for selected
years in the nineteenth
and early twentieth
centuries (females on
the right, age groups as
bottom right)
(after Clegg).

females.[118]) The situation had worsened somewhat since the time of MacKenzie; the incidence of infantile tetanus had risen from about 50 per cent to 70 per cent during the 1860s.[119] Many visitors speculated about the causes of this ongoing medical problem, which was not confined to St Kilda (it occurred in parts of Lewis,[120] and its impact was bad on Faeroe and worse in some parts of Iceland[121]). The situation was deeply depressing, and some families were hit particularly hard. Records show that in the 1860s and early 1870s, Malcolm MacKinnon and his wife Marion, on Croft 13, lost all their nine children in infancy, apart from a son who lived until the age of 20. Over a period of 15 years, Angus and Ann Gillies at Croft 6 had 7 children; they too had one surviving son, who also died at 20.[122]

The effects of the unbalanced sex ratio were becoming increasingly apparent. When Sands was on Hirta, a job for the band of sturdy young unmarried women was to visit outlying islands, catching puffins and plucking them for the feathers. In the summer of 1875, one party was landed on Soay for a three week stay, and the next day another seven, forming a 'detachment of damsels', as Sands charmingly put it, went to Boreray (Figure 72) for the same purpose, taking a turn with the rowing; 'they stepped up the perilous ascent like goats'.[123] They took a smouldering turf for kindling a fire, as well as their bibles; Sands regaled them with laments on the pipes. They soon got to work, dogging puffins out of their burrows, thrusting their hands into holes and wringing necks, moving on to deploy their snares. The following year, a dozen unmarried women went to Boreray for a three-week stay.[124] Given the demographic imbalance, gender roles and gender relations must have been changing, and young women would have been conspicuous as a group. It had been noticed that women who went to Harris to have their babies were more successful in avoiding the eight-day sickness; they mostly seem to have stayed at An-t-Ob (Leverburgh) with Janet MacKinnon, a midwife who eventually trained in Glasgow, and her father Donald, a St Kildan emigré who had become a vet.[125] Probably this was the explanation for the slight fall-off in the incidence of infantile tetanus in the 1870s and 1880s[126] – and another reason why the St Kildans were so keen to get a boat capable of taking them to the Long Island.

Another consequence of the demographic situation was the St Kildans' treatment of children. One of the most evocative of Captain Thomas' photographs is entitled 'three bonnie bairns' (Figure 73). It is a picture of three small boys, snuggled up together, under instructions not to move a muscle until the long time exposure has been completed. But one can see from their faces that these boys are happy, at ease with themselves, and much loved. A couple of

FIGURE 72.
The isle of Boreray.
Note the cluster of
cleits, to the right, and
the three fowlers'
bothies, to the left.

decades later, Sands wrote: 'the few children on the island are idolised. I have frequently sat in a corner and observed a group around an infant, every head, old and young, craned towards it, every face beaming with smiles of delight'.[127] And then there is his description of a woman on the boat returning to Hirta, who had recently given birth on the Long Island, triumphantly holding her baby aloft, long before she could be seen from the shore (and see Figure 68, page 144).[128] Analysis of family records shows that in the year of Sands' first visit, only 8 households contained children; 2 had two children, 6 had only one.[129]

It was hard for young women to find partners on the island. The balance of power in the marriage market was succinctly expressed by the girls who said, on being questioned, 'the lads know best'.[130] The 1852 emigration had reduced the population from about 110 to somewhere between 70 and 80. Young people had to avoid marrying those too closely related to them, and were expected to adhere to a strict code of Christian sexual morality. Births 'out of wedlock' were generally very rare among the *Hirteach* in the nineteenth century, but significantly there were five in the period between 1862 and 1884.[131] Young women were in a desperate situation, and many took the obvious course of action. Clegg's analysis makes it clear: 'of females born between 1856 and 1885 over two thirds received no further mention – they did not marry, they did not die, so they must have emigrated'.[132]

In the year of the 1891 census, the demographic situation looked better – apparently. The male: female ratio had come back into balance, and the number of old people, which had reached a peak at the 1881 census, had declined. More importantly, in this year the minister, Angus Fiddes, who had taken over in 1889 after the 24-year incumbency of MacKay, went to Glasgow to seek detailed medical guidance on midwifery.[133] He took with him the recently-appointed Nurse Chisnhall (whose salary was paid from a fund which he had raised). Next year, four babies were born alive. Two died and two lived; the two survivors were the ones which Nurse Chisnhall had been permitted to attend. The inference was obvious. As soon as Nurse Chisnhall left Hirta, in June 1892, Fiddes hurried back to Glasgow. Failing to recruit a new nurse, he obtained detailed instructions on antiseptic treatment of the umbilical cord and good hygienic practice, went back to Hirta, and started delivering babies himself. In early August he was back in Glasgow, to let the obstetricians know that their advice had been entirely successful, and to thank them.

FIGURE 73. 'Three bonnie bairns' captured by Captain Thomas.

The St Kildans' worst enemy had been vanquished at last. Medical experts were not entirely sure of the cause of the tetanus; it was not until 1928 that Dr George Gibson suggested that Hirta midwives had probably been smearing the rag which dressed the stump of the umbilical cord with fulmar oil, kept in a gannet's stomach. Such a container, frequently refilled, never properly cleaned, would have been an ideal breeding-ground for the tetanus bacillus. 'I would like to have taken that vessel to a bacteriologist', remarked Gibson grimly.[134]

Modernity

While the demographic timebomb was ticking quietly away, the last 50 years of the community's existence saw many improvements in the islanders' quality of life. In summer, regular steamship visits gave Hirta a tourist trade and a market for products such as cloth, knitwear, and birds' eggs; the islanders could also earn money by posing for photographs and putting on displays of climbing, or grinding flour on hand-mills. In 1875 St Kilda produced 227 'yards' (277 m) of tweed and 403 'yards' (496 m) of blanketing (Figure 74). Four years later, 'the annual production was 800 to 1,000 yards, and this quantity was generally booked as sold before its arrival from St Kilda'.[135] The St Kildans had become less reliant on agriculture. By 1885 it was reported that 'the native grain crop is not now largely used as food on the island; a portion of the produce is reserved for seed, and the greater part of the remainder becomes fodder for the stock'.[136] The islanders preferred to concentrate on earning cash (from tourists), or credit (from the estate) for supplying tweed and other commodities, which they used to purchase imported food and other goods. By 1885 it was said that each family had on average £20 in cash savings, and a recent emigrant was said to have taken at least £100 off the island with him.[137] Later literature prefers to characterise the St Kildans as the commercially unadventurous victims of socialism and the Free Church, failing to acknowledge their achievements in the tourist trade, or the fact that, with a little outside assistance, they had effectively turned themselves into a community of weavers.

As usual, the operation of the free market did not automatically take care of necessary infrastructural investment – especially here. For the serious late Victorian Christian conscience, and for governments installed by a more inclusive electorate, social welfare had become a more serious issue. Others have documented the expansion of the St Kildans' educational opportunities, with the appointment of a teacher and the construction of a small schoolroom beside the church in 1898–9; an evocative photograph of the school in action survives (Figure 75).[138] (The foreman of the construction team being a freemason from Skye, the foundation stone was laid 'with full Masonic honours' including the deposition of an old newspaper in which peppermints had been wrapped.[139] Was this when St Kilda gave its name to the Lodge at Portree?) The children picked up English quickly;[140] it was useful in their deal-

FIGURE 74.
By the late nineteenth century, the St Kildans had become a community of weavers.

FIGURE 75.
St Kilda got a purpose-built school in 1899.

ings with tourists, and more or less essential if they eventually decided to emigrate. The appointment of a resident nurse was an important development; nursing cover was effectively continuous during the last 40 years of the community's life.[141] However, the problem of communication with the outside world outside the summer was never solved, except during the First World War.[142]

Living standards improved. The St Kildans were always more 'modern' in their tastes than we might imagine; before the arrival of regular tourist excursions, Hirta boasted such things as a wedding cake with icing on it – as the Duke of Atholl discovered when he stood in as best man – and a correctly adjusted sundial.[143] In 1877 there was a rain-gauge in the garden of the manse, and – perhaps replacing the sundial? – one clock and two watches on the island.[144] The Keartons 'came across things of appalling modernity: such as a woman wearing a Piccadilly fringe, a piece of barbed wire stretched round the minister's garden, and a youth sporting a dicky [a bow-tie]'.[145] Many new products of the industrial age brightened up the final decades of the community's existence. In the summer of 2003 I visited a small, shallow excavation carried out by Susan Bain, the island's archaeology warden, behind one of the houses. I found her carefully brushing the surface of a bright yellow piece of linoleum! Such familiar things often figure in the finds catalogues of St Kilda's archaeologists. The impact of the entrepreneurial vigour and burgeoning social aspirations of later nineteenth-century Britain was felt in the most remote corners of the realm. On Hirta there were marked changes in the decoration of rooms, in furnishings and ornaments, kitchen utensils, diet, and eventually dress styles, as early twentieth-century photographs show. From the 1880s onwards, technological improvements and discoveries of new fishing grounds brought many more trawlers into the north-east Atlantic.[146] The regular visits of fishing and whaling vessels (photographs show a dozen or more sheltering in Village Bay) brought trading opportunities and broadened the islanders' horizons. Apparently the trawlermen's gifts of coal 'and other luxuries' were not entirely disinterested; they were to some extent bribes to stop them being reported for fishing within the three-mile limit.[147] In the Edwardian era, Alice MacLauchlan, the minister's wife, took a liking to the whaler captains, who sometimes helped with the hay-making, and gave her Norwegian lessons; she liked to read about the exploits of the polar explorer Fridjof Nansen.[148]

FIGURE 76. Duirinish parish church, Dunvegan; the tomb of the 25th chief of the MacLeods, who bought back St Kilda in 1871, and faced the onslaught of John Sands not long afterwards. The family motto 'hold fast' has proved highly appropriate.

Tweed and the Edwardians

The last decades of St Kilda coincided with the final years of its lairds. Norman MacLeod, who had bought the islands from a 79-year-old, was 65 when he faced John

Sands' onslaught, and lived to the age of 83. The next laird, his son, inherited in 1895 and died in 1929 at the age of 90; the laird at the evacuation was his younger brother, aged 83. For these elderly men – whose memorials (Figure 76) embellish the east wall of the roofless church of Duirinish parish, at Kilmuir, not far from Dunvegan Castle – the progressive administration of St Kilda is not likely to have been a priority.

In the late 1880s and early 1890s, the average annual turnover of St Kilda had slumped by only 14 per cent, and management costs had been reduced by around £30 a year. Nevertheless the average annual profit slumped to about £66, a fall of 53 per cent, about 15 per cent of turnover. For instance, in 1886 the factor made a loss of £33 on cattle; in 1889 he lost £43 on oil; in 1892 he even lost £1 on tweed.[149] After a gap in the mid 1890s, the records unfortunately become less comprehensive. Mary Harman says that 'for much of the twentieth century the estate was probably providing a welfare service rather than the island paying its way'[150] but it's not clear to me that this was true in the years leading up to the First World War. It depends on what is meant by 'paying its way'. Are landowners an economic necessity? If they are, what level of profit counts as reasonable remuneration? I'm not aware of evidence that the estate was regularly making a loss on St Kilda during this period. The factor continued to operate the truck system, taking the islanders' produce and crediting them with a notional cash sum against the purchase of supplies. The St Kildans' earnings from the estate grew markedly over the first decade of the twentieth century, mostly because many families increased their production of tweed. The peak year was 1911, with a sharp subsequent decline, as Harman's graphs demonstrate.[151] A significant development occurred in 1892,[152] when 20-year-old Alexander (A.G.) Ferguson left Hirta, soon to set up in business at 93 Hope Street in Glasgow to sell tweed and other St Kildan products. In theory, handwoven St Kilda tweed sold at a premium, as an 'exotic' brand, although during the 1890s there was a (temporary) fall in quality which apparently made it 'almost unsaleable' by 1899.[153] Perhaps A. G. Ferguson, who also dealt in Harris tweed, had to cross-subsidise the output of some of his fellow islanders for a while. He came back regularly to Hirta in the summer, ('the proud possessor of the only gun on the island'[154]) and doubtless took the opportunity to explain about quality control. As his successful career shows, he knew what he was doing; indeed he wrote to John MacKenzie in 1903 offering to sell the factor's entire stock of cloth.[155] It is hard, therefore, to believe that the Dunvegan estate did not profit from its ownership of St Kilda during the tweedy Edwardian era. Moreover, right up to the war the factor was still taking feathers, tallow, cattle, fish, and oil from the tenants. Both the market price and MacKenzie's success in selling the goods must have fluctuated (and sometimes inadequately dried fish simply went off), but it seems that he did not seek to close down any of these potential income streams. In accepting these goods for sale, year after year, he is unlikely to have been motivated solely by blind optimism or a charitable disposition.

Harman's figures show rent arrears commencing in the mid 1880s, rising to roughly £400 in little more than a decade, and staying at that level until the war. The loss to the estate looks dramatic, especially when displayed as a histogram.[156] On average, each croft owed around 17 years' rent. However, things are not all they seem. As we have seen, the estate's general policy was to use the value of the products which paid the rents (and the grazing charges) to cover the estate's management costs; once this had been achieved, the islanders' surpluses were booked as credit for imported supplies (sold to them at a profit), and the goods themselves were sold outside (at a larger profit). On the basis of figures for 1900, my calculations show that for the more productive crofters (such as the MacKinnons at no. 1) the rent took up perhaps 5–7 per cent of what they had to sell to the estate. For less productive tenants, such as 70-year-old widow Betsy Gillies at no. 14, the figure was more like 18 per cent. The less productive tenants were usually the widowed, or old couples burdened by the travails of age. Making their rent a first charge against their produce ran the risk of impoverishing them further and antagonising their relatives in the community. It made financial sense for management costs to be covered by the rents paid by richer tenants; at the same time, every 'compassionate' decision to remit the rent of an impoverished household would free up *all* its earning power to be spent as credit at the (profit-making) 'company store'. The wish to channel as much as possible of the island's produce into profit-making concerns may have been the thinking behind the reduction of the rent for a croft from £2 to £1 10s. in 1900,[157] though probably the factor was also under pressure from the St Kildans themselves, who had evidently been told by 'agitators', in Heathcote's phrase,[158] that they might get their rents lowered by the Crofters' Commission.

In the literature, the laird is sometimes commended, by writers of a certain stamp, for his benevolence and enlightened stewardship of St Kilda. Behind the scenes (usually), he and his factor expressed some exasperation with the attitude of the St Kildans, and the exploitation of their high public visibility. We should probably take this with a pinch of salt (followed, perhaps, with its favourite St Kildan antidote, a peppermint). It is likely that the estate was not doing badly. As for the St Kildans, they had largely circumvented their agrarian problems by re-inventing themselves as a community of weavers. In the late Edwardian period, the output recorded by the estate was around 1800 m, over a mile of cloth, more than 100 m per household.[159] This takes no account of tweed sold through other outlets. The establishment of Alexander Ferguson's store must have made a decisive difference. Now the islanders could market their tweed (and other things) in Glasgow (population ¾ million), without going through Dunvegan; and Ferguson, one of their own, was also able to supply the island with imported goods. The great unknown is the volume of the trade – exports *and* imports – passing through 93 Hope Street. When St Kilda was re-provisioned by the Royal Navy, in the years leading up to the First World War, it was Alex Ferguson who normally assembled the supplies.[160] Just after the war – and, presumably, a good deal earlier – Ferguson was supplying groceries in return for dried fish;[161] so he too was operating a truck system, at least to some extent. Ferguson was not in business for philanthropic purposes. But unless he regularly colluded with Dunvegan (and as far as I know, there is no evidence for this) his trading must have been generally beneficial to his fellow-islanders, giving them more options, allowing them to take a more self-confident stance in dealings with a factor whose bargaining position had been weakened. When a St Kildan pleaded poverty, the factor had to tread carefully. Eviction would diminish the viability and productivity of the island community, and probably create a public relations disaster.

World War I and after

In July 1914 there was a crisis. There was bad weather on St Kilda, and a debilitating outbreak of influenza. The estate office could no longer 'see its way' to sending a supply boat. On 9 July, through A. G. Ferguson, the islanders sent a petition to the Highlands and Islands Agricultural Board, now administrators of the Kelsall Fund, asking for 50 pounds for 'some necessaries of life such as meal and flour'. In early August he got a letter saying that there could be no action until the next board meeting in November. Another letter from John MacKenzie the factor, was in traditional vein: the fund was not meant for cases like this, he wrote, since there was no 'acute distress' on Hirta. Furthermore, 'with the exception of Angus Gillies all the signatories are able-bodied men, who are quite able to go where they can get plenty of remunerative employment. When I see some of the signatories travelling 1st class on tourist steamers, and putting up at 1st class hotels on landing, it seems to me unnecessary to offer any opinion on the accuracy of the statements made in the petition'.[162]

When the war broke out, the bottom fell out of the tweed market; additionally, the islanders could no longer afford to buy in superior quality wool from the mainland. By May 1915 the crisis was upon them, and Alexander MacKinnon the minister wrote to the Board asking for £100 worth of provisions, and pointing out that the prices of flour and sugar were now double those of the previous year. The secretary to the Board noted: 'at one time [MacLeod] sent all supplies, but latterly said he could not afford it. Would not send unless they paid, and as they could not pay, two years ago he wanted them to leave the island. This they refused to do. Their income is from tweed. This year very little prospect of sale, as so many customers wearing khaki'.[163] MacKenzie the factor was uncompromising. In May 1915 he suggested that 'many of them are of military age, and might be encouraged to enlist either in the Army or in the Naval Reserve'. In April 1916 he advocated their employment 'at works of national importance in the South'. But in April 1917 MacKenzie was actively trying to secure funding from the Kelsall Fund for buying seed oats and potatoes. The estate had evidently taken a policy decision not to re-supply the island, or at least not at the level of previous years.[164] It was actually the installation of a naval wireless station during the war which guaranteed the islanders' food supplies (and provided an alibi for the inaction of Dunvegan). The establishment and maintenance of the station and the manning of lookout posts provided gainful employment for some of the St Kildans. But after the war, the future looked bleak. In 1919, MacLeod tried to sell St Kilda to Lord Leverhulme, who was in the process of purchasing Harris. Leverhulme was not tempted. The lairds then decided to work together to evacuate Hirta, a project terminated by Leverhulme's death in 1925.[165]

From Mary Harman's graphs it is easy to see the collapse of the system after the First World War – the precipitous fall in the value of goods supplied by the estate; the worsening of rent arrears, before the mini-evacuation of 1924 made the figures look slightly better; the discontinuation of most export commodities apart from tweed – which continued at a level much reduced from the glory days.[166] Persistent contact with representatives of the mainland and its culture tempted the St Kildans to feel that their salvation lay in emigration. The population had been stable since the late 1850s. But after the Great War, people started leaving. By 1925 numbers had plunged to 46.

A detailed study of other Hebridean islands has shown that when the population fell below 40 they were usually deserted.[167] On the eve of the evacuation, Crofts 3, 4, 6, 8 and 10 were already untenanted.[168] St Kilda was finally abandoned because several factors converged to make the future unviable. The government wanted to get rid of a recurring embarrassment, the Dunvegan estate wanted to unburden itself of a property which was no longer profitable, the bottom had dropped out of the market for the islands' exports, and the community itself had become too small to operate, biologically and logistically. To most observers, whether they were having their tea and scones in the Factor's House or at the Scottish Office, evacuation must have seemed the obvious course of action.

Even though they had fully participated in the decision, naturally the emotions of the islanders were more complicated. In the spring of 1937, Lord Dumfries gave an address to the City Business Club of Glasgow, in which, astonishingly, he mentioned 'the probable repopulation of St Kilda in the next few years' and indicated that he was negotiating with a government department about it.[169] One of the club members was the former St Kilda Tweed Factor, Alexander Ferguson. The 65-year-old 'declared that the islanders had been promised the Kingdom of Heaven by the Government then in office. Unfortunately, they found themselves in a fool's paradise, and today they would go back to the island if conditions were similar to those at the time they left'. If the occupation of Hirta had come to appear unviable in the years before the evacuation, life afterwards, on the Scottish mainland, was often disappointing.

CHAPTER NINE

Tales of the Expected

there is something inexpressibly melancholy in these simple
islanders ... being made the victims ... of the controversies which
amuse the leisure of the more cultivated and better provided populations of the mainland.

Sir Charles Trevelyan, in a letter to Norman MacLeod, 25th chief, 18 March 1872 (MM 639/1/6).

FIGURE 77.
'Will no one tell me
what she sings?' A
hundred years after
Wordsworth, young
women like Rachel
Ann Gillies were still
working in the fields.

The St Kilda literature is the basic source for the archipelago's history. But
these texts are important for another reason; they also demonstrate how closely
visitors and even long-term residents interpreted their encounter with these
islands in terms of their own views of the world. In this chapter I want to
show how perceptions of St Kilda were, inevitably, influenced by contemporary intellectual fashions. All visitors to the island had their own
preconceptions and cultural biases. Some were more responsive to their experience than others, who had already decided what they would find on the
islands. Naturally, commentators wanted to write texts which would resonate
with their contemporaries. Visitors and islanders had preconceived ideas about
each other, and were capable of influencing each other's behaviour and attitudes; there was no hard and fast division between observers and observed.
The islanders were very curious about the world beyond their shores; but for
visitors, *they* were the curiosities.

Survivors of the Golden Age

The most celebrated observer of all was Martin Martin. When he came here
in 1697, in his late thirties, he was in a good position to write both authori-
tatively and dispassionately about Hebridean people.[1] He came from the Isle
of Skye and spoke Gaelic; yet he also held a degree from the University of
Edinburgh, and had lived in London. Martin was well aware of the contemporary intellectual agenda, and corresponded with some of the leading scholars
of the day. By the end of the seventeenth century, empirical science had
demonstrated its superior potential not only for understanding the world but
also for changing it. Martin travelled widely in northern Scotland, collecting
information for the scientific community; from time to time the government
made contributions towards his research expenses. As a progressive, scientific
thinker, he suggested various ways of improving the economy of the Hebrides

*St Kilda and the
Wider World: Tales
of an Iconic Island*

– adopting more advanced agricultural methods, metal prospecting, developing a fishing industry, harvesting kelp, and exporting black cattle.[2] But Martin also felt that the knowledge of the Hebrideans themselves should be more widely disseminated. He discussed 'second sight', and argued the scientific case for taking it seriously.[3] He was receptive to the potential of folk medicine, and pointed out that 'a man of observation proves often a physician to himself'.[4] Martin recorded some of the medical remedies employed by the St Kildans. He noted that the islanders' understanding of the infectious nature of the 'boat cold' – the epidemic of coughs and sneezes which followed the arrival of a boatload of visitors, and especially the early season boat of the steward – was based on intelligent observation and inference.[5]

Martin's sympathetic and mostly unromanticised descriptions of the people of Hirta often ring true. But he also wanted to fit his account into a widely-accepted intellectual framework. If one skips the blurb on his title page, the contrast between the text and the author's message, when it eventually arrives, is striking. His conclusion about the St Kildans was this: 'what the condition of the people in the Golden Age is feigned by the poets to be, that theirs really is, I mean, in innocency and simplicity, purity, mutual love and cordial friendship, free from solicitous cares, and anxious covetousness; from envy, deceit and dissimulation; from ambition and pride … they are altogether ignorant of the vices of foreigners, and governed by the dictates of reason and Christianity … their way of living makes them contemn gold and silver, as below the dignity of human nature … they … have no designs upon one another, but such as are purely suggested by justice and benevolence'. Since some of this was quoted on the title page, this glimpse of the Golden Age was obviously intended to be the *Voyage*'s main selling point. Martin was reaching conclusions which his readers were expecting, not to mention mentors such as the influential Geographer Royal, Sir Robert Sibbald.

The concept of the 'Golden Age' was popular in the seventeenth century. In Shakespeare's *Tempest*, written 85 years before Martin's visit, Gonzalo says that if he could populate and rule over the island, he would 'by contraries execute all things'. There would be 'no name of magistrate', no riches or poverty, no agriculture or metal-working, and 'no occupation; all men idle, all; and women too, – but innocent and pure … nature should bring forth … all abundance, to feed my innocent people'. This passage was quoted in relation to St Kilda as recently as 1878.[6] Not long before Shakespeare's time, scholars had rediscovered the literature of classical Greece and Rome, and encountered the 'Fall of Man' view of world history put forward by authors like Hesiod and Ovid, who had posited a gradual descent from a Golden Age through an Age of Silver and an Age of Bronze to the grim realities of their own times – the Age of Iron. This was an interesting variant of the Biblical account of the Fall of Man.[7] In Shakespeare's lifetime, European seamen frequently encountered hitherto 'unknown' peoples in Africa and the New World. How could such people be fitted into existing models of world history, which were based upon the Bible and the classical authors of Greece and

Rome? Sixteenth- and seventeenth-century commentators came to believe that peoples of the New World should be regarded as surviving representatives of the Golden Age. Peter Martyr, discussing the 'Indians' encountered by Columbus, said that 'if they had received our religion I woulde thinke their life most happie of all menne'. So once Martin had chosen to describe Hirta as 'one of the remotest corners of the world' his general approach was predictable. But as we have seen, his text, with its references to sexual jealousy and cunning,[8] does not entirely support the Golden Age model.

In 1758 the Rev. Kenneth MacAulay was sent to St Kilda – in other words, as a missionary to the most remote part of his own parish of Harris. In 1764 he published his *History of St Kilda*. If one discounts Alexander Buchan's not very original early eighteenth-century account, this is the first written description of St Kilda by a resident minister. MacAulay was a shrewd commentator, who took an ethnographic view of the people he called 'these our domestic Indians'.[9] He was well aware of the political and economic pressures which constrained and affected the St Kildans' behaviour: 'the people have their own mysteries of state. In proportion to the number of sheep he possesses, every man must pay a certain heavy tax to the steward; and very few, if any, are scrupulous enough not to practice frauds if they can'. 'Dissimulation, or a low form of cunning, and a trick of lying, are their predominant faults', wrote MacAulay, but he also pointed out that the St Kildans were forced to sell their produce to the steward, the laird's representative, 'whose power is absolute ... while despotism reigns over that little community, industry will be effectually discouraged, and poverty must be the natural consequence of both'. Another thing which exposed the people to the potentially despotic rule of the steward, noted MacAulay, was the fact that they had no access to courts of justice. He was well aware that, given his own dependence on the steward's goodwill, it was 'convenient to look on with a prudent taciturnity', if he intended to remain there for some time, and he diplomatically pointed out that the present steward and his father had relieved the St Kildans from 'many grievous taxes' and 'reformed some old abuses.' Nevertheless MacAulay's sympathies, and his perceptive appraisal of relations of power on Hirta, are quite clear.[10]

The philosophical rhetoric in *History of St Kilda* is reminiscent of Martin's. Apparently the people of Hirta knew nothing of 'the mad quarrels and extravagant frolics of drunkenness, the shameful use of places dedicated to the service of lewdness and folly' and so on. The islanders' lifeways were truly admirable: 'silver and gold, stately houses and costly furniture, together with the fantastic luxury of dress, and the table, they neither have nor desire. To rise in fleets and armies amidst infinite toils and dangers: to earn posts or pensions, after having wriggled themselves into the favour of the great, at the expense of honour and conscience; to create overgrown estates, after having practised all the vile arts of avarice, frauds, extortion and servility, are passions and wishes, which Providence has kindly concealed from them. The humble blessings of bread and wild fowl, of peaceful cottages and little flocks, of angling rods and hunting ropes, are all the riches, honours and profits they aspire after'.[11] The islanders, then, had a winning combination of Christian faith and barbarian simplicity; they were also 'most luckily illiterate enough' to be blissfully free of more subversive casts of mind. Like Martin's St Kildans, they possessed 'as great a share of true substantial happiness, as any equal number of men elsewhere'.[12]

The *History of St Kilda* is a hybrid book.[13] Before it was published, numerous scholarly (and tedious) additions were made to it by Dr John MacPherson of Sleat in Skye (whose book on the origins of the 'Ancient Caledonians'[14] was later to demonstrate the limitations of writing prehistory without understanding the potential contribution of archaeology). It was probably MacPherson who was responsible for claiming that 'the character given to the old Germans, is undoubtedly applicable to this people' (i.e. the St Kildans).[15] This was a reference to the viewpoint of the Roman historian Tacitus. Writing in the first century AD, he had highlighted the decadence of the contemporary Roman aristocracy by praising the barbarian virtues of the Germans. Thus Tacitus eventually made a significant contribution to the ideas which fuelled German nationalism in the nineteenth century and later.[16] So the St Kildans displayed heroic barbarian virtues as well as Golden Age innocence. This sits oddly beside MacAulay's analysis of the economic and political situation of the islanders. If the St Kildans' scope for economic action was constrained by the depredations of the tacksman, and their intellectual freedom was under intermittent pressure from a succession of ministers anxious to indoctrinate them with the correct version of Christian belief and practice, how could he write of them as free agents, who had made admirable moral choices?

Ideologies of Improvement

When Samuel Johnson and James Boswell made their tour of Scotland in 1773, they knew a good deal about St Kilda, because they had been sent a copy of Kenneth MacAulay's book (a good deal of which, they realised, had been ghost-written by someone more scholarly than MacAulay). MacAulay himself was their main adviser on the logistics of the trip, and they called on him at his manse at Cawdor (they had liked the idea of passing through Macbeth country). In the course of their journey, Johnson and Boswell became aware of the growing momentum of economic and social change in Scotland. They stayed at Dunvegan for several days. One morning, after breakfast, MacLeod said: 'A Highland chief should now endeavour to do every thing to raise his rents, by means of the industry of his people. Formerly, it was right for him to have his house full of idle fellows: they were his defenders, his servants, his dependants, his friends ... The system of things is now so much altered, that the family cannot have influence but by riches, because it has no longer the power of ancient feudal times'.[17] Lairds and factors tried hard to make their estates more profitable. They raised rents; they created sheep farms on the better land and moved their tenants onto unviable crofts on the worst soils.

They developed the kelp and fishing industries, making people work long hours in dreadful conditions, to the detriment of their own farming, and for wages most of which were paid back in rent. When they wanted people's labour they prevented them from emigrating; when they wanted their land they evicted them and forced them, sometimes literally, onto ships bound for north America. The story is well known by now.[18] As Pennant commented: 'these gentlemen are for emptying the bag, without filling it'.[19]

The lairds were able to take advantage of the numerous outcomes of the growing scientific curiosity which we have already glimpsed in the writing of Martin. Agriculture became more productive, and the industrial revolution took advantage of the burgeoning commercial expansion of the incipient British Empire. The involvement of the highlands and islands of Scotland in these developments was rather peripheral – but the role they played was in fact very interesting. It is fascinating to notice how the wealthy and powerful during this period were active in several fields of endeavour. Agricultural Improvers also invested in industry, got involved in politics, and were often keen amateur artists with decided views on the aesthetics of landscape. And some of them started to take a distinctly less compassionate, less 'Golden Age' view of people whom they wanted to evict from their land and homes. Conveniently, this perspective could be supported by the authority of scripture. The Bible made it clear that, ever since the Fall, humans have had to accept their own corrupt nature. But 'savages', who were outside the central narrative of Judaeo-Christian history, came to be seen as more degenerate than representatives of mainstream humanity. They came to be regarded as unimprovable, and thus having less right to their portion of God's earth than someone intent on making it more productive.[20] This view provided an excellent pretext for taking over land occupied by native Americans. But identical arguments were deployed in Britain, and for much the same purpose – in order to justify evictions and the enclosure of common lands. It was not at all unusual for the proposed victims – already condemned for fecklessness and inefficient farming – to be compared directly with well-known savage tribes. Thus the commons at Hounslow and Finchley were described as looking 'as if they belonged to Cherokees'.[21]

Thus it is not very surprising to read the comments of young Henry Brougham, who came to St Kilda as a tourist in 1799: 'nothing in Captain Cook's voyages comes half so low. The natives are savage in due proportion ...' Brougham was scathing (and surely incorrect) about St Kildan artefacts; they were 'infinitely coarser and more clumsy, and made in smaller quantity and less variety, than those which navigators have found in any of the Pacific islands, New Holland [Australia] in the south excepted'. Predictably enough, the character of their makers was deeply flawed: 'a total want of curiosity, a stupid gaze of wonder, an excessive eagerness for spirits and tobacco, a laziness only to be conquered by the hope of the above-mentioned cordials, and a beastly degree of filth, the natural consequence of this, render the St Kildian truly savage'.[22] Brougham also complained that 'the natives' were light-fingered; he had to draw and brandish his sword in order to get his boat-cloak back. At one point he excels himself in the role of white man: 'while tea was preparing, I marshalled them thus: servants at my elbow, for aides-de-camp; provender in the rear; male natives in front; female ditto at some distance from our gentlemen – a most necessary precaution to prevent jealousy. To each native I distributed a ration of tobacco and a dram ...'. But he was not too high-minded to find out how much the island was worth; according to him, the tacksman paid £20 to the laird and kept more than twice that amount for himself, a system which Brougham felt was iniquitous and should be abolished.

From the Sublime to the Romantic

Some tourists came for a profound engagement with landscape. In 1757, Edmund Burke, a young Irishman who later had a notable career in British politics, had put forward a systematic analysis of the difference between the Sublime and the Beautiful.[23] Beauty was about pleasure, the Sublime was concerned with that stimulating blend of shock, fear and counter-intuitive delight which children nowadays describe by using the word *scary*. According to Burke, 'whatever ... operates in a manner analogous to terror, is a source of the sublime; that is, it is productive of the strongest emotion which the mind is capable of feeling'. The key words were terror, astonishment, horror, danger, and sudden shock or surprise. Sublime emotions were evoked by a sense of magnificence, vastness, infinity, and darkness – the roar of waterfalls in spate, the raging of storms. Men of cultivated sensibility started to design artificial experiences of the Sublime into their landscaped parks. And they sought sublime scenery in the wild; they wanted to sketch and paint it. One of the most important Sublime tourist destinations in the Hebrides was Fingal's Cave, off the coast of Mull on the small island of Staffa, which had been 'discovered' in 1772 by Joseph (later Sir Joseph) Banks; Mendelssohn came here in 1829, and the painter J. M. W. Turner two years later. Tourists almost always travelled by sea; after 1801 they were able to use the Crinan Canal as a short cut across the neck of the Mull of Kintyre. Edmund Burke contended that 'the ocean is an object of no small terror';[24] so the ultimate Sublime destination, the Mecca of the Ossianic tour, was St Kilda.[25] Visitors not primarily concerned with aesthetic experience were nevertheless drawn into the quest for the Sublime. In the 1820s the Apostle of the North, John MacDonald, described a St Kilda storm as 'a sight awfully grand and sublime'.[26]

By contrast, the geologist John MacCulloch, who came to St Kilda in 1815, was hoping to find the Picturesque. This was an approach to the aesthetics of landscape first popularised by William Gilpin in the 1780s and put forward more systematically in his *Three Essays on Picturesque Beauty* (1792). Appreciating the Picturesque was about understanding precisely which qualities of scenery and artistic composition created the aesthetic satisfaction which

people derived from viewing the landscapes depicted by certain French and
Italian artists (usually in the background of their paintings). However,
MacCulloch was unable to identify the Picturesque at St Kilda. For him, the
strait separating Hirta from Soay (Figure 78) presented, when viewed from
above, 'a scene of singular sublimity, particularly in stormy weather'. But
problems with scale and perspective prevented local seascapes being classified
as picturesque. MacCulloch decided that the sea seen from above, from too
great a distance, and 'dark cliffs beaten by the unceasing surge and lost in the
gloom of the clouds that hang on them' were definitely not 'in the strict sense
of the term picturesque. They are of a higher order, and beyond the narrow
limits of art. Its powers cannot reach these sources of the sublime in landscape'.[27]

When Henry Brougham came here, in early August 1799, his party included
Robert Campbell, who from his infancy had heard of St Kilda as 'a point of
natural grandeur and sublimity nowhere to be surpassed'.[28] But the facetious
Brougham, displaying the too-clever-by-halfness which was later to result in
his fall from high political office, chose to mock the quest for the Sublime.
His party took a trip to Boreray in the islanders' own boat, heavily laden with
10 visitors and 20 St Kildans. On the return voyage, some four and a half
hours after they had set out from Hirta, Brougham woke from a nap to find
himself confronted by precipitous cliffs, with the sea crashing around in 'large,
dark, rough caves', flashes of phosphorescence at every stroke of the oars, and
the keel of the overloaded boat scraping the skerries 'with a heavy and petri-
fying noise' (they were evidently just below the Gap – see Figure 79). At this
point in his account, Brougham turned to satire, improvising a dialogue
between the panic-stricken doctor and himself in the role of enthusiast for the

FIGURE 78.
The Sound of Soay.
Stac Biorach and Soay
Stac, irreverently
known as The Owl and
the Pussycat nowadays,
lie between Soay (left)
and The Cambir
(right).

Sublime. The doctor cries out 'we touch the bottom!' and 'oh dear! I'm sure our boat can't weather it'; the cool tourist counters with 'is not this light delightfully horrible?' and 'by the by, don't Mr Burke reckon terror the basis of the sublime?'

In the landscapes of the Sublime and the Picturesque, humans barely featured. However, the educated classes were soon to take more interest in the people of the Highlands and Islands – mostly because they came to represent a romanticised version of Scottish history. After the Battle of Culloden in 1746 the British government took systematic measures to ensure that Highlanders and Hebrideans would never again pose a military threat (within Britain, that is; Highland regiments would prove excellent soldiers and cannon fodder for wars overseas). But their rehabilitation was at hand, in the form of fantasy history. It all started in 1762, with the publication of *Fingal, an Ancient Epic Poem. Fingal* purported to have been composed in the mists of antiquity by a bard called Ossian, and to have been perpetuated, in fragments, by oral traditions kept alive by Gaelic speakers in the north-west of Scotland. It was retrieved, translated and published by a young man named James MacPherson. In fact, *Fingal* was a fake. MacPherson had struck up an unholy alliance with a namesake, Rev John MacPherson of Sleat in Skye, whom we have met already as the undisclosed co-author of Kenneth MacAulay's book on St Kilda. The material for the Ossian poems was of Irish origin and harked back to the time, around AD 500, when the Irish *Scoti* settled in the west of Scotland. Between them, the MacPhersons fabricated both oral tradition and history, claiming that the re-worked Irish ballads had originated in 'Celtic' Scotland in later prehistory.[29] Almost from the outset, scholars were dubious about Ossian's authenticity; Samuel Johnson, for one, was not taken in.[30] But the poems of Ossian stimulated among contemporary readers the same sort of enthusiasm as J. R. R. Tolkien's *The Lord of the Rings* two centuries later. Ossian was taken very seriously by Dr John MacDonald, the Apostle of the North;[31] in his youth he toured the north-west Highlands, in order to satisfy himself that Ossian was genuinely an ancient poet. These poems brought considerable fame and fortune to James MacPherson, who willed – successfully – that his final resting-place should be Poets' Corner in Westminster Abbey. Ironically, the lays of Ossian were received by many as a powerful validation of the historical and cultural authenticity of the people of the Highlands and Islands. The ripples of the splash made by the Ossian effect travelled ever outwards. In 1778 James MacPherson and John MacPherson's son founded the Highland Society in London, and campaigned successfully for the repeal of the ban on Highland dress. Then came the romantic novels of Sir Walter Scott and, in 1822, a celebrated pageant in Edinburgh organised and choreographed by Sir Walter Scott, and featuring King George IV togged out in the very 'Highland dress' which had until recently been illegal (and which, incidentally, had been created in the 1730s by an Englishman[32]). Dunvegan Castle was involved in this definitive move to reinvent and romanticise the Highland past. Scott, who visited Dunvegan in 1815, wrote to the chief asking him to participate in the Edinburgh festivities, and to look the part by bringing a few clansmen with him.[33] Scott saw a castle which had just been fashionably restyled (on the back of the profits from kelping), and now featured what an estate agent might call a wealth of battlements (Figure 37, page 68) – though the 13 'pepper-pots', the little ornamental turrets costing £100 apiece, were added later, in the 1840s.[34] By this time, 'Highland dress' had caught the Romantic imagination. When John MacDonald first came to St Kilda he was 'somewhat surprised at not finding the kilt and hose among them'.[35] When James Wilson published his account of St Kilda in 1842, he had to add a footnote protesting about one of the illustrations: 'our artist, of his own fancy, has introduced kilted figures to enliven the general aspect of the scene. There are, however, no kilts in St Kilda'.[36]

The epitome of the romanticisation of north-west Scotland was surely Wordsworth's solitary reaper (see Figure 77), whom he encountered in 1803:

> A voice so thrilling ne'er was heard
> In spring-time from the Cuckoo-bird
> Breaking the silence of the seas
> Among the farthest Hebrides.
> Will no one tell me what she sings?
> Perhaps the plaintive numbers flow
> For old, unhappy, far-off things
> And battles long ago.[37]

The young woman noticed by Wordsworth had been forced to seek paid work many miles from her Hebridean homeland; her presence probably reflected the impact of Improvement and the related economic and social changes of the day. In his excellent book, *Improvement and Romance: Constructing the Myth of the Highlands*, Peter Womack has argued that 'officially, Romance and Improvement were opposites ... but in reality they were twins'.[38] The relationship was complex and long-lasting; to some extent it is still with us today. To appreciate the scenery of the Highlands and Islands – especially the human deserts created by the Clearances – was to dramatise and rehabilitate a wilderness which, in other areas, had been conquered by the Improvers: 'on the reverse side of Improvement is written the scenic theme of the sublime'.[39] A mindset developed which overlooked the suffering and humiliation of local communities and portrayed them as Indians preserved in unimproved reservations – authentic survivals from the remote past. In exchange for economic and political weakness, the people of the Highlands and Islanders are allowed to be poetical, to represent organic communities, idealism rather than materialism, heart over head, and so on; they represent the Other (compare the stereotyping of the Irish *vis à vis* the English in the recent film *Titanic*). As Womack notes, the more poignantly gratifying the Highland image's evocation of human nobility becomes, 'the more ruinously it pays for its moral splendour by its separation from practical life'.[40] Eventually, the role of the Highlands and Islands was to provide a *holiday* for

FIGURE 79.
A cave below the Gap,
probably the setting for
Henry Brougham's
satirical account of the
quest for the Sublime.

the Victorian plutocrat, a 'temporary refuge from his rational and profitable mode of life in a sort of anthropological quixotism ... hundreds of miles away from the scenes of work'.[41] The logical culmination of this process saw people dressed as Highlanders manning a stage-set *clachan* at the Glasgow Empire Exhibition of 1938.

So Ossianic mythology and love of the Sublime were not simply the cultural pretensions of artists and intellectuals living in a dreamworld. On the contrary, such worldviews were attractive to men of action, who were running estates, investing in industry, involved in national politics – active supporters and practitioners of science, people who believed in progress and improvement and had self-interested reasons for doing so. Thus Sir Thomas Dyke Acland, one of the St Kilda tourists, was undoubtedly a Romantic, but he also donated money to improve housing conditions on the island. As a politician, he lent his support to various Factory Acts which sought to ameliorate the appalling working conditions in contemporary industry.[42]

Tourists: experience and perception

The tourists who came to St Kilda, then, had various expectations, some potentially self-contradictory. Would they encounter people whose laziness and inefficiency clearly gave them no moral right to continue their un-Improved existence? Or would they discover the wild, romantic Gael? Would they focus on the people as interesting anthropological specimens, or would they find themselves discussing how the island economy ought to be improved? Was St Kilda more interesting to the scientist or to the romantic? The literature reflects such contemporary preoccupations.

In the late eighteenth and early nineteenth centuries, the archipelago certainly inspired those amateur artists who managed to get there, and those who fancied themselves as poets; snatches of verse featuring St Kilda are scattered through the literature. Sir Thomas Dyke Acland, who came here from Devon on a hired yacht in July 1812,[43] qualified under both headings. He had recently taken over family estates in Devon and Somerset, and was soon to begin his political career as one of the two Devon county MPs. A happily married man in his mid-twenties, accompanied by his pregnant wife Lydia and their three-year-old son, he could hardly have foreseen his future as an archetypal Victorian patriarch, rich in years and achievement, surrounded by children and grandchildren, and immortalised as 'the Killerton Oak' in a song composed by the local postmaster (Killerton House, just outside Exeter, was the main family seat). Acland was a keen artist; his sketch-books, featuring pictures of moderate quality done in various combinations of ink, ink wash, charcoal and chalk, are preserved in the Devon County Record Office. Most of his St Kilda drawings are seascapes, featuring towering cliffs and rocks, expressions of the Sublime; people lurk in the background, or take the form of sketchy figures in distant boats. Although he knew the story of Lady Grange, Acland liked the idea that Lydia was the first 'lady' to visit St Kilda (perhaps Scottish ladies did not count), and he wrote a poem about it.[44] It is not great literature (Acland would have been well advised to resist the temptation to find a rhyme for 'St Kilda'). The St Kildans figure in the background; we do not hear much about them except that they are 'unlike the sons of men' and described – with a touch of the Sublime – as 'nurslings of danger'. The Sublimity of the scenery was what was important:

> Few were the pilgrims who tell of its wonders
> Distant and wild the tale that they bear
> Seamen scared by the distant thunders
> Shunn'd the dark rock where the wild waves roar.

A poem published anonymously in 1799, which tries to recreate the feelings of the unfortunate Lady Grange, expresses the complicated thoughtworld of the more sophisticated St Kilda tourist.[45] The poet enrols the people of Hirta as representatives of the Golden Age *and*, because of the dangers of cliff-climbing, as powerful signifiers of the Sublime:

> Far from the crimes and follies that I trace
> Kind Nature holds me midst her favourite race
> Escap'd the fevered world by happy stealth,
> A skiff their navy, and a rock their wealth …

> Nor haughty wealth, with proud contemptuous sneer,
> Nor poverty, the child of wealth, is here
> When now the morning trembles o'er the main,
> Brown Labour calls them to the rocky plain,
> With patient toil each tills his little plot

And Freedom pours contentment on their lot,
O'er the steep rock, with straggling ivy drest,
Clambering, they seek the cormorant's downy nest ...
O'er the high cliff their dangerous trade they urge
Below, tremendous roars the boiling surge:
As pendent from the straining cord they play
I mark their slow descending form decay ...
While far at sea their solitary skiff
The faithful matrons climb the shelving cliff;
With tears of love and anguish heaven implore
To guide the labouring bark to Kilda's shore ...

To a modern reader, the recruitment to these verses of work with serious health and safety implications is shocking, though the imagery of an aristocratic female trapped amongst savages, and of 'simple maids' and 'faithful matrons' exposing themselves to danger on the cliffs adds a psycho-sexual frisson which is entirely in keeping with the Sublime's headiest brews.

One visitor who illustrates the diversity of tourists' attitudes was the geologist John MacCulloch, who visited St Kilda in 1815. He wrote in some detail about geology and mineralogy. As befitted the author of one of the earliest geological maps of Scotland, he accurately identified the contact zone between granophyre and dolerite, a line 'leaving the town and the hill of Conachan on one side, and nearly intersecting the middle of the bay (Figure 23, page 41). The syenite [granophyre] is on the east side of this line and the trap [dolerite] on the west'.[46] However, MacCulloch also appreciated his encounter with the Sublime. At one point he seems to be regressing towards the concept of the Golden Age: 'if [the St Kildan] thinks not his island an Utopia, the pursuit of happiness is indeed a dream'.[47] But MacCulloch also found time for a hard-headed look at the Hirta economy. He argued that the island rent of £40 was low by average standards, and that the remoteness of markets for their produce gave the islanders little disposable wealth to be creamed off in rent rises (but he also notes that 'they make a voyage once or twice in the year to the Long Island, to dispose of that part of their wool, feathers and cheese, which is not required for the payment of rent'). He was also struck by the fact that the St Kildans were apparently prosperous enough to be able to ignore pressure to set up a deep sea fishing industry. Describing them as 'pampered', MacCulloch observes that 'the men are well looking, and better dressed than many of their neighbours of the Long Island; bearing indeed the obvious marks of ease of circumstances both in their apparel and diet'.[48]

Not all visitors romanticised the St Kildans; on a visit to a small island they had no choice but to observe the islanders at close quarters. Reactions of disgust and dismay were quite common. Words like 'wretched', 'miserable', 'poverty' and 'hovel' are commonplace in visitors' descriptions. Commentators did not like the strong smell given off by the people, or their smoky, pokey houses, their internal size seriously reduced by the steaming piles of animal dung which accumulated during the winter. Outsiders felt that some aspects of the St Kildan diet were very much an acquired taste, and that some of the seabirds' eggs on the menu had definitely passed their 'best before' dates; sometimes they had been stored for six or eight months.[49]

It is important, however, not to conclude from these accounts that life on St Kilda was significantly worse than elsewhere in the region. When tourists wrote about other parts of the Highlands and Islands their reactions were similar. Pennant, for instance, described the houses of people in the Cairngorm area as 'shocking to humanity'; in Lochaber they were 'the most wretched that can be imagined'; in Inveraray people lived in 'most wretched hovels'.[50] And the Highlanders were 'indolent to a high degree'.[51]

With the hindsight of history, MacCulloch's remarks about the islanders' alleged laziness and his interest in the economy of Hirta look like the harbingers of a drive for Improvement which came to fruition in Neil MacKenzie's 14-year ministry (1829–43). But Improvement did not stem the flow of adverse comment about the islanders' idleness and ease of circumstances; for instance the naturalist John MacGillivray, who visited Hirta in 1840, said that they were 'well characterised by their extreme laziness'.[52] I think these allegations are partly true, in that the St Kildans' lifeways really *were*, in general, somewhat less onerous than those of other Hebrideans. But they are also predictable expressions of both the Protestant work ethic and the self-interested perspective of the laird. In MacKenzie's day, lairds often paid ministers' salaries; the continuous local presence of an advocate of the Protestant work ethic was clearly to a laird's advantage. One would *expect* to find MacKenzie saying something like: 'the proprietor is very kind to [the islanders], and the small rent they pay barely pays expenses'.[53] The idea that the islanders were incorrigibly lazy was very convenient. It put them on the defensive before the Presbyterian God, and established that they were responsible for their own poverty; the best efforts of a benevolent laird were of no avail, and he was absolved of any blame for their situation.

Paradise lost

It was not until the summer of 1877 that a regular summer steamship service commenced, the *Dunara Castle* and the *Hebridean* each calling twice, as a rule, and later three times, resulting in a roughly fortnightly service during the three months of summer.[54] Some visitors felt that the St Kildans had been thoroughly 'spoiled' by tourism. Amy Goodrich-Freer, writing at the turn of the century, noted that 'St Kilda, like Iona, has become the happy hunting-ground of the Lowland tourist ... we observed from our newspapers that during the fortnight of our solitary stay [in Eriskay], over 300 visitors had arrived in St Kilda'. She went on: 'the natives are deteriorating under the foolish treatment of those who "take an interest" in them; who bring them presents of silver teaspoons, confectionery, silk aprons, mantelpiece ornaments, and silk handkerchiefs of tartans belonging to no known clan in the island. A lady on her return showed me with much delight an old Celtic brooch she had "picked up" for five shillings. It was made, doubtless, in anticipation of such purchasers, out of a brass safety-pin and a penny key-ring (both new). Such an incident, I venture to say, could occur in no other island, not even in Iona'.[55]

Robert Connell, who made two short visits to Hirta in the mid 1880s, was forthright on this matter. He complained about 'the great moral injury that tourists and sentimentalists and yachtsmen, with pocketfuls of money, are working upon a kindly and simple people. They are making the St Kildian a fibreless creature ...'.[56] Connell wrote of beggars who 'have no compunction in proposing to relieve you of everything you are simple-minded enough to part with, from a smoke of tobacco or a lead pencil to a hamper of wines'.[57]

Broadly, there were two kinds of reaction to the St Kildans and their behaviour. Less 'educated' tourists evidently behaved unselfconsciously, buying souvenirs, giving the islanders presents, and treating them as a spectacle. According to Norman Heathcote, who was there in 1898 and 1899, 'many tourists treat [the St Kildans] as if they were wild animals at the zoo. They throw sweets at them, openly mock them, and I have seen them standing at the church door during service, laughing and talking, and staring in as if at an entertainment got up for their amusement'.[58] Tom Steel and Charles MacLean have already explained how, in the summer of 1890, a group of people from Sunderland planned to attend (or rather gatecrash) the wedding of the 'Queen' of St Kilda, and arrived with a pile of wedding presents, to the horror of the *Hirteach*, who refused to let them stay, and held the marriage ceremony after

FIGURE 80.
Interior of an 'Amazon's House' type structure, Gleann Mór.

FIGURE 81.
A probable 'Pictish'
structure just west of
the 'Amazon's House',
Gleann Mór.

they had left the island.[59] More sophisticated tourists were dismayed or horrified by the commercialisation of Hirta, by the encounter with natives whose ethnographic authenticity was so compromised that they required payment to pose for photographs or to stage a cliff-climbing demonstration. Fraser MacDonald has argued persuasively that many of the visitors had a problem with the islanders' piety and rigorous observance of the Sabbath; the St Kildans had captured the spiritual high ground, and outsiders felt themselves under a religious reproach the sharper for being largely unspoken.[60] The temptation was to react by characterising the islanders as fanatical, bigoted extremists.

Many present-day tourists in the Third (or indeed the Second) World will be familiar with these disconcerting experiences. As visitors to the Glasgow Empire Exhibition in 1938 were later to demonstrate, what tourists really wanted, mostly, were unspoilt, ethnographically authentic St Kildans who would never change, who would staff an open-air Museum of Traditional Gaelic Life in perpetuity. But it was not to be. Now we behold a substitute, a set of sepia photographs exuding calm and good ethnographic order, the steady gaze of natives whose co-operation was, in the end, worth paying for. For unlike old Finlay MacQueen and his fellow exiles of the 1930s, these people will not bother us with their pain, their perplexity, their unpredictability; there is no risk that they will turn out to be troublingly inauthentic.

St Kilda and the
Wider World: Tales
of an Iconic Island

Science and literature

There was one kind of visitor who could probably afford to ignore the shenanigans surrounding the tourist trade. Field scientists who work in wild places are fortunate. Generally, they do not have to hurry to 'consume' what they can before their stay comes to an end. They can afford to absorb the atmosphere slowly, waiting to be surprised by serendipitous encounters with nature, drinking in the sheer beauty of the place. In the late nineteenth century, St Kilda became something of a magnet for scientists. In 1884 geological progress was made by Alexander Ross, who had some thin-sections made of the rocks, and then by Sir Archibald Geikie, who visited the archipelago in 1895 and 1896, using a boat to draw the cliff sections (he too recorded the granophyre-dolerite interface where it showed up in the northern cliffs of Hirta[61]). Neil MacKenzie put up two naturalists who were mostly interested in seabirds – George Atkinson in 1831 and John MacGillivray in 1840.[62] The naturalist Richard Kearton and his brother Cherry, an excellent wildlife photographer, came to St Kilda on the *Dunara Castle* in June 1896, leaving on the *Hebridean* ten days later; they had an adventurous and productive stay, which they wrote up in *With Nature and a Camera*.[63] They were curious about the famous St Kilda sub-species of wren, which had made its debut in the scientific literature 12 years before they arrived. The St Kilda sub-species of long-tailed field-mouse was first identified a couple of years after their visit.

Study of the archaeology of the archipelago got off to a rather chequered start, with a series of accidental discoveries triggered by the works initiated by Neil MacKenzie.[64] In the years around 1860 came the work of Captain F. W. L. Thomas, the naval surveyor, who eventually published a long, rambling paper on 'the primitive dwellings and hypogea of the Outer Hebrides',[65] bringing together an extraordinary range of sites – souterrains, wheel-houses, corbelled shielings and houses from all over the Western Isles. Thomas had no real sense of how archaeology might be used to work out the relative ages of these structures, or to distance them from the folk legends attached to them; the paper's strength lay in its measured site plans, which included two of the 'primitive' structures in Gleann Mór (Figures 80 and 81) and two showing the internal fittings of a couple of St Kilda blackhouses (Figure 61, page 130). In 1876 John Sands cleared out part of the Village Bay souterrain, discovering pottery and primitive stone tools amongst other things.[66]

Visitors such as MacDiarmid treated the agriculture of St Kilda from a scientific standpoint.[67] From the 1860s there were also studies of the islanders' medical condition and vital statistics, some of which took advantage of census records.[68] Naturally, interest focused on special St Kilda topics, such as the boat cold; infantile tetanus (*trismus*); the susceptibility of island dwellers to disease; the potentially adverse effects on mental health of marriages within an apparently small breeding population; and the implications of a diet heavily dependent on seabirds and their eggs. Others wrote down folk tales and songs, most notably Neil MacKenzie in the 1830s and the great folksong collector Alexander Carmichael in 1865.[69] St Kilda also attracted photographers – notably Captain Thomas in 1860 and Norman MacLeod in 1886. Sometimes it seems as if just about everyone, however short their stay, felt obliged to write *something* about the lifeways of the islanders!

For the first time since 1764, general books about St Kilda started to appear. There was Sands' *Out of This World: or, Life in St Kilda*, (first published 1876), followed soon by a riposte, George Seton's *St Kilda*, which first appeared in 1878. Then there was Robert Connell's *St Kilda and the St Kildians* in 1887, Kearton's *With Nature and a Camera* in 1897, and Norman Heathcote's *St Kilda*, published in 1900. It is Seton's book, I think, which best reflects the nature of late Victorian debates about St Kilda. The present state and future wellbeing of this small community provided ideal subject matter for the late Victorians, with their earnest Christian ethics, respect for the achievements and potential of science, and growing sense of national political responsibility, as the British state became more democratic and better organised. Britain needed a worldview which would legitimate her control over a global empire and enable her ruling classes to make sense of the world in those terms. Thoughtful people were challenged by the presence of what sounded like a community of anthropological curiosities, a people living 'out of this world' at the edge of the British Isles. Should their anachronistic lifeways be preserved and protected? Or should they be brought into the modern world? If so, how was that to be achieved? In fact the question of St Kilda's future was no more than a sharply-focused, much-debated outcome of much more widespread problems confronting the Highlands and Islands after the bad times of the early nineteenth century. They were addressed by the Napier Commission in 1884 and the MacNeill report in 1886.[70] Just after the First World War a practical experiment took place, Lord Leverhulme making valiant but ill-judged efforts to modernise and revitalise the economies of Lewis, and then Harris.[71]

Leverhulme's project ended in disillusion and failure, and so – for rather different reasons – did the manifold attempts to help the St Kildans during the last 50 years or so of the community's existence. However one interprets the actions which led up to the evacuation, however one assigns responsibility for that event, whether one feels that it was a Good Thing or not, the stark fact is that it happened – a definitive full stop which, as far as many commentators are concerned, brought St Kilda's history to an end.

Paradise regained?

As soon as they got wind of the impending evacuation of Hirta, naturalists could hardly wait to study and record the island's fauna and flora in the wake of the convenient removal of humans and their domestic animals; a research proposal was made at the British Association meeting held at Bristol in 1930.[72] Almost literally, the Oxford and Cambridge Expedition did not let the grass grow under their feet; it took place in the summer of 1931, with the assistance

FIGURE 82.
As the sun shines into the church, the Feather Store and the gun intended to repel further U-boat attacks may be glimpsed through the window.

of five returning St Kildans.[73] Nowadays one struggles to comprehend a world in which an expedition composed entirely of Oxbridge undergraduates could publish so many scientific papers on the basis of three weeks' fieldwork! Some of the expedition's members, however, were later to achieve great distinction – notably David Lack and the extraordinary Tom Harrisson, pioneer of mass observation, under-estimated anthropologist, museum curator and war hero.[74] The expedition included the son and heir of the famous writer John Buchan. The students had seized their chance to explore an archipelago unencumbered by people, the flora of its abandoned arable land as yet ungrazed by Soays. They got to Soay and Boreray, lowered each other down cliffs with ropes, and took a shotgun 'for collecting specimens'.[75]

And then in 1931 the archipelago was purchased by the Bute family (one of whose ancestors had been to St Kilda with Henry Brougham back in 1799). The islands took on a new life as a happy hunting ground for naturalists – those with the right connections, at least – and invited guests (ditto). It was almost as if Hirta had been subjected to a new kind of Clearance – although every summer a few islanders were allowed a temporary return. In another ironic instance of the continuing connection between rampant capitalism and Romanticism, Lord Dumfries (later the Marquis of Bute) – whose immense family wealth derived mostly from the polluted, densely populated zone of mines and dockyards in south Wales – wanted St Kilda to be a wildlife sanctuary. Inspired perhaps by the Duchess of Bedford, who had taken some Soay sheep from Soay to form a parkland flock at Woburn in 1910,[76] he went to considerable trouble in 1932 to get a balanced flock of Soay sheep brought from Soay to Hirta, taking care to keep the breed as 'pure' as possible by systematically removing (by 1937) the few Blackfaces which had escaped the evacuation.[77] In 1936, Michael Powell wanted to make a film based on the story of the last days of St Kilda, and asked permission to shoot it *on* the

FIGURE 83.
The realm of the
gannets.

island. It seems that he planned to repair the houses, and to hire former St Kildans as extras, bringing them over from Lochaline. A friend warned Lord Dumfries that 'you would be absolutely done if you wanted them to accompany you to Borrera or Soay. They would be absolutely the slaves of the Company, and you would have nobody to help you or work our boat'.[78] He was referring to members of the Ferguson family, notably Neil, the postmaster at the time of the evacuation, and his brother Alex the Glasgow tweed merchant. Powell got a dusty answer. Lord Dumfries 'went through all the old arguments: his birds, his holiday, his house [with its recently installed kitchen and bathroom], his privacy ...'. The talented cineast eventually had to make do with Foula in Shetland.[79]

The ideal of the wildlife sanctuary was somewhat compromised. Tourists still wanted to visit St Kilda, and the *Hebridean* and the *Dunara Castle* continued to bring them here. A few St Kildans used this service to get back to Hirta, and gain access to the looms they had left behind; they lived partly by selling things to tourists, and posing for photographs, partly by helping Lord Dumfries and his guests, and partly by taking sea-birds and their eggs, as they had always done. Robert Atkinson, who came here in 1938 just a couple of years after graduating from Oxford, has left an entertaining account of his experiences.[80] He shared the island with old Finlay MacQueen (Figure 1, page xiv; Figure 21, page 36) who was in his element, catching puffins, salting down fulmars and drying fish for the winter; old Mrs Gillies (Figure 34, page 60), who never stopped working – scrubbing and baking, carding and spinning wool, knitting, and scraping crotal off the rocks to make red dye; and her son Neil, who spent a lot of time smoking and staring into the fire. Then a 42-year-old bachelor, he had been a shipyard worker in Glasgow for some years before being paid off; he was later appointed caretaker of St Kilda by Lord Dumfries, who wanted to put a stop to the depredations of foreign trawlermen.[81] The St Kildans sold postcards, socks and gloves, and birds' eggs; they still held services in the church and observed the Sabbath. The 76-year-old Finlay MacQueen, who allegedly didn't speak much English (but was apparently capable of conversing in Gaelic with Breton fishermen using their own *patois!*[82]), posed for photographs with a stuffed gannet (Figure 21), or sometimes a stuffed puffin;[83] he was notorious for concealing stashes of tobacco about his person and then exhibiting the emptiness of his pockets, or the bowl of his pipe, in quite shameless attempts to cadge some more. In 1918 he had been all for trying to row out and obtain tobacco from the German U-boat (see Figure 82) which was just about to open fire on the radio station![84] MacQueen, whose earlier life had included acting as midwife at the birth of his nephew,[85] was an epic figure, 'on his broad bare feet with the well-spread toes' carrying 'a fowling rod, a hoe, opera glasses, a sack and a coil of rope'.[86] When the bird census was being taken in 1939, the St Kildans evidently waited until Lord Dumfries had left and then took a boat over to Dun 'and came back with *baskets* of eggs – razorbills, guillemots, puffins etc – and about 100 fulmars. Davie [one of the naturalists] protested and said to Gillies "I thought you were bird watchers not destroyers" or words to that effect – and Neil hummed and hawed and said oh yes but you allowed him to have a dozen fulmars or so'.[87] A letter to Lord Dumfries from the estate office in July 1939 complains, '[the St Kildans] are not playing the game. Apparently they make the holiday at St Kilda a purely business trip . . .'.[88]

Doubtless at the centre of many of these exploits was the redoubtable A. G. (Alexander) Ferguson, the St Kildan who had become a Glasgow tweed merchant, and was now in his sixties. It was he who had the marble 'open book' monument placed at the centre of the Hirta graveyard, in memory of his parents; in his early eighties he still visited St Kilda regularly on his motor yacht.[89]

Lord Dumfries installed modern amenities in the former manse, got himself some dye-stamped notepaper headed 'Oiseval House', and in 1936 had Mass said on the island. His conduct as guardian of Hirta's wildlife might raise a few eyebrows nowadays. Shooting seals was very much on the agenda,[90] followed up by an order for a sealskin sporran. In 1939 a 'huge' walrus made a few appearances; Lord Dumfries wanted to shoot it, and A. G. Ferguson took a couple of pot-shots. The estate was relaxed about the use of firearms. It was not very easy to get permission to carry out scientific work on Hirta, and Lord Dumfries insisted on vetting any proposed publication. In 1948 he asked an expedition of naturalists to bring back some live gannets and gulls for Glasgow Zoo![91] But birds were ringed and traps were set; wildlife censuses were carried out in 1931, 1939, and 1947.[92]

After the war, St Kilda's role as a nature reserve was taken more seriously (Figure 83). In the climate of opinion which saw the election of a socialist government with a large Parliamentary majority, the private ownership and management of nature reserves of national importance started to seem problematic. A new generation of more professional scientists started to visit St Kilda. Some of the best naturalists of the day found good reasons (or excuses?) for visiting the archipelago – men of the calibre of James Fisher, Kenneth Williamson, Frank Fraser Darling, and John Morton Boyd. The scientists were enthusiastic supporters of the Bute vision (as, of course, they had to be). Williamson and Boyd, who were consultants and observers in April 1957 when the Ministry of Defence bulldozers started to roll (Figure 4, page 3), prayed that: 'some day, let us hope, the needs of defence will permit St Kilda to be left again to the sea-birds and the seals'.[93]

The death of history?

Most people, I suppose, believe that St Kilda's history came to an end with the evacuation (although accounts of the late twentieth-century experiences of the military are beginning to appear[94]). Present-day visitors are not necessarily well-prepared for the idiosyncrasies of today's lively community of transients – engineers, managers, support staff, summer wardens, researchers and work party members. It must have been quite a shock, in the late 1990s, to bring a yacht into Village Bay on a beautiful summer evening (Figure 85), contemplating the poignant sight of the abandoned village, a study in Celtic twilight – to be greeted by a deeply sun-tanned figure daubed in war-paint, clad only in a leopard-skin loin-cloth and a necklace of sheep metatarsals, brandishing a spear and speaking pidgin English – and then to go ashore and get caught up in an instant Roman Toga party. When the late twentieth-century story of St Kilda comes to be told, the propensity of patrons of the Puff Inn for fancy dress, among many other aspects of their lifeways, will require some kind of anthropological explanation.

Of course, St Kilda's history has not ended. More people are concerned about conservation and management issues than ever before; in these days of the internet and the webcam, this group of islands can be 'virtually' visited by thousands of people all over the world, and many can air their views on the world wide web. Managers walk on eggshells. St Kilda is what archaeologists have come to call a contested landscape. There are still those who consider human beings a non-native species on St Kilda, who would like nothing better

FIGURE 84.
The Base. Note the early head dyke, running like a switchback above the 1830 dyke, and then below it for a short stretch just before both are truncated by the cliff-edge.

than to bulldoze the base and return to the nature reserve of the early 1950s. Perhaps some day the radar station and its support facilities will become redundant, and their vision may become a reality. Until then, we would do well to treat the archipelago respectfully, but not over-reverentially, opening our minds to new cultural and artistic possibilities, as the old St Kildans assuredly would have done.

CHAPTER TEN

In Conclusion:
The Cunning of the St Kildans

Look at their sly, assuring mockery.
They are aware of what we are up to
With our internal explorations, our
Designs of affluence and education
They know us so well, and are not jealous

D. Dunn, St Kilda's Parliament, 1879–1979 *(1981)*.

FIGURE 86.
The spinner.

In Britain – perhaps especially in England – various rural places have had their histories written meticulously, often affectionately. But St Kilda is not just another Wigston Magna, another Wharram Percy. This tiny archipelago in the north-east Atlantic has become a historical drama queen; in more than a mere geographical sense it has become the Ultima Thule of local studies. As we have seen, the prior expectations of commentators have encouraged them to emphasise and exaggerate the exoticism of its people and their lifeways, and the historical consequences of the islandness and geographical remoteness of St Kilda. In the later twentieth century, writers have gone further, writing history as classical tragedy. The 'Fall of Man' model within the Hardrock Consensus was founded upon ideas which had a long ancestry among Hirta's observers. The 'Golden Age' concept established the primal innocence of the St Kildans. At the same time, the habit of referring to them as 'natives' and making comparisons with Hottentots, Kaffirs, Indians, and South Sea islanders fuelled the myth of their inability to adapt to the modern world. Like various peoples familiar to British colonial administrators, the St Kildans could be portrayed as doomed losers in a perpetual struggle for survival, based on 'laws of nature' unjustifiably extrapolated from the scientific ideas of Charles Darwin. Not many commentators pointed out that the *Hirteach* were pretty much like humans the world over. On the contrary, Tom Steel specifically states that 'the St Kildans can only be described as St Kildans' and that 'the history of the St Kildans shows the folly of thinking of the islanders as similar to ourselves'.[1]

From this point of view it has been hard to avoid classifying the 'premodern' St Kildans as part of the natural history of the archipelago. The extinction of the community has been seen simultaneously as nature taking its course *and* as an illustration of the essentially '*un*natural' ecological and social vandalism perpetrated by the modern world. Once the St Kildans had 'lost their innocence', they became essentially decadent; for Williamson and Boyd their fate was starkly symbolic of the plight of the planet. The global situation has worsened, of course, since the days of Operation Hardrock, and even more since 1972, when Charles MacLean was arguing that the survivors of a future ecological Armageddon might need to replicate the modes of social existence developed and practised by the St Kildans over the centuries.

With our ancestors, we might choose to believe that we have been created – or have evolved – 'in the image of God', set on this planet in fulfilment of some divine design, given a license to kill off other species or consume global 'resources' at will in a drive for 'progress', in accordance with a divine

FIGURE 87.
A young man photographed by Captain Thomas.

purpose which in other contexts is regarded as mysterious and unfathomable. From a more contemporary perspective, it is difficult not to agree with the proposition that humans *are* and always have been part of the 'natural' world, and that ultimately we ignore ecological principles at our peril. A future commentator from another galaxy, writing *The Life and Death of Planet Earth*, will surely have to set what we call 'history' within the larger frame of natural ecology. We may find ourselves in sympathy with this long-term view of planetary history, and dismayed by the ecological vandalism of the twentieth century. It is tempting to look for small-scale allegories, miniature versions of such a grand narrative, as Paul Bahn and John Flenley did in their book *Easter Island Earth Island*. It is even more tempting to find an island which 'fast forwards' human history at a scale which we can comprehend.

This question of historical scale is an interesting one. Our narratives of the 'death' of this island community might choose to concentrate on individual events – occasions like the fateful 'tea and scones' meeting at the Factor's House, for instance. But we might also choose a wider perspective, and regard St Kilda as a casualty of demographic realities, capitalist market forces, or failures of administration. And as we have seen, it is possible to select an even more long-focus lens, and think globally. But before recruiting St Kilda as a global allegory for human history writ at the largest imaginable scale, we should bear in mind that this place was not truly an 'island' in the required sense. As we have seen, most of the cultural and historical horizons regularly recognised within northern Scotland are represented here – stone tools of the Bronze Age (and perhaps also the later Neolithic), burnt mounds, a souterrain and wheelhouses from the Iron Age, probable Pictish structures, early

Christian chapels and carved stones, and then Norse burials and placenames. The odd sherds of Hebridean Ware and a pollen signature may be all that survive (at present) to represent the earlier Neolithic (how far would we really expect a megalithic tomb or its cairn to survive in a place like this, where stone is frequently recycled?). And it would not be surprising to find fragmentary evidence for an Atlantic roundhouse. From Skaill knives to steatite, the theme of links with the Northern Isles – perhaps especially Shetland – self-evidently involving passages by sea, recurs like a persistent drum-beat, albeit muffled at times by archaeologists' uncertainties. Sea-knowledge endures. St Kilda possessed what outsiders wanted or needed, whether it was abundant and unusual food resources at certain seasons (for visiting retinues), shelter and hospitality (deep sea fishermen from at least 'Pictish' times) or spiritual nourishment (seekers of the Sublime).

Our possession of historical hindsight does not make the 'death' of this community inevitable. One could easily envisage different decisions being made in 1930, decisions just as explicable in early twentieth-century terms as the ones which *were* taken. 'Modernity' – or relatively rapid and disorienting cultural change – formed part of the context in which St Kilda was evacuated, although I don't believe that such an abstraction should be taken to 'explain' this event (Figure 88). If we choose an individual casualty of capitalism and make it a symbol of the human historical predicament at a global scale, we should be very aware of what we are doing. Grand historical themes are illuminating and thought-provoking, but they do not really help us to write history at a familiar human scale.

Some readers may find this a pedantic point of view. They may prefer to embrace and continue the frequent use made of St Kildan history and culture, over the past three centuries, to reflect and illustrate philosophical propositions of the day. And maybe there *are* certain places – especially places endowed with dramatic ruins, breath-taking scenery, and not too many tourists – which

FIGURE 88.
The radar station on Mullach Mór symbolises both the face of modernity and St Kilda's current involvement with the wider world.

should be reserved and preserved as locations especially suited to philosophical reflections on human history. Perhaps this should be one of St Kilda's most significant roles in the future, as a World Heritage Site not inscribed only for its wildlife.

Domination and resistance?

If naturalists had been serious about treating *Homo sapiens* as part of St Kilda's natural history, they would have had to deal with questions of intra-specific predation. The patterns and hierarchies of dominance known to students of the higher primates, which are often established and renewed on a face-to-face, confrontational basis, are now represented, in most human societies, by institutionalised structures of power. On St Kilda, vicissitudes of climate and weather may have caused trouble from time to time. But they were surely a less significant threat to the well-being of the islanders, with their diversified, storage-focused economy, than the behaviour and attitudes of the chief (and later the laird) and the tacksman (later the factor), especially in the days when they were accompanied by substantial retinues. If St Kilda's distant location exposed its inhabitants to less frequent predation (by pirates and assorted foreigners as much as by lairds and their representatives) they were nonetheless vulnerable to the designs and desires of those who did make the voyage.

There is much to admire, it seems to me, about the 'cultural competence' of the St Kildans – the effectiveness of their economic strategies, the many skills which men and women had to master, their ingenious and creative use of raw materials, and so on. They had a remarkable range of regulations and institutions which seem 'designed' (but actually must have evolved) to reduce social disharmony to manageable proportions – the famous self-regulated communitarian 'republic'. But this was no inward-looking commune, for the St Kildans participated in the affairs of the wider world, and they developed an effective 'foreign policy' to cope with everything from the chance visits of outsiders to the more systematic, recurrent relationship with the chiefdom or estate. Of course, it is probably the case that most other Hebridean and northeast Atlantic communities could be described in much the same terms; what distinguishes St Kilda is mostly the richness of its documentation. The lifeways of the *Hirteach* form a powerful reminder of the cultural competence of pre-Enlightenment societies in general.

But if the St Kildan 'culture' formed an impressive set of resources and practices which sustained the community over the long term, a cultural repertoire which was always available, it is also striking how intelligently and effectively the islanders dealt with new challenges presented by the external world. They were 'cunning' not only in the sense that they were good at haggling and striking bargains with the tacksman, concealing the true numbers of their sheep, or shaming tourists into paying them more than they had intended; they were 'cunning' in the older sense of the word, meaning intelligent or knowing. Martin noted their sense of solidarity when confronted by the steward, their resistance to new taxes, their willingness to protest to Dunvegan if they felt an injustice was being perpetrated.[2] One of the most telling anecdotes relates to the year 1886. The St Kilda literature often notes the islanders' thirst for news; their recorded enquiries after the health of the monarch and the vanquishing of Britain's foes make them sound like paid-up members of the Conservative party (and apparently they were great admirers of Queen Victoria[3]). However, when Connell visited them, the questions they asked were 'How is the crofter question getting on?' 'What are the landlords doing?' 'Have their heads been chopped off yet?'[4]

For much of the time period under consideration, it is impossible to work out the balance of advantage between the island and the laird (and the tacksman); we do not have complete or trustworthy figures for the amount or cash value of what Hirta produced each year, what proportion (in cash or kind) of this income went in rent or other payments, how far the amounts to be paid were adjusted to take account of good and bad harvests, and how far the tacksman or factor operated on his own account, beyond the reach of Harris or Dunvegan. But if the basic economic facts are difficult to ascertain, it is hard to avoid noticing the political battles which the St Kildans won, and some of their achievements. While other Scottish communities were exposed, figuratively speaking, to the chill winds of nineteenth-century capitalism and global economics, the St Kildans were often able to turn to their advantage their own exposure to real storms. They were not driven from their lands, or forced to rely for food mainly on the potato. They farmed their own crofts and lived in 'modern' houses long before most other Hebrideans. They won their battle to convert manse and church into Free Church properties, and had their laird chasing halfway across the country in a vain attempt to prevent an emigration to Australia. They charmed numerous outsiders, from Captain Otter to John Sands, into taking up the cudgels on their behalf. Many others were persuaded that St Kilda was a worthy charitable cause; they offered their expertise and scientific knowledge, donated money, and paid for new boats for the islanders. The near-monopoly power of the laird and his factor was diminished by the St Kildans' taking advantage of the summer steamship services and the opportunities presented by tourism, their conversion into a community of weavers, and trading through A. G. Ferguson's emporium in Glasgow. By the Edwardian period the *Hirteach* and their advocates were in a position to seek and obtain practical support from various government departments and agencies as well as publicity-seeking captains of commerce and industry and popular newspapers like the *Daily Mirror*. The estate had become vulnerable to bad publicity; Dunvegan, on the defensive, was now in a politically-weak position, with no real sanction against tenants who pleaded poverty and accumulated rent arrears, while selling tweed to Alex Ferguson and buying supplies from him. For the last 70 years of the community's existence, laird and factor had to play their traditional 'paternalistic' role for public consumption (and they clearly made a favourable impression on some of the audience) whilst harbouring feelings of frustration and resentment against the islanders.

The things which went wrong were mostly beyond the St Kildans' control. They could not have been expected to realise the demographic consequences of the 1852 emigration, or to predict the collapse of the market for much of their produce in the early twentieth century. The St Kildans only came into contact with those who administered and delivered government policy; they were not in a good position to influence those who made decisions in government and the civil service, or to recognise that official attitudes and priorities might change. During the 1920s, the islanders' ability to influence events was rapidly slipping away from them. These anthropological curiosities, survivals from a vanished age, had played their cards rather well. Eventually, however, emigration, as a decision taken by individuals or families and then finally by the community, was the only card left to play.

In conclusion

As we have seen, there have been various approaches to the St Kilda community and

FIGURE 89.
Framing St Kilda.

interpretations of its history. In this book I have taken issue with some of them. I have ended by stressing the cultural competence of the St Kildans, and their determination to achieve their goals within contemporary constraints. I am not suggesting that this made them special, or distinguished them from other small-scale human communities, and I am well aware that my own account may turn the historical St Kildans into figures just as symbolic and archetypal as those created by earlier narratives. Nevertheless, I contend that as one reads between the lines to gain some sense of the people, looking beyond the bemusement and condescension of the commentators, one can discern the genius of the *Hirteach*, and through them, that of many human societies. And if the world community decides to celebrate the history of these islands, and to enhance their World Heritage Site status, perhaps we should accept the honour without cavil, on behalf of quietly determined and hard-working people the world over.

Notes

Notes to Chapter 1:
Prologue: Reopening the Inquest

1. Fisher 1948, 108.
2. Williamson and Boyd 1960, 12.
3. Williamson and Boyd 1960, 32–4.
4. Mathieson 1928.
5. Williamson and Boyd 1960, plate 9; Atkinson 1949, plate XXIX.
6. Williamson and Boyd 1960, 11.
7. Williamson and Boyd 1960, 15.
8. Atkinson 1949, 220, 224.
9. Crampsey 1988, 54.
10. Borthwick 1988, 19–20.
11. Kinchin and Kinchin 1988, 82.
12. Williamson and Boyd 1960, 31.
13. MacGregor 1960, 1, 13.
14. MacGregor 1960, 33, 35, 36, 45.
15. MacGregor 1960, 40, 42, 45.
16. MacGregor 1960, 42.
17. MacGregor 1960, 46.
18. Steel 1994, 9, 51, 53, 94, 192.
19. Connell 1887, 61.
20. Steel 1994, 277.
21. Steel 1994, 192.
22. Steel 1994, 123, 155.
23. Steel 1994, 136, 190.
24. Steel 1994, 139.
25. Steel 1994, 91.
26. Steel 1994, 93, 98, 102, 122, 129–33, 135, 180, 182.
27. Hoskins 1955, 232.
28. MacLean 1987, 143–54.
29. Löffler 1983.
30. Rainbird 1999.
31. Martin 1986, 1.
32. MacKenzie 1911, 28–9.
33. Evans 1973.
34. Bahn and Flenley 1992.
35. e.g. Hau'ofa 1993, Gosden and Pavlides 1994, Broodbank 2000.
36. Fleming 1999.
37. Pennant 1790, 213.
38. e.g. Kearton 1897, 27.
39. e.g. Ramsay 1888, 399–400.
40. Martin 1981, 372.
41. Pennant 1790, 214.
42. Landt 1810, Annandale 1905, Williamson 1948, Fenton 1978.
43. Fenton 1984.
44. Martin 1986, 63.
45. MacCulloch 1819, 31.
46. Quine 1988, Chalmers 1996, Steel 1994.
47. Taylor 1968, 120–1.
48. Steel 1994, 49.

Notes to Chapter 2:
The Qualities of the Isle

1. Wilson 1842, 59; Kearton 1897, 93.
2. Harman 1997, 258.
3. Steel 1994, 193.
4. Fisher 1952, 132.
5. Martin 1986, frontispiece.
6. Munro 1961, 78.
7. Quine 1988, 218.
8. Martin 1986, 15.
9. See Parker Pearson et al. 2004, 106-14.
10. Campbell 1974, 31.
11. Jewell, Milner and Boyd 1974.
12. Chambers Edinburgh Journal 1838, 331.
13. MacKenzie 1911, 44.
14. MacAulay 1974, 209.
15. Atkinson 2001, 61.
16. Quine 1988, 122.
17. MacAulay 1974, 186–7.
18. MacKenzie 1911, 15–16; Elliott 1895, 126.
19. Ross, NTS STK 3/22.
20. Ross, NTS STK 3/22.
21. Martin 1981, 299; Milner 1848, 2061; Elliott 1895, 125.
22. MacGillivray 1842, 56; Connell 1887, 125.

23. MacKay 2002, 3.
24. Heathcote 1985, 96–7; Steel 1994, 108.
25. Seton 1980, 115; Sands 1878, 165.
26. Connell 1887, 19–20.
27. Ross, NTS STK 3/22.
28. Fisher 2001, 11.
29. Mentioned in Parker Pearson *et al.* 2004, 156–8; and *pers. comm.*
30. *Martin 1986, 44; MacAulay 1974, 71.*
31. Parker Pearson *et al.* 2004, 156–8.
32. Martin 1986, 44.
33. Martin 1986, 46.
34. MacAulay 1974, 71.
35. MacAulay 1974, 76–7.
36. Taylor 1968.
37. Harman 1997, 80–1.
38. Munro 1961, 78; Martin 1986, 58–9.
39. Harman 1997, 73.
40. Taylor 1969.
41. Coates 1990, 46–49.
42. Harman 1997, 84–5.
43. Dodgshon 1998, 59, 105–7.
44. Martin 1986, 10, 48.
45. Martin 1986, 10.
46. See Fisher and Vevers 1943, 189–90 for general scepticism about Martin's estimates.
47. Harman 1997, 88–90, 126–7.
48. Domhnall Uilleam Stiùbhart *pers. comm.*
49. Johnson and Boswell 1984, 281–300.
50. Grant 1981, 494–7.
51. Johnson and Boswell 1984, 297.
52. Harman 1997, table 1.
53. MacLeod of MacLeod 1928, 104.
54. Bray 1996, 134–40.
55. Knox 1975, 158–60.
56. Reproduced in Bray 1996, 138.
57. Knox 1975, 160.
58. Campbell 1799, 48–9.
59. MacCulloch 1819, 27.
60. Campbell 1799, 11, 45.
61. Harman 1997, 98–101.
62. Nicolson 2000, 224.
63. Otter 1825.
64. Otter 1825, 346, 350, 367.
65. Brougham 1871; Campbell 1799.
66. Quine 1988, 7–10.
67. DCRO 1148M add. 23 F12–22.
68. Richards 1992b, 59.
69. Hunter 2000.
70. Steel 1994, 180.
71. Harman 1997, 251.
72. Holohan 1986.

73. Steel 1994, 189.
74. MacAulay 1974, 40; Brougham 1871, 106–7.
75. Harman 1997, 256–9.
76. Steel 1994, 158.
77. Harman 1997, 275.
78. Harman 1997, 264–5.
79. Seton 1980, 235.
80. A very full list is in Fisher 1952, 125–6.
81. Geikie 1897, 405–17.
82. MacNeill 1886.
83. MacKay 2002, 35–6.
84. Steel 1994, 162.
85. Harman 1997, 279.
86. MacKay 2002, 38–52.
87. MacGregor 1931; Steel 1994.

Notes to Chapter 3:
Men of Stone

1. Fossitt 1996.
2. e.g. in South Uist: Brayshay and Edwards 1996, 17–20.
3. Henshall 1972.
4. Fossitt 1996.
5. Brayshay and Edwards 1996, 20–26.
6. Ritchie 1985, 174.
7. Henshall 1972, 257–64; Müller 1988, 32–36.
8. Sheridan 2003.
9. Serjeantson 1990, 11.
10. Fleming and Edmonds 1999, 153.
11. Walker 1984, 107–8.
12. Cottam 1979.
13. Stell and Harman 1988, end paper.
14. Fleming 1995; Fleming and Edmonds 1999.
15. Fleming 1995.
16. Williamson & Boyd 1960, 32–4.
17. Fisher 1948, 93.
18. Walker 1984.
19. MacKenzie 1911, 8.
20. Dickson 1992; Parker Pearson *et al.* 2004, 97.
21. Miket 2002, 81.
22. Sands 1878, 78.
23. Clarke 1995.
24. Whittle 1986, 133.
25. See e.g. Calder 1965; Rees 1979, 1986; Clarke 1995.
26. Clarke 1995.
27. Annandale 1903, 1905.
28. e.g. Martin 1986, 39; Atkinson 2001, 43.

29. Kearton 1897, 52.
30. Kearton 1898, 76.
31. MacGregor 1931, 279.
32. Clarke 1995.
33. e.g. Whittle 1986, 45–58; Edwards and Whittington 1998; Calder 1965.
34. Harman 1997, 39.
35. Stell and Harman 1988, 26.
36. Harman 1997; Emery 1996.
37. Buckley 1990; Hodder and Barfield 1991.
38. Burt 1754, 279.
39. Kearton 1897, 13–14.
40. Sands 1877, 187.
41. Hunter 1996, 62.
42. Armit and Braby 2002.
43. Parker Pearson *et al.* 2004, 85–7.
44. MacKenzie 1911, 10.
45. Barfield & Hodder 1987.
46. Armit 1996, 109–35.
47. Parker Pearson *et al.* 2004, 84.
48. Miket 2002, 81; Crawford 2002, 119.
49. Armit 2002.
50. Martin 1981, 28; MacAulay 1974, 48.
51. Miket 2002.
52. Mathieson 1928, 124.
53. Quine 1988, 219, quoting from the diary of the botanist John Gladstone.
54. Thomas 1870, 172.
55. Parker Pearson *et al.* 2004, 98–9.
56. Martin 1986, 24.
57. MacAulay 1974, 54–5; Kennedy in 1862, quoted in Thomas 1874, 705.
58. Thomas 1870, 175.
59. And see Taylor 1968, 129–31.
60. Crawford 2002, table 14.
61. Parker Pearson *et al.* 2004, 102.
62. Coates 1990, 77.
63. Cartledge and Grimbly 1999; Serjeantson 1988.
64. Serjeantson 1988, 213.
65. Pennant 1790, 60–1; MacCrie 1848, 386, 393–4, 402; Williamson 1908, 38.
66. Serjeantson 1988, Fuller 1999, 350–1.
67. Boyd and Boyd 1990, 204.
68. Parker Pearson and Sharples 1999, 10–15; Armit 2002.
69. Murphy and Simpson 2003, 109.
70. Serjeantson 1988, 221.

Notes to Chapter 4: The Interdependence of Islands

1. See Parker Pearson *et al.* 2004, 110–14 and especially fig. 61.
2. Parker Pearson *et al.* 2004, 121–3.
3. Sharples and Parker Pearson 1999; Parker Pearson *et al.* 2004.
4. Parker Pearson *et al.* 2004, 143.
5. Coates 1990, *passim*; MacAulay 1974, 32.
6. Taylor 1968, 126; Coates 1990, 148–52.
7. Harman 1997, 70.
8. Graham-Campbell and Batey 1998, 77; Harman 1997, 69–71.
9. Emery 1996, 179–80.
10. Fagan 2000, 65, 83–4.
11. Coates 1990, 79.
12. Martin 1986, 13; 1981, 281; MacAulay 1974, 48.
13. Heathcote 1985, 48.
14. Berry 1969; Berry 1979, 36.
15. Sands 1878, 44.
16. MacQueen and MacQueen 1995, 11.
17. Sands 1878, 44.
18. Quine 1989, 141.
19. MacKenzie 1911, 15; MacDiarmid 1877, 245.
20. Hastrup 1985, 1990.
21. Coates 1990, 148–52; Taylor 1968, 128–9.
22. And see Baldwin 1996.
23. Taylor, 1968, 125, 143; Coates 1990, 41.
24. MacLeod of MacLeod 1927, 185.
25. MacLeod of MacLeod 1928, 1–2.
26. Dodgshon 1995, 1998.
27. Burt 1754, 158–9.
28. Dodgshon 1998, 88–9.
29. Burt 1754, 107.
30. Burt 1754, 158, 228.
31. Martin 1981, 101.
32. MacDonald 1997, chapter 8.
33. Simpson 1938; Miket and Roberts 1990, 8–9.
34. Rixson 1998, 49.
35. Rixson 1998, 99.
36. Martin 1981, 286.
37. Quine 1988, 105.
38. MacKenzie 1911, 48; Kearton 1898, 74; Sands 1877, 287.
39. MacAulay 1974, 195.
40. Grant 1981, 60.
41. MacLeod of MacLeod 1928, 52.
42. Grant 1981, 65.
43. Grant 1981, 45.

St Kilda and the
Wider World: Tales
of an Iconic Island

44. MacLeod of MacLeod 1928, 70.
45. MacLeod of MacLeod 1928, 75–6.
46. MacLeod of MacLeod 1928, 76.
47. MacLeod of MacLeod 1928, 95–6.
48. Grant 1981, 404.
49. Allowing for the mid eighteenth-century shift to the Gregorian calendar; Martin 1986, 286.
50. Allowing for the calendar shift; Martin 1981, 9.
51. Martin 1986, 48, 28.
52. Martin 1986, 10, 41.
53. Rixson 1998, 98.
54. Martin 1986, 10.
55. Martin 1981, 95.
56. Burt 1754, 42–3, 56, 88.
57. *King Lear* I. IV. 247–49.
58. Pennant 1790, 215.
59. Martin 1981, 103–4.
60. Martin 1986, 62.
61. Moray 1678, 927.
62. Beatty 1992.
63. Munro 1961, 88.
64. Munro 1961, 88, 81, 77.
65. Martin 1981, 60–3.
66. Monro 1961, 131.
67. Martin 1986, 26, 55–6.
68. Moray 1678, 928.
69. Martin 1981, 16–18.
70. Martin 1981, 291.
71. Martin 1981, 17.
72. O'Hanlon 2003, 9.
73. Martin 1981, 96–7.
74. Coates 1990, 63.
75. Martin 1986, 19.
76. Martin 1986, 47.
77. Otter 1825, 359–60.
78. MacAulay 1974, 81, 216.
79. Martin 1986, 49.
80. Brougham 1799, 107; MacAulay 1974, 207; Buchan 1974, 20; Martin 1986, 76.
81. Martin 1986, 50.
82. Martin 1986, 48.
83. MacAulay 1974, 204, 94.
84. Martin 1981, 97–8.
85. Lawson 2002, 47.
86. Lawson 2002, 56, 59.
87. e.g. MacAulay 1974, 271; MacCulloch 1819, 26; Napier Commission, 864.
88. MacAulay 1974, 265.
89. Martin 1986, 38, 48.
90. Martin 1986, 50.
91. Martin 1986, 49.
92. Martin 1981, 94.
93. MacAuley 1974, 245.
94. Fleming 2000.
95. Martin 1981, 323.
96. Burt 1754, 135.
97. MacKenzie 1911, 30.
98. MacLean 1838, 21.
99. MacKenzie 1911, 20.
100. Marcus 1998, 125–54.
101. Martin 1981, 283; 1986, 28–9.
102. Gauld 1989.
103. Gauld 1989, 50–1; Taylor 1969, plates VII and VIII.
104. See, e.g., Alice MacLauchlan's diary in the Edwardian era – Quine 1988, 53–108.
105. MacKenzie 1911, 27.
106. Martin 1986, 45.
107. Martin 1986, 45.
108. Marcus 1998, 161.
109. Martin 1986, 46.
110. Martin 1986, 66.
111. Buchan 1974, 36; Harman 1997, 84–5.
112. Harman 1997, 91.
113. Connell 1887, 20–1; Kearton 1897, 38.
114. Sands 1878, 82.
115. Martin 1986, 46.
116. Martin 1986, 38.
117. Campbell 1799, 92.
118. Brougham 1871, 106; MacKenzie 1911, 29; Connell 1887, 56.
119. Campbell 1799, 25.
120. MacKenzie 1911, 29.
121. Johnson and Boswell 1984, 237; Otter 1825, 348.
122. Durrenberger 1992, 39.
123. Sharples and Parker Pearson 1999.
124. Sharples *pers. comm.*
125. Moray 1678, 927.
126. Graham-Campbell and Batey 1998, 76.
127. Morrison 1968, 17; Haswell-Smith 1998, 220.
128. Dodgshon 1998, 75, 111, 133, 213.
129. Walker 1808, 23.
130. Haswell-Smith 1998, 220.
131. Anon 1577–95 in Skene 1890, 431.
132. Harman 1997, 231.

Notes to Chapter 5: A Study in Cultural Competence

1. Heathcote 1985, 71.
2. *Glasgow Herald* 24 Sept 1926.
3. Dodgshon 1998, 12.

Notes

4. Hordern and Purcell 2000, 74, 182.
5. Anon 1577–95 in Skene 1890, 431.
6. MacAulay 1974, 38.
7. Harman 1997, 100.
8. Harman 1997, 323.
9. Harman 1997, 97.
10. Martin 1986, 18.
11. MacAulay 1974, 36.
12. MacCulloch 1819, 27; Atkinson 1838, 224.
13. MacAulay 1974, 33–4.
14. Martin 1986, 18; MacAulay 1974, 44–5.
15. MacAulay 1974, 11 fn, 34–5.
16. Buchan 1974, 25.
17. Martin 1986, 19.
18. Quine 1989, 181.
19. Martin 1986, 39, 58; Quine 1989, 195–6.
20. Martin 1981, 374.
21. MacKenzie 1911, 7–8.
22. MacAulay 1974, 28–30.
23. Martin 1986, 18.
24. MacDiarmid 1877, 243–6.
25. Martin 1986, 21; MacAulay 1974, 130.
26. Atkinson 1838, 223.
27. MacCulloch 1819, 29.
28. Seton 1980, 129.
29. MacPherson 1897, 474–5.
30. Fisher 1952, 141; Fisher and Vevers 1943, 185–6; MacKenzie 1911, 15.
31. Boyd and Boyd 1990, table 11.1.
32. Serjeantson 1988.
33. Fisher and Waterston 1941.
34. Atkinson 1838, 221.
35. Seton 1980, 235–6.
36. MacLeod n. d., 183–5. His visit took place in 1746.
37. Harvie-Brown and Buckley 1888, lxxxv; Coates 1990, 167.
38. Serjeantson 1988; Fuller 1999, 350–1.
39. Fuller 1999.
40. MacLeod *c.* 1756–1775.
41. Heathcote 1985, 175.
42. MacLean 1838, 10.
43. Atkinson 1838, 222.
44. Quine 1988, 158.
45. MacKenzie 1905, 50–53.
46. Pennant 1790, 146.
47. Martin 1986, 23.
48. MacLeod *c.* 1756–1775.
49. Munro 1961, 78; Buchanan 1762, 78.
50. Martin 1986, 19.
51. Kearton 1897, 48.
52. Campbell 1974, 25.
53. Anon in Skene 1880, 431.
54. Céron-Carrasco and Parker Pearson 1999.
55. e.g. Martin 1981, 284; MacCulloch 1819, 26; Heathcote 1985, 207–11.
56. See, e.g., Sands 1878, 59.
57. MacKenzie 1911, 24.
58. Quine 1988, 105.
59. MacKenzie 1911, 14–15.
60. NTS STK 3/2.
61. MacGillivray 1842, 62.
62. MacNeill 1986, 7.
63. Seton 1980, 343.
64. Martin 1986, 37, 38.
65. Martin 1986, 39–42.
66. Harman 1997, 128.
67. Martin 1981, 14.
68. MacAulay 1974, 212.
69. MacCulloch 1819, 25.
70. MacDiarmid 1877, 236.
71. Seton 1980, 91–2.
72. Sands 1878, 23.
73. Harman 1997, 280–3.
74. Cumming 1886, 136.
75. MacKenzie 1885–6, 9–11.
76. Martin 1986, 38.
77. Seton 1980, 298.
78. MacKenzie 1911, 12.
79. MacLean 1838, 22, 41.
80. Harman 1997, 201.
81. MacKenzie 1911, 20, 52–3.
82. Martin 1986, 10.
83. Harman 1997, 193.
84. MacAulay 1974, 182.
85. Martin 1981, 295; 1986, 54.
86. Martin 1986, 11.
87. MacKenzie 1911, 20.
88. Martin 1986, 54.
89. Harman 1997, 167, 171.
90. MacPherson 1897, 206–7.
91. Martin 1986, 57.
92. Kearton 1897, 80.
93. MacKenzie 1921, 88.
94. Harman 1997, 171.
95. MacPherson 1897, 206–7.
96. Brewer 1830, 452.
97. Harman 1997, 206, 215.
98. Moray 1678, 929.
99. Moray 1678, 929; Martin 1986, 54–5; MacAulay 1974, 182; Otter 1825, 372; Atkinson 1838, 220; Wilson 1842, 52–5.
100. Wilson 1842, 53–4.
101. MacFarlane 2003, 84.
102. MacKenzie 1911, 23–4.
103. Seton 1980, 207, 211.

104. Martin 1981, 295.
105. MacDiarmid 1877, 244, 250; Heathcote 1985, 211.
106. MacKenzie 1911, 10–11.
107. Landt 1810, 135–6.
108. MacCulloch 1819, 27.
109. MacKenzie 1911, 11; MacAulay 1974, 44–5.
110. MacDiarmid 1877, 251.
111. Hordern and Purcell 2000, 176–8.
112. Martin 1981, 289–90.
113. e.g. MM 633/1.
114. Stell and Harman 1988, 4–13.
115. Harman 1997, 327.
116. Hunter 1996, 146–50.
117. Harman 1997, 61.
118. Buchan 1974, 27.
119. Martin 1986, 17.
120. Moray 1678, 928.
121. Martin 1981, 295.
122. Buchan 1974, 24.
123. MacAulay 1974, 125.
124. Quine 1988, 139.
125. MacAulay 1974, 40.
126. MacAulay 1974, 128.
127. Moray 1678, 928.
128. MacAulay 1974, 216.
129. MacKenzie 1911, 8.
130. MacKenzie 1911, 8.
131. MacKenzie 1911, 9.
132. MacAulay 1974, 216.
133. Martin 1986, 63.
134. MacKenzie 1911, 12.
135. Martin 1986, 57.
136. MacAulay 1974, 214; MacKenzie 1911, 12.
137. Martin 1981, 15.
138. See Harman 1997, 152.
139. As documented by Sands 1878.
140. Martin 1986, 63.
141. Martin 1986, 55.
142. MacAulay 1974, 191.
143. MacFarlane 2003, 72–7.
144. MacKenzie 1681–4, 29.
145. Martin 1986, 60–1.
146. Martin 1986, 61.
147. Carmichael 1994, 362–3.
148. Harman 1997, 239.
149. Carmichael 1994, 361.
150. Summarised in Fleming 2001, 13–14.
151. e.g. Cashdan 1990.
152. Kaplan *et al.* 1990, 117.
153. Martin 1986, 25.
154. MacDiarmid 1877, 245; MacQueen and MacQueen 1995, 10.
155. Quine 1988, 192.
156. Wilson 1842, 50–1; Seton 1980 opp. p. 198.
157. Martin 1986, 55.
158. Seton 1980, 197–8, quoting Morgan.
159. Atkinson 1838, 220.
160. Wilson 1842, 51–5.
161. Seton 1980, 199.
162. Martin 1986, 20.
163. See Harman 1997, 47; *pace* Coates 1990, 63–4.
164. Cuthbertson 1996, 56.
165. Moray 1678, 928.
166. Moray 1678, 928.
167. Atkinson 2001, 66–8.
168. MacAulay 1974, 119–20.
169. Martin 1986, 38.
170. Campbell 1799.
171. MacDonald 1825, 32.
172. MacKenzie's Journal, quoted in Seton 1980, 300.
173. Martin 1986, 57–8.
174. MacKenzie 1911, 14.
175. MacAulay 1974, 186.
176. Quine 1988, 192.
177. Campbell 1799, 46.
178. Sands 1878, 108.
179. Martin 1986, 44.
180. Martin 1986, 45.

Notes to Chapter 6: The Social Psychology of the St Kildans

1. Martin 1986, 66.
2. Martin 1986, 59.
3. MacLean 1838, 46.
4. Martin 1986, 60.
5. Elliott 1895, 118.
6. Martin 1986, 54.
7. Martin 1986, 53.
8. Quine 1988, 122.
9. Quine 1988, 139.
10. Martin 1986, 44–5, 10.
11. Martin 1986, 10, 48.
12. Ross, NTS STK 3/22.
13. Heathcote 1985, 70.
14. Martin 1986, 51–2.
15. Östrom 1990.
16. Martin 1986, 49.
17. Martin 1986, 52.

18. Buchan 1974, 27–8.
19. Buchan 1974, 27.
20. NAS CH 1/2/32 f. 477.
21. Ibid, ff. 202–204.
22. Ibid, f. 472.
23. Fleming 2000.
24. Harman 1997, 163–5.
25. Allen 1880; Fenton and Hendry 1984.
26. Campbell 1799, 59; Kearton 1897, 12; Steel 1994, 73.
27. Fenton and Hendry 1984, 11.
28. Harman 1997, 163.
29. Seton 1980, 109.
30. Kearton 1897, 12.
31. Muir 1858, 13.
32. Fleming 2000, 357–9.
33. MacAulay 1974, 275.
34. Martin 1986, 46.
35. Seton 1980, 102.
36. MacAulay 1974, 33.
37. Fleming 2000, 357.
38. Martin 1981, 120–3.
39. Campbell 1902; see also Ross 1976.
40. MacCulloch 1819, 31.
41. Martin 1986, 78, (mis-labelled as p. 70); Seton 1980, 259–60, quoting MacKenzie's journal.
42. MacDonald 2001, 163–8.
43. Martin 1986, 52.
44. Martin 1986, 43.
45. MacAulay 1974, 243.
46. Baillie 1875, 256.
47. e.g. Quine 1988, 155.
48. Martin 1986, 43–4, 47, 52.
49. Martin 1986, 43.
50. Quine 1988, 129, 138.
51. Martin 1986, 62.
52. Martin 1986, 7.
53. See Parker Pearson *et al.* 2004, 196–201 for the antiquity of this mindset.
54. MacKenzie's journal, quoted in Seton 1980, 301.
55. Martin 1986, 43.
56. MacAulay 1974, 95.
57. MacAulay 1974, 84.
58. See the photograph in Heathcote 1985, 19.
59. Fisher 2001, 9.
60. Harman 1997, 228.
61. Fleming 2001, fig. 2.
62. Harman 1997, 228.
63. Harman 1997, 228.

64. Harman 1997, 233.
65. MacGregor 1929, 128–46.
66. Thomson 1996, 165–9.
67. MacGregor 1929, 128–46.
68. Löffler 1983: 29, 280 ff.
69. MacAulay 1974, 6.
70. MacGregor 1929, 144.
71. Mellars 1987, 265–73.
72. Thomson 1996, 175.
73. Fleming 2004b.
74. Coates 1990, 118, 93, 105, 135.
75. Coates 1990, *passim.*
76. *Mason 1936, 63.*
77. Wilson 1842, 30–1.
78. Malaurie 1982, 141–4.
79. Martin 1986, 44; 1981, 295.
80. MacAulay 1974, 81–2; Martin 1981, 295.
81. See Fleming 1999, 197 for a summary of these customs in Martin's writings.
82. MacGregor 1929, 124–5.
83. Fleming 1999, 197.
84. Ramsay 1888, 438–9; MacKenzie 1906, 2.
85. Ross 1976, 119–23.
86. MacLeod 2002, 160–9.
87. Martin 1986, 44; MacAulay 1974, 76–7.
88. Elliott 1895, 119–20.

Notes to Chapter 7:
A Man with a Mission

1. Sinclair 1793, 212.
2. NSA 1845, vol. 13, 363–80.
3. Kennedy 1932, 71.
4. Brown 1893, 693.
5. Brown 1893, 692–3.
6. MacDonald 1823, 29.
7. MacDonald 1823, 25.
8. MacDonald 1823, 32–3.
9. Cook 1982, 129.
10. Harman 1997, 252.
11. MacKenzie 1911, 3.
12. Cook 1982, 129.
13. Harman 1997, 251.
14. MacLean 1838.
15. MacGillivray 1842, 68.
16. Seton 1980, 58.
17. MacLeod 1898, 166–7.
18. MacQueen and MacQueen 1995, 15.
19. MacQueen and MacQueen 1995, 16.
20. MacLean 1838, 39.
21. Harman 1997, 104–5.
22. Wilson 1842, 23–4.

23. Connell 1887, 36–7.
24. NTS STK 3/18.
25. Wilson 1842, 23.
26. Cook 1982, 128.
27. Wilson 1842, 17.
28. MacKenzie 1911, 20.
29. Connell 1887, 142.
30. MacKenzie 1911, 22.
31. MacKenzie 1911, 21–2; Wilson 1842, 13, 36.
32. MacLean 1838, 45.
33. Atkinson 1838, 216.
34. Ross NTS STK 3/22.
35. MacKenzie 1911, 22–3.
36. Buchanan 1983, 16–17.
37. MacKenzie 1905, 398.
38. Quine 1989, 75.
39. Wilson 1842, 22.
40. MacLean 1838, 41.
41. Harman 1997, 254.
42. Wilson 1842, 10.
43. Seton 1980, 243.
44. Seton 1980, 57.
45. MacKenzie 1911, 52.
46. MacKenzie 1911, 23.
47. MacKenzie 1905.
48. Wilson 1842, 74–81.
49. Milner 1848, 2060.
50. MacLean 1838, 38, 40.
51. Williamson and Boyd 1960, 54–66.
52. MacAulay 1974, 101.
53. MacAulay 1974, 42.
54. e.g. Harman 1997, 142.
55. Atkinson 2001, 42.
56. Turner 1999.
57. Stell and Harman 1988, 41–2.
58. Mathieson 1928, 132.
59. MacLean 1838, 46.
60. e.g. Stell and Harman 1988, 23.
61. MacCulloch 1819, 29.
62. Grant 1981, 401.
63. Stell and Harman 1985, 39.
64. Emery 1996, 82–4.
65. MacKenzie 1911, 19.
66. MacKenzie 1911, 19.
67. Martin 1981, 43.
68. MacDonald 1823, 24; Harman 1997, 67–8.
69. MacKenzie's Journal, quoted in Seton 1980, 301.
70. Seton 1980, 97, quoting Sands.
71. Martin 1986, 63.
72. Atkinson 2001, 44.
73. Kearton 1897, 53.
74. And see Lawson 1993, 15, 29, 33.
75. Buchanan 1983, 16–17.
76. MacKenzie 1911, 38.
77. Wilson 1842, 74–81.
78. MacKenzie 1911, 32–8.
79. Fuller 1999, 56, 73.
80. MacLeod 1898, 232.
81. Seton 1980, 266.
82. Brown 1893, 21–2.
83. Details from Brown 1893.
84. Brown 1893, 653.
85. Brown 1893, 695.
86. Wilson 1842, 23.
87. Connell 1887, 87–8.
88. e.g. MacKenzie 1911, 16–17.
89. Seton 1980, 206.
90. Milner 1848, 2057, 2060.
91. Brown 1893, 695–6.
92. MacQueen and MacQueen 1995, 14–18.
93. Richards 1992a.
94. Napier Commission, 870.
95. MM 639/1/6.
96. NAS GD 371/231/1–2.
97. MacQueen and MacQueen 1995, 20.
98. Brown 1893, 699.
99. MacKay 1974, 6–7.
100. Cook 1982.
101. Cook 1982.
102. NSA 1845, vol. 7, 374–6.
103. MacKay 1974, 14.

Notes to Chapter 8: From MacLeod's Prison to Fool's Paradise

1. NTS STK 3/1.
2. NTS STK 11/1.
3. NTS STK 3/2.
4. Seton 1980, 102.
5. NTS STK 4/1.
6. Morgan 1861.
7. NTS STK 4/4, 4/5.
8. Brewer 1830, 451.
9. Thompson 1969, 59.
10. NAS GD 492/12/47.
11. MacDiarmid 1877, 242.
12. *Scotsman* 12 and 22 Oct 1860.
13. NTS STK 4/6.
14. NTS STK 4/7.
15. NTS STK 4/9.
16. NTS STK 11/4.
17. NTS STK 7/7.
18. NTS STK 4/4, 4/5.

19. NTS STK 4/9.
20. *The Scotsman*, 7 November 1860.
21. NTS STK 4/9.
22. NTS STK 3/6.
23. NTS STK 3/6, 3/7.
24. NTS STK 4/10.
25. NTS STK 4/11.
26. NTS STK 3/7.
27. NTS STK 3/7.
28. NTS STK ¾.
29. NTS STK 3/8.
30. NTS STK 3/7.
31. NTS STK 3/8.
32. NTS STK 3/9, 3/12.
33. Smith 1875, 144.
34. Quine 1989, 72.
35. Harman 1997, 109.
36. Harman 1997, 273.
37. NTS STK 4/14.
38. STK 3/8.
39. NTS STK 3/11.
40. NTS STK 3/12.
41. Seton 1980, 61.
42. NTS STK 4/19.
43. NTS STK 4/20.
44. Seton 1980, 61.
45. Seton 1980, 59–6.
46. Harman 1997, 134.
47. Morgan 1862, 178.
48. Thomas 1870, plate XXVIII.
49. Letter in NTS STK – locus not recorded.
50. MacDiarmid 1877, 239.
51. In a letter to the *Times* in August 1871, quoted in Turner 1895, 164.
52. Harman 1997, 110.
53. Sands 1877.
54. MacDiarmid 1877, 247–8; Seton 1980, 134; Sands 1878, 74.
55. Seton 1980, 134.
56. NAS GD 403/50/1–12.
57. *Scotsman* 12 March 1877.
58. NAS GD 403/50/1–12.
59. Sands 1878, 109.
60. Seton 1980, 66.
61. NAS GD 403/50/1–12.
62. Sands 1878, 128–9.
63. *Scotsman* 5 March 1877.
64. Harman 1997, 111.
65. Sands 1878, 130.
66. *Scotsman*, 10/5/1877.
67. Seton 1980, 117.
68. Seton 1980, 117.
69. Seton 1980, 343.
70. Seton 1980, 162, 170, 198.
71. Seton 1980, 183, 255.
72. Seton 1980, 316–7.
73. GD 403/50/1–12; Seton 1980, 56.
74. Sands 1878, 96.
75. Sands 1878, 14.
76. Sands 1878, 99, 109; *Scotsman* 1 March 1877.
77. *Scotsman* 1 March 1877; Sands 1878, 113.
78. *Scotsman* 9 March 1877.
79. *Scotsman* 1 March 1877.
80. *Scotsman* 9 March 1877.
81. *Scotsman* 9 March 1877.
82. *Scotsman* 12 March 1877.
83. *Scotsman* 10 March 1877; Sands 1878, 122.
84. *Scotsman* 1 March 1877.
85. Sands 1878, 108.
86. *Scotsman* 7 March 1877.
87. *Scotsman* 12 March 1877.
88. Sands 1876, 28.
89. NTS STK 7/25.
90. NTS STK 7/41.
91. NTS STK 7/43.
92. NTS STK 7/27.
93. *Scotsman* 10 March 1877.
94. *Scotsman* 10 March 1877.
95. NTS STK 7/46.
96. *Scotsman* 1 March 1877.
97. *Scotsman* 27 Feb; 7 March; 16 March, 1877.
98. *Scotsman* 12 March 1877.
99. *Scotsman* 13 March 1877.
100. NTS STK 7/28.
101. *Scotsman* 16 March 1877.
102. The figures in this paragraph are based on my own analysis of data in MM 630 and 631.
103. Sands 1878, 120.
104. *Scotsman* 7 March 1877.
105. Sands 1878, 120.
106. Sands 1878, 126.
107. MacDiarmid 1877, 242.
108. Scott 1914, 37.
109. MM 626/1.
110. NTS STK 7/63, 7/64.
111. MacDiarmid 1877, 247.
112. MacNeill 1886, 6.
113. MacKenzie 1885–6, 9–11.
114. Nicolson 1937.
115. Clegg 1977, 1984.
116. Seton 1980, 156–7, 206–13.
117. *Scotsman* 27 Feb 1877.
118. MacAulay 1974, 211.

119. Collacott 1981, Table 1.
120. Ferguson 1958, 142.
121. Gibson 1928, 54.
122. Lawson 1993.
123. Sands 1876, 76.
124. Sands 1878, 49–53, 84.
125. Holohan 1985, 52.
126. Collacott 1981, Table 1.
127. Sands 1878, 22.
128. Sands 1878, 72.
129. Lawson 1993.
130. Seton 1980, 297.
131. Connell 1887, 137; see also Clegg 1977, 304.
132. Clegg 1984, 9.
133. Turner 1895, 166.
134. Gibson 1928, 59.
135. Scott 1914, 36.
136. MacNeill 1886, 6.
137. MacNeill 1886, 7.
138. Harman 1997, plate 42.
139. Heathcote 1985, 95.
140. MacDiarmid 1877, 241; Connell 1887, 149; Steel 1994, 118, quoting George Murray's diary.
141. Harman 1997, 265.
142. MacKay 2002, 38–52.
143. Morgan 1861, 105, 108.
144. MacDiarmid 1877, 240.
145. Kearton 1897, 22.
146. Fisher 1952, 441–2.
147. Heathcote 1985, 208.
148. Quine 1988, 83, 89, 99.
149. MM 633/1.
150. Harman 1997, 114.
151. Harman 1997, 116–7.
152. Steel 1994, 189.
153. Scott 1914, 70.
154. Heathcote 1985, 186.
155. MM 632.
156. Harman 1997, 115.
157. Harman 1997, 100.
158. Heathcote 1985, 207.
159. Harman 1997, 117.
160. NTS STK 9.
161. Quine 1988, 114, 129.
162. NTS STK 9.
163. NTS STK9.
164. And see Harman 1997, 113.
165. Nicolson 2000, 224–5.
166. Harman 1997, 113–7.
167. Moisley 1966, 52–3.
168. Lawson 1993.
169. Oban Times, '50 Years Ago', 9/4/87.

Notes to Chapter 9: Tales of the Expected

1. Withers 1999.
2. Martin 1981, 336–49.
3. Martin 1981, 300–35.
4. Martin 1981, xii.
5. Martin 1986, 38–41.
6. Seton 1980, 345.
7. Levin 1970.
8. Martin 1986, 38.
9. MacAulay 1974, ii.
10. MacAulay 1974, 124–9, 245–7, 274.
11. MacAulay 1974, 275.
12. MacAulay 1974, 276–7.
13. Powell 1940.
14. MacPherson 1768.
15. MacAulay 1974, 221.
16. Schama 1995, 75–134.
17. Johnson and Boswell 1984, 297.
18. See, e.g., Hunter 2000.
19. Quoted in Johnson and Boswell 1984, 291.
20. Hodgen 1964, 377–411.
21. Scrutton 1887, 56–68.
22. Brougham 1871, 105.
23. Burke 1757.
24. Burke 1757, 43.
25. MacDonald 2001.
26. MacDonald 2001, 160.
27. MacCulloch 1819, 52–3.
28. Campbell 1799, 1.
29. Trevor-Roper 1983.
30. Johnson and Boswell 1984, 208, 303.
31. MacDonald 2001, 158–60.
32. Trevor-Roper 1983.
33. MacLeod of MacLeod 1928, 106.
34. Simpson 1938.
35. MacDonald 1825, 25.
36. Wilson 1842, 35.
37. See Bray 1996, 161–79.
38. Womack 1988, 3.
39. Womack 1988, 72, 86.
40. Womack 1988, 169.
41. Womack 1988, 165.
42. Acland 1981, 68.
43. Acland 1981.
44. DCRO 1148 M add/36/141–60.
45. Anon 1799.

46. MacCulloch 1819, 57.
47. MacCulloch 1819, 29.
48. MacCulloch 1819, 25–9.
49. Martin 1986, 36; MacAulay 1974, 143.
50. Pennant 1790, 132, 239, 229.
51. Pennant 1790, 214.
52. MacGillivray 1842, 55.
53. MacKenzie 1911, 17.
54. Napier Commission 865; Heathcote 1985, 204.
55. Goodrich-Freer 1902, 390–1.
56. Connell 1887, 164.
57. Connell 1887, 56.
58. Heathcote 1985, 69–70.
59. Steel 1994, 134–5; MacLean 1987, 130–1.
60. MacDonald 2001.
61. Geikie 1897, 405–17.
62. Atkinson 2001, MacGillivray 1842.
63. Kearton 1897.
64. MacKenzie 1905.
65. Thomas 1870.
66. Sands 1878, 78–80.
67. MacDiarmid 1877.
68. Morgan 1862, Mitchell 1865.
69. Harman 1997, table 20.
70. Summarised by Connell 1887, 28.
71. Nicolson 2000.
72. MacGregor 1931, 169.
73. Tweedsmuir 1953, 135–42.
74. Heiman 1999.
75. Tweedsmuir 1953.
76. Williamson and Boyd 1960, 79.
77. Fisher 1948, 107.
78. NTS STK 4/2 letter 22/5/36.
79. Powell 1990, 31–48.
80. Atkinson 1949.
81. Quine 1988, 38–9.
82. Tweedsmuir 1953, 141.
83. MacGregor 1931, 274; MacGregor 1969, opp. p. 129.
84. Quine 1988, 125.
85. Quine 1988, 150.
86. Atkinson 1949, 259.
87. NTS STK 4/6.
88. NTS STK 4/7.
89. MacKay 1963, 35.
90. Quine 1988, 176.
91. Boyd 1986, 220.
92. Fisher 1951, 39.
93. Williamson and Boyd 1960, 13.
94. e.g. MacKay 2002.

Notes to Chapter 10: In Conclusion: The Cunning of the St Kildans

1. Steel 1994, 9, 11.
2. Martin 1986, 38, 49, 5l; 1981, 290.
3. Seton 1980, 247–8.
4. Connell 1887, 33.

Bibliography

Acland, A. (1981) *A Devon Family: the Story of the Aclands*, Chichester.

Allen, J. R. (1880) 'Notes on wooden tumbler locks', *PSAS* **14**, 149–62.

Annandale, N. (1903) 'The survival of primitive implements, materials and methods in the Faroes and South Iceland', *Journal of the Anthropological Institute*, 246–59.

Annandale, N. (1905) *The Faroes and Iceland: Studies in Island Life*, Oxford.

Anon (1799) *Epistle from Lady Grange to Edward D____, Esq: Written During Her Confinement in the Island of St Kilda*, Edinburgh.

Armit, I. (1996) *The Archaeology of Skye and the Western Isles*, Edinburgh.

Armit, I. (2002) 'land and freedom' in B. Smith and I. Banks eds *In the Shadow of the Brochs*, Stroud, 15–26.

Armit, I. (2003) *Towers in the North: The Brochs of Scotland*, Stroud.

Armit, I. and Braby, A. (2002) 'Excavation of a burnt mound and associated structures at Ceann nan Clachan, North Uist', *PSAS* **132**, 229–58.

Atkinson, G. C. (1838) 'An account of an expedition to St Kilda in 1831', *Transactions of the Natural History Society of Northumberland, Durham and Newcastle* **2**, 215–225.

Atkinson, G. C. ed. D. Quine (2001) *Expeditions to the Hebrides*, Waternish, Isle of Skye.

Atkinson, R. (1949) *Island Going*, London.

Bahn, P. and Flenley, J. (1992) *Easter Island Earth Island*, London.

Baillie, Lady (1875) 'Visit to St Kilda – by a lady', *Church of Scotland Home and Foreign Missionary Record*, January 1, 254–7.

Baldwin, J. R. (1996) 'Heaps, humps and hollows on the Foula Skattald' in D. J. Waugh ed. *Shetland's Northern Links: Language and History*, Edinburgh, 205–29.

Barfield, L. and Hodder, M. (1987) 'Burnt mounds as saunas: An exercise in archaeological interpretation', *Antiquity* **61**, 370–9.

Beatty, J. (1992) *Sula: The Seabird Hunters of Lewis*, London.

Berry, R. J. (1969) 'History in the evolution of *Apodemus sylvaticus* (Mammalia) at one edge of its Range', *Journal of the Zoological Society of London* **159**, 311–28.

Berry, R. J. (1979) 'The Outer Hebrides: Where genes and geography meet', *Proceedings of the Royal Society of Edinburgh* **77B**, 21–43.

Borthwick, A. (1988) *The Empire Exhibition: Fifty Years on*, Edinburgh.

Boyd, J. M. (1986) *Fraser Darling's Islands*, Edinburgh.

Boyd, J. M. and Boyd, I. L. (1990) *The Hebrides: A Natural History*, London.

Bray, E. (1996) *The Discovery of the Hebrides*, Edinburgh (first published 1986).

Brayshay, B. and Edwards, K. (1996) 'Late-Glacial and Holocene Vegetational History of South Uist and Barra' in D. Gilbertson *et al.* eds *The Outer Hebrides: The Last 14,000 Years*, Sheffield, 13–26.

Brewer, Sir D. (1830) *The Edinburgh Encyclopedia*, London (St Kilda entry is in volume XII, pp. 450–2).

Broodbank, C. (2000) *An Island Archaeology of the Early Cyclades*, Cambridge.

Brougham, Henry (1871) *Memoirs of the Life and Times of Lord Brougham Written by Himself*, London.

Brown, C. G. (1997) *Religion and Society in Scotland since 1707*, Edinburgh.

Brown, T. (1893) *Annals of the Disruption*, Edinburgh.

Buchan, A. (1974) *A Description of St Kilda alias Hirta*, Aberdeen (first published 1727).

Buchanan, G. (1762) *The History of Scotland*, Edinburgh.

Buchanan, M. (1983) *St Kilda: A Photographic Album*, Edinburgh.

Buckley, V. ed. (1990) *Burnt Offerings*, Dublin.

Burke, E. (1757) *A Philosophical Enquiry into the Origin of our Ideas of the Sublime and Beautiful*, London.

Burt (1754) *Letters from a Gentleman in the North of Scotland*, London.

Calder, C. (1965) 'Cairns, Neolithic houses and burnt mounds in Shetland', *PSAS* **96**, 37–86.

Campbell, J. G. (1902) *Witchcraft and Second Sight in the Highlands and Islands of Scotland*, Glasgow.

Campbell, R. (1799) *An Account of the Island of St Kilda and Neighbouring Islands*, NLS ms. 3051.

Campbell, R. N. (1974) 'St Kilda and its sheep' in P. Jewell, C. Milner and J. M. Boyd eds: *Island Survivors: The Ecology of the Soay sheep of St Kilda*, London, 8–35.

Carmichael, A. (1994) *Carmina Gadelica: Hymns and Incantations*, Edinburgh (first published 1899).

Cartledge, J. and Grimbly, C. (1999) 'The Bird Bones' in M. Parker Pearson and N. Sharples *Between Land and Sea: Excavations at Dun Vulan, South Uist*, Sheffield, 282–88.

Cashdan, E. ed. (1990) *Risk and Uncertainty in Tribal and Peasant Economies*, Boulder, USA.

Céron-Carrasco, R. and Parker Pearson, M. (1999) 'The fish bones' in M. Parker Pearson and N. Sharples *Between Land and Sea: Excavations at Dun Vulan, South Uist*, Sheffield, 274–82.

Chalmers, N. (1996) 'St Kilda' in B. Kay ed. *The Complete Odyssey: Voices from Scotland's Recent Past*, Edinburgh, 27–35.

Clarke, P. A. (1992) 'Artefacts of coarse stone from Neolithic Orkney' in N. Sharples and A. Sheridan eds *Vessels for the Ancestors*, Edinburgh, 244–58.

Clarke, P. A. (1995) *Observations of Social Change in Prehistoric Orkney and Shetland based on a Study of the Types and Context of Coarse Stone Artefacts*, M. Litt thesis, University of Glasgow.

Clegg, E. J. (1977) 'Population changes in St Kilda during the 19th and 20th Centuries', *Journal of Biosocial Science* **9**, 293–307.

Clegg, E. J. (1984) 'Some factors associated with island depopulation and the example of St Kilda', *Northern Scotland* **6**, 3–11.

Coates, R. (1990) *The Place-names of St Kilda*, Lampeter.

Collacott, R. A. (1981) 'Neonatal tetanus in St Kilda', *Scottish Medical Journal* **26**, 224–7.

Connell, R. (1887) *St Kilda and the St Kildians*, London.

Cook, A. L. M. (1982) *A Family Saga*, typescript ms, NAS GD 1/980/10.

Cottam, M. B. (1979) 'Archaeology' in A. Small ed. *A St Kilda Handbook*, Edinburgh, 36–61.

Crampsey, R. (1988) *The Empire Exhibition of 1988; The Last Durbar*, Edinburgh.

Crawford, B. (1987) *Scandinavian Scotland*, Leicester.

Crawford, I. (2002) 'The wheelhouse' in B. Smith and I. Banks eds *In the Shadow of the Brochs*, Stroud, 111–28.

Cumming, C. F. G. (1886) *In the Hebrides*, London.

Cuthbertson, D. (1996) 'Natural born climbers', *On the Edge*, December 1996/January 1997, 52–7.

Darling, F. (1955) *West Highland Survey*, Oxford.

Bibliography

Devine, T. (1994) *Clanship to Crofters' War: The Social Transformation of the Scottish Highlands*, Manchester.

Dickson, J. (1992) 'North American driftwood, especially *Picea* (spruce), from archaeological sites in the Hebrides and Northern Isles of Scotland, *Review of Palaeobotany and Palynology* **73**, 49–56.

Dodgshon, R. A. (1995) 'Modelling chiefdoms in the Scottish Highlands and Islands prior to the '45'' in B. Arnold and D. B. Gibson eds. *Celtic Chiefdom: Celtic State*, Cambridge, 99–109.

Dodgshon, R. (1998) *From Chiefs to Landlords*, Edinburgh.

Dunn, D. (1981) *St Kilda's Parliament, 1879–1979*, London.

Durrenberger, E. P. (1992) *The Dynamics of Medieval Iceland*, Iowa, Iowa City, U. S. A.

Edwards, K. J. and Whittington, G. (1998) 'Landscape and environment in prehistoric West Mainland, Shetland', *Landscape History* **20**, 5–17.

Elliott, J. S. (1895) 'St Kilda and the St Kildans', *Journal of the Birmingham Natural History and Philosophical Society* **1**, 113–35.

Emery, N. (1996) *Excavations on Hirta 1986–90*, Edinburgh.

Evans, J. D. (1973) 'Islands as laboratories for the study of culture process' in C. Renfrew ed. *The Explanation of Culture Change*, London, 517–20.

Eyre-Todd, G. ed. (1888) *Poems of Ossian, Translated by James Macpherson*, London.

Fagan, B. (2000) *The Little Ice Age*, New York.

Fenton, A. (1978) *The Northern Isles: Orkney and Shetland*, Edinburgh.

Fenton, A. (1984) 'Northern links: continuity and change' in A. Fenton and H. Palsson eds. *The Northern and Western Isles in the Viking World*, Edinburgh, 129–45.

Fenton, A. and Hendry, C. (1984) 'Wooden tumbler locks in Scotland and beyond', *Review of Scottish Culture* **1**, 11–28.

Ferguson, T. (1958) 'Infantile tetanus in some Western Isles in the second half of the nineteenth century', *Scottish Medical Journal* **3**, 140–6.

Fisher, I. (2001) *Early Medieval Sculpture in the West Highlands and Islands*, Edinburgh.

Fisher, J. (1948) 'St Kilda: a natural experiment', *The New Naturalist*, 91–104.

Fisher, J. (1951) *Portraits of Islands*, London.

Fisher, J. (1952) *The Fulmar*, London.

Fisher, J. and Vevers, H. (1943) 'The breeding distribution, history and population of the North Atlantic gannet (*Sula bassana*)', *Journal of Animal Ecology* **12**, 173–213.

Fisher, J. and Waterston, G. (1941) 'The breeding distribution, history and population of the fulmar (*Fulmarus glacialis*) in the British Isles', *Journal of Animal Ecology* **10**, 204–72.

Fleming, A. (1995) 'St Kilda: stone tools, dolerite quarries and long-term survival', *Antiquity* **69**, 25–35.

Fleming, A. (1999) 'Human ecology and the early history of St Kilda, Scotland', *Journal of Historical Geography* **25**, 183–200.

Fleming, A. (2000) 'St Kilda: family, community and the wider world', *Journal of Anthropological Archaeology* **19**, 348–68.

Fleming, A. (2001) 'Dangerous islands: fate, faith and cosmology', *Landscapes* **2.1**, 4–21.

Fleming, A. (2004a) 'St Kilda: the pre-Improvement *Clachan*', *PSAS* **133**, 375–89.

Fleming, A. (2004b) 'The skerry of the son of the King of Norway' in E. Carter and O. Lelong eds. *Modern Views, Ancient Lands*, Oxford. 65–70

Fleming, A. and Edmonds, M. (1999) 'St Kilda: quarries, fields and prehistoric agriculture', *PSAS* **129**, 119–59.

Fleming, J. (1848) 'Zoology of the Bass Rock' in T. McCrie *The Bass Rock*, Edinburgh, 385–408.

Fossitt, J. A. (1996) 'Late Quaternary vegetation history of the Western Isles of Scotland', *New Phytologist* **132**, 171–96.

Fuller, E. (1999) *The Great Auk*, privately printed.

Gauld, W. (1989) 'In the lee of Rockall', *Northern Studies* **26**, 43–55.

Geikie, A. (1897) *The Ancient Volcanoes of Great Britain*, London.

Gibson, G. (1925) 'The black houses of the Outer Isles', *Caledonian Medical Journal* **12**, 364–72.

Gibson, G. (1928) 'The tragedy of St Kilda', *Caledonian Medical Journal* (April), 50–62.

Goodrich-Freer, A. (1902) *Outer Isles*, Westminster.

Gosden, C. and Pavlides, C. (1994) 'Are islands insular? Landscape vs. seascape in the case of the Arawe Islands, Papua New Guinea', *Archaeology in Oceania* **29**, 162–71.

Graham-Campbell, J. and Batey, C. (1998) *Vikings in Scotland: An Archaeological Survey*, Edinburgh.

Grant, I. F. (1981) *The MacLeods: The History of a Clan*, Edinburgh (first published 1959).

Harman, M. (1997) *An Isle called Hirte: History and Culture of the St Kildans to 1930*, Isle of Skye.

Harvie-Brown, J. A. & Buckley, T. E. (1888) *A Vertebrate Fauna of the Outer Hebrides*, Edinburgh.

Hastrup, K. (1985) *Culture and History in Medieval Iceland: An Anthropological Analysis of Structure and Change*, Oxford.

Hastrup, K. (1990) 'Cosmology and society in medieval Iceland: A social anthropological perspective on world-view' in K. Hastrup ed. *Island of Anthropology*, Odense, 25–43.

Haswell-Smith, H. (1998) *Scottish Islands: A Comprehensive Guide to Every Scottish island*, Edinburgh.

Hau'ofa, E. (1993) 'Our sea of islands' in E. Waddell, V. Naidu and E. Hau'ofa eds. *A New Oceania: Rediscovering our Sea of Islands*, Fiji, 2–16.

Heathcote, N. (1985) *St Kilda*, Edinburgh (facsimile of 1900 edition).

Heiman, J. (1999) *The Most Offending Soul Alive*, Honolulu.

Henshall, A. (1972) *The Chambered Tombs of Scotland*, vol. 2, Edinburgh.

Hodder, M. and Barfield, L. eds (1991) *Burnt Mounds and Hot Stone Technology*, Sandwell.

Hodgen, M. T. (1964) *Early Anthropology in the Sixteenth and Seventeenth Centuries*, Philadelphia.

Holohan, A. M. (1985) 'St Kilda: Childbirth and the women of Main Street', *Scottish Medical Journal* **30**, 50–3.

Holohan, A. M. (1986) 'St Kilda: emigrants and disease', *Scottish Medical Journal* **31**, 46–49.

Hordern, P. and Purcell, N. (2000) *The Corrupting Sea: A Study of Mediterranean History*, Oxford.

Hoskins, W. G. (1955) *The Making of the English Landscape*, London.

Hunter, J. R. (1996) *Fair Isle: The Archaeology of an Island Community*, Edinburgh.

Hunter, J. (2000) *The Making of the Crofting Community*, Edinburgh.

Jewell, P., Milner, C. and Boyd, J. M. eds. (1974) *Island Survivors: The Ecology of the Soay Sheep of St Kilda*, London.

Johnson, S. and Boswell, J. (1984) *A Journey to the Western Islands of Scotland* and *The Journal of a Tour to the Hebrides*, London (first published 1775 and 1786).

Kaplan, H. *et al.* (1990) 'Risk, foraging and food sharing among the ache' in E. Cahsdan ed. *Risk and Uncertainty in Tribal and Peasant Economies*, Boulder, 107–43.

Kearton, R. (1897) *With Nature and a Camera*, London.

Kearton, R. (1898) 'The strange life of lone St Kilda', *World Wide Magazine*, 69–97.

Kennedy, J. (1932) *The Apostle of the North: the Life and Labours of Rev. John MacDonald, D. D., of Ferintosh*, Inverness.

Kinchin, P. & Kinchin, J. (1988) *Glasgow's Great Exhibitions*, Bicester.

Knox, J. (1975) *A Tour Through the Highlands of Scotland and the Hebride Isles in 1786*, Edinburgh (first published 1787).

Landt, G. (1810) *A Description of the Feroe Islands*, London.

Lawson, W. (1993) *Croft History: Isle of St Kilda*, Stornoway.

Lawson, W. (2002) *Harris in History and Legend*, Edinburgh.

Levin, H. (1970) *The Myth of the Golden Age in the Renaissance*, London.

Löffler, C. (1983) *The Voyage to the Other World Island in Early Irish Literature*, Salzburg.

MacAulay, K. (1974) *The History of St Kilda*, Edinburgh (facsimile of 1764 edition).

MacCrie, T. (1848) *The Bass Rock*, Edinburgh.

MacCulloch, J. (1819) *A Description of the Western Isles of Scotland*, London.

MacCutcheon, C. (2002) *St Kilda: A Journey to the End of the World*, Stroud.

MacDiarmid, J. (1877) 'St Kilda and its inhabitants', *Transactions of the Highland and Agricultural Society* **10**, 232–54.

MacDonald, F. (2001) 'St Kilda and the sublime', *Ecumene* **8**, 151–74.

MacDonald, J. (1823) *Journal and Report of a Visit to the Island of St Kilda*, Edinburgh.

MacDonald, J. (1825) *Report and Journal of Two Visits to the Island of St Kilda in the Years 1822 and 1824*, Edinburgh.

MacDonald, R. A. (1997) *The Kingdom of the Isles*, East Linton.

MacFarlane, R. (2003) *Mountains of the Mind*, London.

MacGillivray, J. (1842) 'Account of the island of St Kilda, chiefly with reference to its natural History', *Edinburgh New Philosophical Journal* **32**, 47–70.

MacGregor, A. A. (1929) *Summer Days among the Western Isles*, Edinburgh.

MacGregor, A. A. (1931) *A Last Voyage to St Kilda*, London.

MacGregor, A. A. (1969) *The Farthest Hebrides*, London.

MacGregor, D. R. (1960) 'The island of St Kilda: a survey of its character and occupance', *Scottish Studies* **4**, 1–48.

MacKay, J. A. (1963) *St Kilda – its Posts and Communications*, Edinburgh.

MacKay, J. (2002) *Soldiering on St Kilda*, Honiton.

MacKay, M. S. (1974) *Kilchrenan Kirk*, privately printed.

MacKenzie, G. (1681–4) 'An account of Hirta and Rona' in W. MacFarlane ed. *Geographical Collections*, Edinburgh, vol. 3, 28–9.

MacKenzie, H. R. (1885–6) 'St Kilda', *The Celtic Magazine* **11**, 9–16; 62–9; 120–5.

MacKenzie, J. B. (1905) 'Antiquities and old customs in St Kilda, compiled from notes made by Rev. Neil MacKenzie', *PSAS* **39**, 397–402.

MacKenzie, J. B. (1906) '*Bardachd irteach*: St Kilda verses', *Celtic Review*, April, 1–16.

MacKenzie, J. B. (1911) *Episode in the Life of Rev. Neil MacKenzie at St Kilda from 1829 to 1843*, privately printed.

MacKenzie, O. H. (1921) *A Hundred Years in the Highlands*, London.

MacLean, C. (1987) *Island on the Edge of the World*, London (first published 1972).

MacLean, L. (1838) *Sketches on the Island of St Kilda*, Glasgow.

MacLeod, J. N. (1898) *Memorials of the Rev. Norman MacLeod*, Edinburgh.

MacLeod, N. (n. d., *c.* 1756–1775) NLS Adv ms 21.1.5 ff 183–85.

MacLeod, N. (2002) *Morvern: A Highland Parish*, Edinburgh (first published 1867).

MacLeod of MacLeod, R. C. (1927) *The MacLeods of Dunvegan*, Edinburgh.

MacLeod of MacLeod, R. C. (1928) *The MacLeods: Their History and Traditions*, Edinburgh.

MacNeill, M. 1886. *Report of Malcolm MacNeill, Inspecting Officer of the Board of Supervision, on the Alleged Destitution in the Island of St Kilda, in October 1885. Presented to both Houses of Parliament by Command of Her Majesty, March 1886*, London.

MacPherson, J. (1768) *Critical Dissertations on the Origin, Antiquities, Language, Government, Manner and Religion of the Ancient Caledonians*, London.

MacPherson, H. A. (1897) *A History of Fowling*, Edinburgh.

MacQueen, K. and MacQueen, E. G. (1995) *St Kilda Heritage*, Edinburgh.

Malaurie, J. (1982) *The Last Kings of Thule*, London.

Marcus, G. J. (1998) *The Conquest of the North Atlantic*, Woodbridge (first published 1980).

Martin, M. (1981) *A Description of the Western Isles of Scotland*, Edinburgh (facsimile of 2nd edition, 1716; first published 1703).

Martin, M. (1986) *A Voyage to St Kilda*, Edinburgh (facsimile of 4th edition, 1753; first published 1698).

Mason, T. H. (1936) *The Islands of Ireland*, London.

Mathieson, J. (1928) 'The antiquities of the St Kilda Group of Islands', *PSAS* **62**, 123–32.

Mellars, P. (1987) *Excavations on Oronsay*, Edinburgh.

Miket, R. (2002) 'The souterrains of Skye' in B. Smith and I. Banks eds. *In the Shadow of the Brochs*, Stroud, 77–110.

Miket, R. and Roberts, D. (1990) *The Medieval Castles of Skye and Lochalsh*, Portree.

Milner, W. (1848) 'Some account of the people of St Kilda, and of the birds in the Outer Hebrides', *The Zoologist* **6**, 2054–2062.

Mitchell, A. (1865) 'Consanguineous marriages on St Kilda', *Edinburgh Medical Journal* **10**, 899–904.

Mitchell, A. (1868) 'On some remarkable discoveries of rude stone implements in Shetland', *PSAS* **7**, 18–34.

Moisley, H. A. (1966) 'The deserted Hebrides', *Scottish Studies* **10**, 44–68.

Moray, R. (1678) 'A description of the Island Hirta', *Transactions of the Royal Society* **12**, 927–9.

Morgan, J. E. (1861) 'The falcon among the fulmars', *Macmillan's Magazine* (June), 104–11.

Morgan, J. E. (1862) 'The diseases of St Kilda', *British and Foreign Medico-Chirurgical Review* **29**, 176–91.

Morrison, A. (1968) 'The island of Pabbay', *Clan MacLeod Magazine* **5**, 16–19.

Muir, T. S. (1858) *St Kilda: A Fragment of Travel by Unda*, privately printed.

Müller, J. (1988) *The Chambered Cairns of the Northern and Western Isles*, Edinburgh.

Munro, R. W. (1961) *Monro's Western Isles of Scotland and Genealogies of the Clans*, Edinburgh.

Murphy, E. and Simpson, D. (2003) 'Neolithic Northton: a review of the evidence' in I. Armit *et al.* eds *Neolithic Settlement in Ireland and Western Britain*, Oxford, 101–11.

Napier Commission (1884) *Evidence taken by Her Majesty's Commissioners of Inquiry into the Condition of the Crofters and Cottars in the Highlands and Islands of Scotland*, Vol. II, Edinburgh.

New Statistical Account of Scotland, vol. 7: Renfrew – Argyle, (1845), Edinburgh.

New Statistical Account of Scotland, vol. 13: Banff – Elgin – Nairn, (1845), Edinburgh.

Nicolson, J. (1937) 'John Sands', *Shetland Times*, 3rd July.

Nicolson, N. (2000) *Lord of the Isles*, Stornoway (first published 1960).

O'Hanlon, R. (2003) *Trawler: A Journey Through the North Atlantic*, London.

Östrom, E. (1990) *Governing the Commons: the Evolution of Institutions for Collective Action*, Cambridge.

Otter, W. (1825) *The Life and Remains of Edward Daniel Clarke*, London (2 volumes).

Parker Pearson, M. and Sharples, N. (1999) *Between Land and Sea: Excavations at Dun Vulan, South Uist*, Sheffield.

Parker Pearson, M., Sharples, N. and Symonds, J. (2004) *South Uist: Archaeology and History of a Hebridean Island*, Stroud.

Pennant, T. (1790) *A Tour in Scotland*, London (first published 1769).

Bibliography

Pennant, T. (1998) *A Tour in Scotland and Voyage to the Hebrides 1772*, Edinburgh (first published 1774 and 1776).

Powell, L. F. (1940) 'The history of St Kilda', *Review of English Studies* **16**, 44–53.

Powell, M. (1990) *Edge of the World: The Making of a Film*, London (first published 1938).

Quine, D. A. (1988) *St Kilda Portraits*, Ambleside.

Quine, D. A. (1989) *St Kilda Revisited*, Ambleside (first published 1982).

Rainbird, P. (1999) 'Islands out of time: towards a critique of island archaeology', *Journal of Mediterranean Archaeology* **12**, 216–34.

Ramsay, J. (1888) *Scotland and Scotsmen in the Eighteenth Century*, Vol. 2, Edinburgh.

Rees, S. (1979) *Agricultural Implements in Prehistoric and Roman Britain*, Oxford.

Rees, S. (1986) 'Stone implements and artefacts' in A. Whittle *Scord of Brouster: An Early Agricultural Settlement on Shetland*, Oxford, 75–91.

Richards, E. (1992a) 'St Kilda and Australia: emigrants at peril, 1852–3', *Scottish Historical Review* **71**, 129–55.

Richards, E. (1992b) 'The decline of St Kilda: demography, economy and emigration', *Scottish Economic and Social History* **12**, 55–75.

Ritchie, W. (1985) 'Inter-tidal and sub-tidal organic deposits and sea level changes in the Uists, Outer Hebrides, *Scottish Journal of Geology* **21(2)**, 161–76.

Rixson, D. (1998) *The West Highland Galley*, Edinburgh.

Ross, A. (1976) *The Folklore of the Scottish Highlands*, London.

Russell, M. (2002) *A Different Country: The Photographs of Werner Kissling*, Edinburgh.

Sands, J. (1877) 'Life in St Kilda', *Chambers's Journal*, 284–7, 312–6, 331–4.

Sands, J. (1878) *Out of This World; Or, Life in St Kilda*, Edinburgh.

Sayers, W. (1993) 'Spiritual navigation in the Western Sea: *Sturlunga Saga* and Adomnán's *Hinba*', *Scripta Islandica* **44**, 30–42.

Schama, S. (1995) *Landscape and Memory*, London.

Scott, W. R. (1914) *Report to the Board of Agriculture for Scotland on Home Industries in the Highlands and Islands*, Edinburgh.

Scrutton, Sir T. E. (1887) *Commons and Common Fields; or, The History and Policy of the Laws Relating to Commons and Enclosures in England*, Cambridge.

Serjeantson, D. (1988) 'Archaeological and ethnographic evidence for seabird exploitation in Scotland', *Archaeozoologia* **II/1.2**, 209–24.

Serjeantson, D. (1990) 'The introduction of mammals to the Outer Hebrides and the role of boats in stock management', *Anthropozoologica* **13**, 7–18.

Seton, G. (1980) *St Kilda*, Edinburgh (facsimile of 1878 edition).

Sharples, N. and Parker Pearson, M. (1999) 'Norse Settlement in the Outer Hebrides', *Norwegian Archaeological Review* **32**, 41–62.

Sheridan, A. (2003) 'French connections I: Spreading the *Marmites* thinly' in A. Armit *et al.* eds *Neolithic Settlement in Ireland and Western Britain*, Oxford, 3–17.

Simpson, W. D. (1938) 'Dunvegan Castle' in R. C. McLeod of McLeod ed. *The Book of Dunvegan*, Aberdeen, xv–xlvi.

Sinclair, Sir J. (1791–1799) *The Statistical Account of Scotland, 1791–1799*, Edinburgh.

Skene, W. F. (1880) *A History of Celtic Scotland*, Edinburgh, 3 vols.

Smith, R. A. (1875) 'A visit to St Kilda in 1873', *Good Words*, 141–44, 264–9.

Smout, C. (1983) 'Tours in the Scottish Highlands from the eighteenth to the twentieth centuries', *Northern Scotland* **5**, 99–121.

Steel, T. (1965) *The Life and Death of St Kilda*, Edinburgh.

Steel, T. (1994) *The Life and Death of St Kilda*, London (reprint of 1988 edition).

Stell, G. and Harman, M. (1988) *Buildings of St Kilda*, Edinburgh.

Taylor, A. B. (1968) 'The Norsemen in St Kilda', *Saga Book of the Viking Society*, **17**, 116–43.

Taylor, A. B. (1969) 'The name "St Kilda"', *Scottish Studies* **13**, 145–58.

Thomas, F. W. L. (1870) 'On the primitive dwellings and hypogea of the Outer Hebrides', *PSAS* **7**, 153–95.

Thomas, F. W. L. (1874) 'Letter from St Kilda by Miss Anne Kennedy, communicated with notes', *PSAS* **10**, 702–11.

Thompson, F. (1969) *Harris Tweed: The Story of a Hebridean Industry*, Newton Abbot.

Thomson, D. (1996) *The People of the Sea*, Edinburgh (originally published 1954).

Trevor-Roper, H. (1983) 'The invention of tradition: The Highland tradition of Scotland' in E. Hobsbawm and T. Ranger eds *The Invention of Tradition*, Cambridge, 15–41.

Turner, G. A. (1895) 'The successful preventive treatment of the scourge of St Kilda (*Tetanus Neonatorum*), with some considerations regarding the management of the cord in the new-born Infant', *Glasgow Medical Journal* **43**, 162–74.

Turner, R. (1999) 'Locating the Old Village in Village Bay', *St Kilda Mail* **23**, 30.

Tweedsmuir, Lord (1953) *Always a Countryman*, London.

Walker, J. (1808) *An Economical History of the Hebrides and Highlands of Scotland*, Edinburgh.

Walker, M. J. C. (1984) 'A pollen diagram from St Kilda, Outer Hebrides, Scotland', *New Phytologist* **97**, 99–113.

Whittle, A. (1986) *Scord of Brouster: An Early Agricultural Settlement on Shetland*, Oxford.

Williamson, A. (1908) *The Bass Rock: Its Historical and other Features*, Edinburgh.

Williamson, K. (1948) *The Atlantic Islands: A Study of the Faroe Life and Scene*, London.

Williamson, K. and Boyd, J. M. (1960) *St Kilda Summer*, London.

Williamson, K. & Boyd, J. M. (1963) *A Mosaic of Islands*, Edinburgh.

Wilson, J. (1842) *Voyage Round the Coasts of Scotland and the Isles*, Edinburgh.

Withers, C. (1988) *Gaelic Scotland: The Transformation of a Culture Region*, London.

Withers, C. (1999) 'Reporting, mapping, trusting: making geographical knowledge in the late seventeenth century', *Isis* **90**, 497–521.

Womack, P. (1988) *Improvement and Romance: Constructing the Myth of the Highlands*, London.

Index

*St Kilda and the
Wider World: Tales
of an Iconic Island*

Illustration Acknowledgements

The Publishers wish to thank the following organisations for granting us permission to reproduce in this book images for which they own the copyright: The National Trust for Scotland, for Figures 5, 7, 21, 34, 42, 51, 54, 55, 58, 68, 75, 77 and 86; The Royal Commission on the Ancient and Historic Monuments of Scotland, for Figures 35, 38 and 56; The National Archives of Scotland, for Figures 57, 73 and 87; The George Washington Wilson Collection, Aberdeen University Library, for Figures 10 and 52; The School of Scottish Studies, University of Edinburgh, for Figures 48 and 74; The Ordnance Survey, for Figure 11; The Ministry of Defence for Figure 25, which is Crown Copyright; The National Museums of Scotland, for Figure 60; Devon County Record Office, for Figure 64. Figure 70 is out of copyright.

All other images in this book are copyright its author, Andrew Fleming.